Madison Avenue Entertainment
The Book Publishing Division
P.O. Box 908
Roosevelt, New York 11575
877-507-5841
This book is a work of facts and should be presented and
published as nonfiction. It is based on a true story. The
transcripts that appear in the appendix section of this book
are accurate and exact copies of the transcripts that are
provided to us by official Court Reporter, Debra Dunn.
They have not been altered in any way. The same is with
respect to the exhibits and all relevant documents.
Madison Avenue Entertainment Group at 877-507-5841 or
MadisonAvenueEntertainmentGroup.com
Manufactured in the United States of America
ISBN 978-1456381097

CONTENTS

Chapter 1
The Most Controversial Person You Never Heard Of.   1.

Who is Nicholas Willis/Zimmerman, Sean Williams and Puzz Pacino? I get
"very personal" with Mr. Controversial.

Chapter 2
The Credit Card King (A borderline genius)   16.

Wanna learn how to steal 600,000 from American Express, MasterCard, Visa,
Discover, Western Union.... Just ask the Credit Card King.

Chapter 3
Prison Politics (A report from behind the wall)   39.

The Blood's, The Crips and America's Misconception about Prison Life.

Chapter 4
C.E.O Sean Williams (An underground success)   50.

Bobby Simmons introduces Latashé, Freaky Tah's last performance, Tyrese is a
no show, and Canibus rips the mic.

Chapter 5
How I Was Wrongfully Convicted   67.
(A nightmare I never woke up from)

Sean's Lawyers and Private Investigator
uncovers a ton of evidence that proves his
innocence. Why won't Judge Rosengarten listen
to them?

5A.
More than (7) seven alibi witnesses account   74.
for Sean's whereabouts on September 19, 1998

5B.
Sean's lawyer waives the most important motion   92.
in his case.

5C.
Sean gets into a heated discussion with   97.
Judge Rosengarten at his sentencing court date.

5D.
Sean's Private Investigator, Kevin W. Hinkson,   135.
finds out that Nakia was forced to identify him at trial.

5E.
The Criminal Injustice System turns   148.
a blind eye to all of Sean's evidence.

Chapter 6
The Escape Attempt   163.

Sean plans one of the biggest escape attempts
in New York State history, or did he?

6A.
Did Nicholas Zimmerman and Steven Finley know   179.
that Tony Dubose was breaking into Sing Sing C.F.?

6B.
Sean is placed in solitary confinement in   184.
violation of his Constitutional Rights

6C.
How strong is Pirro's case against Sean   198.

6D.
What was Jeanine Pirro's true intention   204.
in bringing this case?

APPENDIX pg.218

Transcripts:

Arraignment Transcripts; Sean's lawyer waives all motions.	Arraignment Transcripts 1-8
Sandoval Transcripts; Leigh Bishop exposes Sean's criminal background	Sandoval Hearing Transcripts 29-37
Adjournment Transcripts; Judge Rosengarten denies the request for the adjournment	Proceedings Transcripts 18-19
Karisha Braithwaite's Trial Testimony	Transcripts 288-313
Julia Hosein's Trial Testimony	Transcripts 318-331
Nakia Stubbs Trial Testimony	Transcripts 365-445
Detective Christian Kanehl's Trial Testimony	Transcripts 453-479
Jatanya Belnavis's Trial Testimony	Transcripts 503-519
Proceedings Transcripts; Judge Rosengarten denies Sean's witnesses.	Transcripts 561-569
Katiuscia Brifils Trial Testimony	Transcripts 571-583
Sentencing Transcripts; Sean gets into a heated discussion with Judge Rosengarten	Transcripts 1-26

Exhibits

- Exhibit A. Detective Muldoon Report   1
- Exhibit B. Detective R. Aiello Report   4
- Exhibit C. Inspector Defuria Report   6
- Exhibit D. Notice of Alibi   10
- Exhibit E. Barry Alexander Affidavit   11
- Exhibit F. Latina Boyd's Affidavit   13
- Exhibit G. Samuel Belnavis Affidavit   14
- Exhibit H. Natasha Dockery Affidavit   15
- Exhibit I. Nakia Stubb's Affadavit   16
- Exhibit J. Haron Wilson Affidavit   18
- Exhibit K. Theophulus Brown Affidavit   19
- Exhibit L. New Paper Article about Jeanine Pirro   21
- Exhibit M. New Paper Article about Jeanine Pirro   22
- Exhibit N. Administration Segregation Report   23
- Exhibit O. June 2003 Sing Sing Article   24
- Exhibit P. People v. Zimmerman Indictment   25
- Exhibit Q. Sing Sing Article   40
- Exhibit R. Sing Sing Article   42
- Exhibit S. Sing Sing Article   44
- Exhibit T. Grievance Committee Article Pirro   46

Chapter 1

The Most Controversial Person

You Never Heard Of

Before I started the interviews, the drafting, and the writing for this book, I took some time to ask myself if this is really something I wanted to do. This being my first project, I wanted it to be my best project. Following in the footsteps of Biggie, Jay-Z, and Nas, all of their first albums were classics. I wanted this to be my "classic album."

However, at the present time, the subject of this book is under a major investigation (and I emphasize the word "major") by the Westchester County District Attorney's Office, The New York State Police, the Queens District Attorney's Office, The Department of Corrections and the Federal Bureau of Investigations. In other words, everyone is pretty much out to get him.

I knew because of the controversy surrounding his name the book would do an impressive first week of sales. What I wasn't ready for is for me to somehow become involved in his investigation. I must admit that I was warned by several people that writing a book about his situation might not be a good idea at this time.

Upon visiting him at Shawangank Correctional Facility in Wallkill, N.Y., a correctional officer handed me a visitors request form that all visitors must fill out in order to visit an inmate. After completing the form with all of the inmates information of whom I was there to see, I handed it back to the officer and waited for my name to be called. I don't think it was more than 30 seconds before that officer called me back up to the desk.

"Excuse me Ms. Hughes" the officer said: "I don't mean to be nosy or anything but are you sure you want to visit Inmate Zimmerman?" Before I could ask the officer why he was whispering, and to confirm that yes, I was sure I wanted to visit Zimmerman, he interrupted me with "I'm only trying to warn you that all of his visitors are arrested after they visit him."

I'm not sure what I said in response to his statement but I do remember my mind going completely blank after that. "Arrest me for what, what did I do, I ain't got nothing to do with no escape attempt, I just wanna visit him and see how he is doing." All of the normals ran through my mind that would run through anyone elses mind if they had just been told that they might be arrested.

The officer stated that he would continue to process the paperwork if I still "truly wanted to visit Zimmerman." Answering with a dry throat, I responded: "Yeah, I still wanna see him." Taking what seemed to be a mile long walk back to my seat, I remember thinking to myself, "Uh huh, you done got yourself in trouble again. Ain't nobody gonna bail you out if you get arrested. Your boyfriend don't even know that you're up at some jail seeing some inmate. Your name is gonna probably wind up in the newspapers next to all his other girlfriends. And then you're gonna be serving time for a crime you didn't commit just like the inmate you're here to visit."

Just as I was going to pick up my bag and walk out the front door, an officer

2

yelled out "Alright, who's here to see Zimmerman?" I didn't respond right way but it didn't matter because all the other female visitors looked in my direction as if to say "she is, take her away."

It was too late to turn back now. If I tried to walk out of the building that would look really suspicious, so I had no choice but to continue on with the visit. The situation I was in reminded me of a conversation I had with a colleague of mine, in which he stated that the government would go to any extent to cover up internal corruption. Perhaps maybe, the Correction Officer who "warned me" that I might be arrested only said that to scare me off so that I wouldn't visit Zimmerman. Maybe there is some corruption going on inside (the prison).

The thought that the officer's statement might only be a scare tactic relaxed me a little, but I was still nervous, my palms were still sweating and this was my very first project. On top of that, I was minutes away from meeting a young brother that has the world on his shoulders. He doesn't know me, and I don't know him, so I don't know how he might react to my questions. He told me in letters that I could get as personal as I want, but personal to me might be disrespect to him. Whatever the case, I came here today to get my "classic album," even if I have to risk being arrested to get it.

I know with his controversy and my investigative skills we could put together a really good book - or - be put in jail for exposing the government, which ever came first. In any event, I was willing to risk that.

3

I was literally taken through a maze to get to him. The officer that escorted me through the prison informed me that the person I was visiting was so "high profile" that they turned an old hospital office into a personal visiting room just for him. "Larry Davis is here too, and he don't even get treated like this" the officer said. Just as I was searching my vocabulary for the nicest way to say "thanks idiot for making me as nervous as possible" we arrived at the personalized visiting room.

He wasn't in the room when I first got there, which was good because it gave me time to collect my thoughts and relax. The officers noticed that I was nervous. They were watching me, and in turn, I was watching them. To break the silence one of the officers said "Zimmerman will be here shortly." As I nodded my head and said "thank you" I heard what sounded like a knock on a door and keys jingling.

As I stared nervously through the window, about six more corrections officers appeared and along with them was a dark skinned, six foot, medium build (very attractive I might add) young brother. I remember thinking to myself "damn, six officers had to transport him down here, and now they are gonna stick him in the room with me, alone." Why do they need so much security around him? I have heard all types of crazy stories from my girlfriends about how their man be flipping out on them when they go to see them. I hope this guy doesn't mistake me as one of his girlfriends.

I noticed that he was wearing handcuffs. He stood motionless as the other officers removed them, not saying a word. Another officer tried to make small talk

4

with him. He just stared at him as if the officer didn't even exist. I wondered what was wrong with him but then again rumor has it that he is in prison for a crime he didn't commit. So he has a right to be upset. I figured I rather not ask that question. When he looked in the direction of the visiting room and noticed I was sitting there he waved and gave me one of the nicest smiles a brother in prison can give. I waved and smiled back and then he came into the room:

(Interview Opens)

N.Z.   Good morning.

K.L.   Good morning.

N.Z.   I appreciate your coming to see me.

K.L.   Ok that's alright.

N.Z.   Was it a long ride?

K.L.   No, actually it wasn't that long, less than two hours I believe.

N.Z.   Yeah. It shouldn't be that long. Did I take a long time to come down?

K.L.   No, not really. I just got here.

N.Z.   Oh, okay. Was any of the officers disrespectful to you when you were being processed?

K.L.   Disrespectful?

N.Z.   Yeah you know, did they say anything to you out of line?

K.L.   Well, not disrespectful, but one of the officers said I might be arrested when

5

I leave here.

N.Z.   Arrested? (laughs)

K.L.   Yeah, arrested, that's what he said. (slight smile)

N.Z.   Why would they arrest you? (more laughs)

K.L.   I don't know.

N.Z.   Nah, no one is going to arrest you. The government is in enough trouble with me. Trust me, no one is going to arrest you when you leave here.

K.L.   Then why would he say that?

N.Z.   Well, it's a long story and I guess throughout our conversations I will be filling you in, but their ultimate goal is to stop people from coming to see me so that's how they scare them. Did they scare you?

K.L.   No, not really. (lying)

N.Z.   Well, that's the way they scare people into not wanting to visit me. They were expecting you to turn around and walk out the door.

K.L.   (Thinking to myself "He just doesn't know how close I was to walking out that door.")

K.L.   How did you know that they would say something to me in the processing room?

N.Z.   They pretty much try to intimidate anybody new that tries to visit me. They know this is your first time here, so I figured they would say something to you.

6

K.L.   But that's wrong isn't it? I mean, they shouldn't be harassing your visitors.

N.Z.   Yeah it's wrong, but no one ever blamed the Department of Corruption of being

right. They are following order's from the "higher up's" in Albany to harass me

and my family and to make my life hell. That's all, it's nothing new. I'm not

surprised.

K.L.   Excuse me, did you say the Department of "Corruption"?

N.Z.   Yeah (smile)

K.L.   What's that?

N.Z.   Well, to you they are known as the Department of Corrections. You know,

you see them out there in their uniforms and they seem to be working hard

at keeping the violent criminals in prison, and away from society, and keeping

the citizens of the State of New York safe. Well, I'm sorry, but I just don't

see it like that.

K.L.   Well, what do you see?

N.Z.   I see one of the most powerful, most corrupt organizations in all of the 50

states. I see a system and a game plan that was put together long before

me and you were even thought of. I see, and have experienced, a

brotherhood that is so secret and quietly kept, that there is no such definition

to the phrase "Criminal Justice." Some people use the phrase "Justice is

Blind." I disagree. Justice isn't "Blind", as a matter of fact "Justice" can see

very well, it probably has 20/20 vision. But Justice only sees what it wants

7

to see and closes it's eyes to what is doesn't. So there is absolutely nothing wrong with "Justice's" vision.

K.L. Um. That's deep.

N.Z. Yeah, and it gets deeper than that sis. You know, one of the reasons why I agreed to do this book with you is not because of the money that was offered or the publicity that came with it, but I thought to myself that I have been blessed with a rare opportunity to let the public (as a whole) know what really goes on in the prisons that they pay taxes for, and exactly how the Criminal Injustice System gets their convictions.

K.L. "Criminal Injustice System"? (laughs)

N.Z. Yeah, Criminal Injustice. (laughs) I guess you're going to be quoting me on all my little phrases. It's all good. (laughs)

K.L. Did you come up with them on your own?

N.Z. Yeah. Either that or I heard them from another prisoner.

K.L. O.K. Well at least your honest.

N.Z. Yeah, no need in me taking credit for something I didn't create.

K.L. Well before we get too far into the interview I wanted to start off the book by introducing you to everyone. You know, all your "fans." (laughs)

N.Z. Fans? (laughs) I didn't know I had fans?

K.L. Oh yeah, you've got fans brother. All my girlfriends are in love with you. (laughs)

N.Z. (blushing) Oh, O.K. Well tell them I said hi and thanks, I guess ... (laughs)

K.L. I will. But like I said I want to introduce you to everyone. I want to ask you some questions. You know, a lot of people talk about you but no one knows who you are. You had an album out in 2001, a video, you are hated by almost every law enforcement agency, yet no one knows who you are. You're the most controversial person that no one has ever heard of. And on top of that you go by twenty different names. So I wanna ask you brother, what is your name? (laughs)

N.Z. I guess you were serious when you said you wanted to get personal. (laughs)

K.L. Oh yes, very personal. (laughs)

N.Z. O.K. Well a deal is a deal. So I'll stick to it.

K.L. So what is your real name?

N.Z. My mother born and raised me Nicholas Willis.

K.L. O.K.

N.Z. My father's last name was Zimmerman ...

K.L. Was?

N.Z. Yeah, he is no longer with us.

K.L. Oh I'm sorry, my condolences.

N.Z. Thank you. So normally, since my father's last name is Zimmerman, I have identification under Willis and Zimmerman. So the first time I was arrested I had identification on me under the name Willis, so the cops took my

9

pedigree information under the name Willis. The next time I was arrested, I had identification under the name Zimmerman so the cops booked me as Zimmerman.

K.L. Oh. O.K., so Zimmerman is not a fake name?

N.Z. Nah, that's my name.

K.L. Well how did your father get a white name?

N.Z. (laughs) What do you consider a white name?

K.L. Zimmerman! (laughs)

N.Z. Well, it's actually Jewish but ...

K.L. Yeah, Jewish white! (laughs)

N.Z. Yeah, well if you look at it that way. I never really got the chance to research my family tree but I plan to do it when I go home.

K.L. O.K. Now, who is Sean Williams?

N.Z. That's my D.B.A. name (Doing Business As). I did most of my business under that name when it came to the music industry.

K.L. Is that legal?

N.Z. Yeah, people in the music business never use their real names. Like Jamie Fox's name is Eric Bishop and Courtney Love's real name is Love Michelle Harrison, you know, my business name was Sean Williams.

K.L. And everyone knows you as Sean?

N.Z. Yeah, I've went by that name so long that everyone calls me Sean.

K.L.　O.K., makes sense. And Puzz Pacino?

N.Z.　That's my stage name as a rapper.

K.L.　Oh O.K. Now the D.A. is trying to say that you have so many different aliases that you can't be trusted cause they don't know your real name.

N.Z.　I couldn't care less what a D.A. thinks about me or my name. I will only be judged by one person when I leave this Earth, so I live my life for him.

K.L.　Is that God?

N.Z.　Yes ma'am.

K.L.　So you believe in God?

N.Z.　Lately, that's all I believe in.

K.L.　Um.

N.Z.　Do you believe in God?

K.L.　Does it make a difference if I did or didn't?

N.Z.　No, I'm just asking.

K.L.　O.K. well, I'm giving the interview, so I'll do the asking. (smile)

N.Z.　O.K., fair enough. (smile)

K.L.　Where are you from?

N.Z.　Africa.

K.L.　(laughs) Africa?

N.Z.　Yeah, Africa (laughs)

K.L.　You know what I mean. (laughs)

N.Z.   Well you got smart with me so I'm getting smart with you. (laughs)

K.L   Oh, alright, well no more getting smart.

N.Z.   O.K.

K.L.   Now, I'm going to ask you again, where are you from?

N.Z.   I'm originally from Bushwick, Brooklyn. I started hanging out in East New York

Brooklyn when I was 15 or 16 and I made lots of friends out there, so that was

my hood. Also around the time my moms and me moved to Rosedale, Queens

so that's why I knew some people in Queens.

K.L.   Oh, O.K. Age?

N.Z.   Twenty- eight (28), but who knows how old I will be tomorrow.

K.L.   Why do you say that?

N.Z.   I read a newspaper article a couple weeks ago that said I was 33. I couldn't

Believe it. (smile)

K.L.   Oh. How about school. Did you finish?

N.Z.   Nah I left school in the eleventh grade. I was one of those brothers that

always felt I was ahead of my time. I couldn't sit still in the classroom.

I couldn't sit in one spot for seven (7) hours a day without some type of

progress being made. I felt like school was holding me back. I'm feeling the

results of that decision now.

K.L.   So you regret not finishing school?

N.Z.   I wouldn't say regret but I would have done things a lot differently if given the chance. I'm handling my business now as far as school goes, so its all good. A lot of things I already know, but there are so many little perks and extras that you can pick up on by sitting in a room with twenty (20) other individuals that all want to learn the same subject. People are constantly asking questions and bouncing different theories off of each other, so for me, that is the benefit of school. I missed that, but I'm going to take care of it now.

K.L. Girl friend?

N.Z. Nah. Unfortunately I'm a little unemployed right now.

K.L. Unemployed?

N.Z. Yeah, my girl friend fired me a couple of years back when all this nonsense took place. So I lost my job as her man.

K.L. You mean the escape thing at Sing Sing?

N.Z. Yeah.

K.L. O.K., I want to get into that a little later, but you're saying that you're single. What kind of lady are you looking for?

N.Z. Well, right now I'm just chillin. I was in my last relationship for ten (10) years so it would be kind of hard to just jump into another relationship. She meant a lot to me and I don't know if anyone could replace that. I have a few friends but that's about it.

K.L. Well my friends are going to be very upset. (laugh)

N.Z. I'm sorry ... (smile)

(Interview Closed.)

As I started to get deeper into the conversation with him I started to relax and get a little more settled. His responses and answers to my questions were interesting. His attitude was positive and he was focused in the right directions. To say the least, the interview was turning out better than I thought.

There were some questions that I had in mind that I felt might offend a person in a situation that he is in. But once I was finally face to face with him and could actually hear him speak, I felt comfortable asking my "personal" questions. It kind of felt like I was speaking with an old friend that I haven't seen in a while. For instance, when he asked me did I believe in God, I told him that "I was giving the interview and that I would be asking the questions from now on." Now, there is no question that I believe in God, but that was my little test to see if he would get upset at the fact that I was getting smart with him. I wanted to see if he had the "temper" the District Attorney said he had and if so, the interview would have probably ended there. But he didn't even frown at my statement, much less get upset. In fact, he got smart with me, in a playful mood.

This guy was no "gangsta'," and if he was, he was good at hiding it. We were already into the first two hours of the visit but there were so many questions that I had not asked yet. (Visits in Shawangank C.F. are from 8:45 a.m. to 2:30 p.m.) Something tells me that I will have to visit him again, but for some reason, I didn't mind.

Chapter 2

The Credit Card King

A Borderline Genius

In March of 1997, Nicholas (or Sean, whichever sounds best) was the focus of yet another "major" investigation by the Queens District Attorney, the Federal Bureau of Investigation, the Postal Inspectors and the Secret Service. It was alleged (and he was convicted of) stealing some $600,000 from American Express, MasterCard, Visa, Discover, Sony, The Wiz, Western Union, (and the list goes on)...

The Daily News, Newsday, The New York Times and The Post covered the story, labeling Sean (or Nicholas) the new "Credit Card King" surpassing his competition, a 27 year old bank teller convicted of stealing some $400,000 a year earlier. At press time, Queens District Attorney Richard Brown stated that as a result of a search of Sean's car and house, The F.B.I., The Secret Service, and the Postal Inspectors unit were able to uncover and shut down a "credit card and check manufacturing plant."

Among the items seized from Sean's house was two credit card encoding machines used to demagnetize the magnetic strip found on the back of credit cards, and to re-magnetize the magnetic strip with a new credit card number, giving the credit card an unlimited spending power. But when the spending spree was over, the person actually using the credit card wouldn't get the bill, the person's credit

16

card number that was re-magnetized into the new card would. (sounds confusing huh, well I'm a little dazed myself so I figured I would ask the "Credit Card King" in my next interview.)

Also recovered was two check encoding machines used to reproduce and manufacture company checks of unsuspecting businesses, over 150 credit card numbers, 2000 sheets of check printing paper, 30 manufactured (ready to use) credit cards, 70 manufactured (ready to use) checks, 20 manufactured (ready to use) money orders, hundreds of PIN numbers, security codes and classified information for every major credit card company in America. (See Exhibit A. Detective Muldoon's report/Exhibit B. Detective Aiello's report/Exhibit C. Postal Inspector Defuria's report)

After the investigation was completed, the government admitted "that there is no way to estimate the amount of damage Nicholas caused with his operation." Upon his arrest, Nicholas was held on a half of a million dollar bond and housed on Rikers Island in Queens N.Y. Unable to come up with the bail money, Nicholas eventually pleaded guilty to the charge of possession of a forgery device and received a 1 1/2 to 4 1/2 year sentence. Included in the plea agreement was the provision that Nicholas would serve time for his girlfriend, who would have been arrested if Nicholas did not plead guilty immediately. (The same girlfriend who is no longer with him.)

17

(Interview Open)

K.L.   All right, I want to ask you a few questions about your 1997 conviction for "possession of a forgery device."

N.Z.   All right.

K.L.   You were convicted of stealing an estimated $600,000 from MasterCard, Visa, American Express, Discover ...

N.Z.   Uh ... First let me say this. I need your readers to know that in no way am I glorifying or encouraging that type of life style. That's my past, and I'm not proud of it. I probably would not even discuss that part of my life with you if the rest of my life didn't depend on it. I only agreed to talk about this because I need people to know the real reason why I am in prison, and why the D.A. did everything and anything unconstitutional to put me here. But I would not suggest that type of life for anyone, you are constantly looking over your shoulder.

K.L.   O.K., that's stated for the record.

N.Z.   All right.

K.L.   O.K., I want you to explain to me exactly what was going on in 1997.

N.Z.   I got caught up in a lot of things I should not have. Like any other kid coming up in the ghetto or in a rough neighborhood I was trying to find a way out. We didn't have much coming up and my moms did the best she could raising us. She worked two jobs, taking care of six kids by herself, so it was hard on

18

her. I always wanted to do something to take care of my moms so she wouldn't have to work so hard. So she could take it easy once in a while. So I somehow got caught up in the paper game.

K.L. "Paper Game?" Explain that.

N.Z. It's just a slang word for it. It's not drugs and it's not robbery or violence so it's referred to as the paper game.

K.L. O.K. Now you say "Somehow got caught up." Are you saying that this wasn't planned?

N.Z. Nah. It definitely wasn't planned. As a matter of fact I can't even remember where or when I started that lifestyle or where I picked up on it. I just know I was young. Real young.

K.L. How young?

N.Z. Uh ... Maybe 15, 16 ...

K.L. Wow, that's young!

N.Z. Yes it is.

K.L. O.K. Now, back to March of 1997. I want you to try to reconstruct the day when all these agencies show up to your front door. I want you to take me through it step by step if you can.

N.Z. All right, I'll try, but it was a while back.

K.L. That's O.K.

N.Z.   All right. I remember I over slept that day and I didn't wake up until about

10:00 a.m. I woke up to the sound of the bell ringing and I was wondering

why no one was answering the door. I got up and answered the door and it

was the mailman. A mailman I never saw before and I was kind of familiar

with all of the mailmen that worked my street. I remembered that he had

been ringing my door bell for the past ten minutes and usually when the

mailman rings your bell twice, and you don't answer your door, then he's

gone. He is not going to wait around., Whatever he has for you, you will get

it tomorrow, when he comes back. So that felt kind of strange to me.

K.L.   O.K.

N.Z.   So I opened the door, and right away he says I have your mail for you. Now

there is three things strange about this mailman. One, I've never seen him

before. Two, he has been ringing my bell for ten minutes. And three, he is

(personally) trying to give me mail, in my hand, when there is a perfectly

working mailbox sitting to the left of him.

K.L.   Umm ... So what did you say?

N.Z.   Well, I didn't take it. I don't know what it was but something told me not to

take it.

K.L.   All right.

N.Z.   So now this guy is getting kind of pushy with me and he is like "man, just

take the mail!" So as he is holding the mail in his hand, with his arm extended in my direction, I looked at the name on the envelope and realized it's not addressed to me or anyone in my family.

K.L. Who's name was on it?

N.Z. It's the name of a person who's credit card I was familiar with.

K.L. "Familiar with?"

N.Z. Yeah ...

K.L. What does that mean?

N.Z. (Familiar with) don't worry, you will figure it out later.

K.L. O.K. (smiles)

N.Z. So I pretty much figured out, at that point, that this guy was a cop. He wasn't to good at posing undercover. A dead giveaway at that point.

K.L. So what were you thinking at that point?

N.Z. I just knew I wasn't going to touch that mail.

K.L. O.K., so what happens next?

N.Z. Well, he is still being pushy about taking the mail so I say "Why don't you just leave it in the mailbox, it doesn't have my family's name on it, it probably belongs to the people downstairs"?

K.L. Oh, so you lived in a duplex or something?

N.Z. Yeah, it was a three level house.

K.L. O.K. and ...

N.Z. So the phony mailman says, "why don't you just hold it in your house until they get home?" So at that point I got a little upset and said, "just leave it in the box" and I closed the door.

K.L. Well, did he leave it in the mailbox?

N.Z. You know after all that, he didn't even put it in the box. He just walked away. That confirmed that he was definitely a cop.

K.L. Well, why was he trying to get you to take the mail?

N.Z. Hold on, I'm getting to the point. It will all make sense when I'm finished.

K.L. All right. (curious)

N.Z. So I closed the door and go upstairs to look out the window to see where he went and I seen him walk up the block and get into an undercover police car. And since I know of no mailman that delivered mail from a police car, I knew something was very, very wrong.

K.L. Um ...

N.Z. So I got dressed because I wanted to go to a friend of mines house to tell him what just happened and to be careful. I figured it wouldn't be smart for us to use the phone.

K.L. O.K.

N.Z. Now, this friend lived around the corner from me, and we were really close at the time. And regularly we would switch up cars, you know, I would drive his and he would drive mines.

K.L.   What kind of cars did you two have?

N.Z.   Back then, I had a Mitsubishi Diamante, I forget what kind of car he had.

K.L.   O.K.

N.Z.   So the night before all this happened, I had given him my car but I didn't take his. I didn't plan on going anywhere the following day, so I didn't need his car. He said he was going to see a girl and he wanted to show her he had two cars, so he took mine.

K.L.   O.K.

N.Z.   So the next morning, when the phony mailman came to my house, I noticed that my car was parked in my driveway. But this wasn't unusual, because he always put my car in my driveway when he was finished with it and then he would walk around the corner to his house. So when I seen my car was in the driveway I got dressed and I went around the corner to tell him what happened.

K.L.   And ... (still curious)

N.Z.   Well, when I got in my car, and drove around the corner to his house, there was about 10 to 15 police cars waiting for me.

K.L.   Oh ...

N.Z.   You know, flashing lights, sirens, bullhorns, the works. The government really knows how to make you look dangerous.

K.L.   Yeah, I see the way they brought you to the visiting room.

23

N.Z. Yeah, that's how they convince you that I am a criminal and violent, and that they are there to protect you from me.

K.L. Yeah, I know brother.

N.Z. O.K. Now. They order me to stop the car and to get out with my hands up and everything, so I do it. I didn't put up a fight. One of the officers came over to me and said just calm down "Nicholas," everything is going to be alright.

K.L. How did they know ...

N.Z. I'll get to that (smile)

K.L. All right (very curious)

N.Z. So the officer asks me, "where are you going" and I say "to see a friend of mine". And he says, "so what do you have in your (trunk)?" Now when he said that, right away I new something was up because he didn't say what do you have in your (car), like most officers. He was more specific, asking what do I have in my (trunk), as apposed to (the entire car).

K.L. Um.

N.Z. I wasn't that worried because I knew nothing was in my trunk, so I just told him "nothing is in my trunk." He asked could he search my car and I said "Nah, I'm in a rush to get somewhere ...

K.L. If you didn't have anything why didn't you just let him search your car?

N.Z. Well, the law says if the police stop you without reason to do so, then you

24

don't have to let them search you or your car. So at that time, I felt that they stopped me for no reason.

K.L. Oh O.K.

N.Z. So one of the cops grabbed the keys to the car out of my hand and said "we will search the car if we want." Before the cop even began to search the car, the other two officers were already putting handcuffs on me and starting to read me my rights. So at this point I'm saying to myself, "wait a minute, what is going on here?"

K.L. What were you being charged with?

N.Z. Absolutely nothing at that point.

K.L. Um.

N.Z. So now, as I am being read my rights, the officer that took the keys from me went straight for the trunk of the car and opened it, but he never searched the inside of the car, it seemed like he was only interested in the (trunk) of the car. So he opens the trunk, goes in it, and says "yeah, we got him" and as he is saying this he pulls a brown duffle bag out of the trunk of the car and I am looking at the bag like "who the hell bag is this?" (laughs)

K.L. (laughs)

N.Z. So before he even opened the bag and went through it, he was telling the other officers to arrest me. It was like he already knew something was in the bag. So at this point I am being driven back around the corner to my house

25

and I'm being asked the usual police questions, "do I wanna make any statements that could help me out later on, was anyone else involved in this?"

K.L. And what were you saying?

N.Z. I keep asking them "what's in the bag?" But they never answered me, they just kept saying, "come on Zimmerman, you know what's in the bag."

K.L. Um.

N.Z. So now we are back in front of my house and they are asking me if anything else was in the house because they are going to get a search warrant and find out anyway, so I better just tell them. And I am like, "anything else like what?"

K.L. O.K.

N.Z. So this goes on for about two hours and eventually they go and get a search warrant and search my house.

K.L. Did they find anything?

N.Z. Yeah, they find an old broken gun that didn't even work that a friend of mine left at my house a few years ago. I didn't even know the thing was still in my house. And they found like $500 or $1000 in my room, that was it. Now what they found in the bag was a different story.

K.L. What was in the bag?

N.Z. In the bag was two credit card demagnetizing machines, two check encoding machines, 1 money order embossing machine, they say it was a couple

hundred credit cards, checks, money orders, pin numbers, bank codes, etc...

K.L.   O.K. Now, this is the part where I am completely lost and I am sure my

readers are too. So I need you to explain to me; what is a credit card

d-e-m-a-g-n-e-t-i-z-e-r machine and what does it do? (laughs)

N.Z.   (laughs) All right, I'll explain. A credit card demagnetizer machine is a

machine that (demagnetizes) credit cards or any card with a magnetic strip

for that matter. Do you know what a magnetic strip is?

K.L.   Uhh... (laughs)

N.Z.   All right, I'll show you. Do you have your credit card with you?

K.L.   Yes.

N.Z.   Let me see it.

K.L.   (searching purse for credit card, credit card found, handing over credit card).

N.Z.   O.K., you see this black strip on the back of your credit card?

K.L.   Uh huh - (curious again)

N.Z.   This black strip is what is known as a "magnetic strip." In this strip, is your

credit card number, your expiration date, and your bank routing numbers.

When you go to a store and you buy something using your credit card, the

cashier swipes this magnetic strip through the cash register and the

computer in the cash register is able to read the magnetic strip and obtain

your information. So, the purpose of the (mag) strip is to provide convenience

27

for the cashier so she doesn't have to manually type in people's long credit card number all the time. She can just swipe it.

K.L.   O.K., I follow.

N.Z.   Now the machine that (I was convicted of being in possession of) was also able to read the magnetic strip on the credit card but this machine was a little different, it did a little bit more.

K.L.   O.K. (being nosy)

N.Z.   Not only did it read the mag strip on the card but with the push of a button, it was also able to erase whatever information that was already in the strip, and with another push of a button, it was able to put whatever information I wanted it to back on to the strip, without anyone ever noticing a change in the card.

K.L.   Well why would you want to change the information on the strip, how would that help you.

N.Z.   Well say, for instance, you came to me one day and you said "Sean, I want to go shopping, but I don't have any money on my credit card, can you help me?" The government alleges that I would then take your credit card, put it through my machine and erase your information from your card and replace it with someone else's credit card information. Someone with a lot more money than you. Then, when you go shopping and the cashier swipes (your) card, she is actually charging and billing the person's credit card account that

28

I put the mag strip, and not you. But you are still using your credit card, and the face of your card still bares your name. So you're still you, just the person being billed is not you.

K.L Ohhhhhhhhhhh!!!! (Big Laughs!) And you were able to do this with anyone who had a credit card?

N.Z. Yeah, that's what the government alleges.

K.L. Umm Hmm! Now I see why they call you the Credit Card King!

N.Z. Yeah, but I am done with that part of my life.

K.L. So what did the check machine do?

N.Z. It basically was the same thing, only for checks. On the bottom of your check, you can find your account number, bank routing number, and your check number. But these numbers are printed in a funny looking text that no normal computer or machine can print. So I was (convicted of being in possession of a machine that can print those special numbers.

K.L. And you basically would put someone else's account number on the bottom of my check and I would be spending their money?

N.Z. Yeah that's what the Government alleges.

K.L. Oh O.K. I follow you. But how did that bag get in the trunk of your car?

N.Z. Good question. This is where things get a little interesting.

K.L. Oh it gets more interesting? (laughs)

N.Z.　(laughs) Yeah, just a little more.

K.L.　O.K.

N.Z.　Now after I was arrested I hired a lawyer and he was able to find out that the feds had been investigating me for the last six months or so, along with the Queens District Attorney's office. They had been following me, taking pictures, listening to my phone calls, etc. ... Allegedly, they were getting so many complaints from the credit card companies that people were getting monthly credit card bills in the mail from purchases that they never actually made. Some of the people would live as far away as California but their credit card was being used in N.Y., all while the they still had the original card in their hand. American Express, MasterCard, Visa could not understand how this was happening, so they called the F.B.I. in N.Y. for help. So the F.B.I. see that something really big is going on here because there are a couple hundred thousand dollars missing from people's accounts but these people couldn't have made the charges because they lived in completely different states. So now the F.B.I. are investigating, and when these guys come into the picture someone is going to go to prison. You can count on that.

K.L.　Um.

N.Z.　So the F.B.I. and the D.A. get a lucky break one day. Allegedly a young lady was using one of our cards in the store one day and she got arrested with the card on her.

K.L. Why was she arrested?

N.Z. Well by that time, the F.B.I. had already teamed up with MasterCard, Visa,

etc. ... and they told them to alert the store owner whenever one of our cards

was used. So, as soon as this young lady used the card, a flag went up in

the computer telling the cashier to alert security, security then called the

cops, and the cops held her until the F.B.I. picked her up.

K.L. O.K.

N.Z. Now when the young lady is arrested, she starts to tell the F.B.I. about my

friend that lives around the corner from me. She says she got the card from

him and that he has machines in his house that makes credit cards and

checks, etc. ...

K.L. She is telling everything?

N.Z. Yeah, pretty much. At least according to the government.

K.L. Wow.

N.Z. So based on what she tells them, they obtain a warrant to search his house

and when they do, they find all the machines and credit cards, etc. ...

K.L. Well if they found everything in his house what does that have to do with you?

N.Z. Well the girl that had been arrested had already told the F.B.I. that my friend

wasn't the head guy in charge, and that his friend was, which would be me.

And when they investigate, they pretty much want the head guy in charge.

So when they went to his house, they went with the intention of finding out who I was. It wasn't long before they found that out.

K.L. (laughs)

N.Z. So according to my lawyer, my friend gives me up immediately. Also when they searched his house they find some I.D. cards with my face on them with different names of people, so they knew what I looked like to.

K.L. I would have just said he put my face on there, I didn't tell him to do it.

N.Z. You're exactly right and that is why they didn't arrest me because they knew that just because my face was on the I.D.'s that wasn't enough. So from what I understand my friend was arrested about a week prior to me being arrested. They had already searched his house, found all the machines and charged him. But I never knew nothing about his arrest, he never told me that he had been arrested. He was released after he agreed to work with the District Attorney's office to entrap me into his case.

K.L. Um.

N.Z. I remember the entire week before I was arrested my friend had been calling me on my house phone trying to get me to talk to him about certain things and that was unusual because he never liked to talk on the phone about nothing. This guy hated talking on the phone, so that was strange. But I never thought in a million years that this guy would work with the police and plus I didn't even know that he had been arrested. So all the conversations

32

we had that week were taped by the D.A.'s office and in each conversation my friend keeps asking me do I "want him to bring the (bag over"). And I'm like, "nah just hold it over there, just keep it at your house." Then he would call back the next day and say, "Yo, I'm going away for a couple of days, you sure you don't want to hold the bag until I come back." And I'm like, "Just hold it over there, it will be alright. If I need to get it later I got the key, I'll just get it myself."

K.L.   He was trying to get you to talk about the bag on the phone?

N.Z.   Yeah, but in all the conversations I never said, "bring me the bag." I guess God was walking with me or something.

K.L.   Um hum.

N.Z.   So now the cops realize that I am not saying anything incriminating on these tapes so they don't have a case against me at this point, and legally their investigation against me should have stopped, but it didn't. This is where they start to bend the law. My friend tells the cops that he can get my car from me and that he would leave the bag in the trunk for them and then all they have to do is wait for me to come out and get in the car and they got me. So now they got me in <u>my</u> car, with a bag of I.D.'s, with <u>my</u> face on it and two or three forgery machines. There was absolutely no way I was going to beat that case so I had to plead guilty.

K.L.   Damn, that's messed up.

N.Z. Yeah, it is. I am actually working to get that conviction off of my record right now. What the police did in reality was enter into a conspiracy with my friend to plant illegal evidence in my car in order to set me up and arrest me, this is exactly what the law says they <u>can not</u> do. So they broke that law. I'm trying to prove that in court, I have a long battle ahead of me but I won't stop until I win.

K.L. Why didn't you prove all of this in court back in 1997? Why did you wait so long?

N.Z. I was only 21 when I was arrested. I knew absolutely nothing about the constitution, my rights, the law, etc. I'm from East New York, Brooklyn. I didn't even know a constitution existed. (laughs) Like I said, that's the benefit of school. I missed that.

K.L. Yeah, but you knew how to ("demagnetize a credit card") (laughs)

N.Z. Yeah, I was smart in some areas, and a fool in others (laughs).

K.L. Well, the lawyer you had, shouldn't he had found out if the police set you up?

N.Z. That is exactly my argument in court. Had my lawyer done his job I would not have had to plead guilty to that case, the evidence would have been suppressed.

K.L. Um.

N.Z. You know, you are pretty good, you sure you're not a lawyer? (laughs)

K.L. Yeah, I'm from Hughes and Associates. Do you want me to represent you?

34

(laughs).

N.Z. (laughs) Nah, I had my share of lawyers. I don't want anymore.

K.L. All right now. Your girlfriend was also arrested in relation to this case?

N.Z. Nah, she was never arrested. I agreed to plead guilty so that they wouldn't bother her. They wanted to give her like 6 months or something, so I took it. They just tacked it on to my case.

K.L. What did she have to do with your case?

N.Z. My friend that was arrested told the cops that she use to help me make cards and stuff like that. So that was it.

K.L. O.K. now. How did you only receive 1 1/2 to 4 1/2 years in prison for such a big case?

N.Z. The laws back then for paper crimes wasn't strict. I plead guilty to (possession of a forgery device). That's a "D" felony. They dropped it down to an "E" felony and since it was my first felony conviction, I only got 1 1/2 to 4 1/2 years in prison.

K.L. How long did you do out of that sentence?

N.Z. About fourteen months, and then I went to work release.

K.L. O.K., and how did the (Secret Service) get involved? (smile) Aren't they suppose to watch the President?

N.Z. (laughs) You know, still to this day none of us has figured out why the Secret

Service was there. But that's a good question? I'll look into that. (laughs)

K.L. Did you do Federal or State time?

N.Z. I went to the State. Actually, from what I understand there was some type of battle over who would get the conviction because both the state and the F.B.I. participated in the investigation. I think the state had jurisdiction over the situation.

K.L. O.K. Now, I'm sure all the readers want to know what is a brother from East New York doing walking around with a "credit card demagnetizer." Not too many brothers have one of those, so where did you get yours?

N.Z. You know that is the first thing the D.A. asked me when we finally met face to face.

K.L. Did you tell him where you got it?

N.Z. (laughs)

K.L. What's so funny?

N.Z. Nah, its nothing. (laughs)

K.L. So why are you laughing?

N.Z. I laugh to keep from getting upset.

K.L. Upset at what?

N.Z. Upset at the fact that you would even ask me something like that. (no more laughs)

K.L. Oh, I'm sorry.

N.Z.   Nah, It's all right. Just please try not to ask me anything like that again.

K.L.   O.K.

(Interview Closed)

The next sixty (seconds) in that room felt like sixty (minutes). There was complete silence. He took a sip of the juice I had bought him and then stared off into space. It was like he left the room or something. I didn't look in his direction and he didn't look in mines. His arms were folded, and he had a look on his face similar to a father who had just caught his two year old playing with matches, after he warned her about how dangerous they were. The only difference was he wasn't a father and there wasn't any two year olds around.

I obviously upset him by asking him did he tell the D.A. where he got the machines from. Guys in his position usually don't talk to law enforcement agencies and it is a complete insult if anyone even accuses them of doing so (or in this case even asking if they did.) I apologized once again and he accepted. The rest of the conversation was nice.

He mostly talked about his nieces and nephews and how much he wished he could be there for them right now. We spoke about his favorite foods and hobbies and before you knew it the visit was over. Before I left I told him that I wasn't completely finished with the interview and that I might come back next week.

He said "He would love to have me back," like a gentlemen would. I felt

37

wrong leaving him there like that. Almost guilty, like it was my fault he was there.

Generally, he was a nice person and very, very smart and his conversation was

interesting. Something tells me my first project is going to be a classic.

Chapter 3

A Report From Behind the Wall

As scheduled, our interview continued the following week and because the last visit went fairly well I was a little more focused and relaxed this time. I was excited to see him again. I wondered what his week was like and what he's been up to since I last seen him. I knew he had his hands full with all the legal work he is preparing. Working on appeals, lawsuits and constructing a website by hand keeps him busy. With so much going on in his life I wondered if the book we are working on crossed his mind at all this week, or if I even crossed his mind for that matter.

During the ride to the facility, a news report came over the radio about his case. The host of the show reported in a humorous way that he had been indicted on charges of attempting to escape from Sing Sing Correctional Facility. "Man, I don't know who Nicholas Zimmerman is, but the brother had four women break into Sing Sing C.F. to help him escape. They had guns, Corrections Officers uniforms, the blueprints to the prison, the works. (Four women) tried to break into that jail, I can't even get one woman to come to my house" the host said.

There was some other females riding in the van I was in that transported us to the facility. There were all very familiar with "Sean's" situation and they actually started to clap for him when the host of the show reported the story. "That's right Sean" one of the females said. "Don't never stop fighting for your freedom" yelled

39

another. They all spoke of "Sean" as if they actually knew him personally, but neither of the females had ever met him. That didn't matter to them because they were all too familiar with his struggle and his pain. Judging from the fact that they were also on the way to visit a loved one in prison, they too, probably one time or another, encountered some corruption by the hands of law enforcement. They identified and accepted Sean as one of their own and so he was the topic of discussion for the rest of the ride.

We finally arrived at the facility just minutes before 9:00 a.m. I was filling out the visitors request form when I noticed the officer from last week that "warned me" that I might be arrested after the visit.

"Good morning Ms. Huges" the officer said. "Did we have a good visit last week with Zimmerman?"

I wanted to say "none of your damn business," but instead I just smiled and nodded my head in the affirmative. I was taken through the same maze to get to the (personalized visiting) room but this time he was already there. He stood as I walked into the room and kissed me on the cheek while shaking my right hand and placing his left on my back. I felt that he respected me as a woman and I liked that. He thanked me for the blueberry muffin and orange juice I brought him and then we started to converse.

K.L.   They were talking about your case on the radio a little while ago.

N.Z.   Yeah.

K.L.   They said you were indicted on the escape attempt charges in Sing Sing.

N.Z.   Oh. O.K. That's good, that's good.

K.L.   That's good?

N.Z.   Um hum. (muffin in mouth)

K.L.   I thought being indicted was a bad thing?

N.Z.   (finishing muffin) In some cases it's bad, but in my case it's good.

K.L.   You wanna explain?

N.Z.   Well, if the news is correct and I have been indicted then I can now file a motion to dismiss the indictment and to throw out the entire case. I couldn't do that before because there wasn't an indictment to dismiss. So we kind of been waiting for this.

K.L.   Do you think the indictment will get dismissed?

N.Z.   Oh yeah, it will get dismissed. We're not worried about that. As long as they follow the letter of the law it will get dismissed. I start to worry when they don't follow the law, that's the problem.

K.L.   Um.

N.Z.   But everything should be alright.

41

K.L.   O.K. I wanted to start the interview off by asking you what prison life is like

for you and what goes on behind these walls? What have you learned from

prison and how would you describe it to someone who has never been there?

N.Z.   I think the average American citizen has a big misconception about what

prison life is actually about and what goes on in here. Granted that you have

violence, homosexuality, drugs, and gangs, somewhere in all of that you can

find some of the most intelligent brothers in prison. Some brothers actually

come here and use their time wisely. Researching different aspects of the

law, getting their G.E.D., college degree, whatever.

K.L.   You being one of those brothers, how do you stay focused on your law work

in a place like this.

N.Z.   Well for me, it's about how bad do you wanna go home. You can hang out

with your homies kicking it about nothing and stay in prison and not learn

anything, or you can hit the law books hard and find the keys that are going

to open the door to your freedom. For me, I want to go home to my family so

I know the faster I finish that appeal, the faster I go home, it's that simple.

K.L.   Now, you said something about drugs being in the prison. How does drugs

get in to the prison?

N.Z.   Next question!

K.L.   Uh. O.K. Um ... (thinking of next question) Well what about the violence in prison, how do you manage to stand clear of any violence?

N.Z.   In that aspect it's all about the individual. If you come in this place thinking you are a gangsta', there's always gonna be another gangsta' who's thinking you are trying to outdo him or his gang. Now you got two gangsta's trying to outdo each other. That ain't about nothing. They either wind up killing themselves or getting years in solitary confinement. The individual that comes in here, minds his business and stays to himself nine times out of ten won't have any problems, but once again, it's all about the individual.

K.L.   Have you had any problems since you been in prison?

N.Z.   Nah, fortunately God has managed to keep me safe and focused on my journey through life and through prison. So I've been blessed not to get into anything thus far.

K.L.   If you were to have any problems how would you handle it?

N.Z.   Next question!

K.L.   If there was one thing you could change about prison what would that be?

N.Z.   Oh wow, that's a good question. I don't know if it is one thing I could narrow it down to. I would change so many things, I don't know where to start. I guess one of those things would be the attitude of the correctional officers.

K.L.   What about it?

N.Z.   You know, I would say 60% to 70% of most of the problems that occur in

43

prison is attributable to the correctional officer. In some ways, it is almost certain that the C.O.'S started the problem. In Sing Sing, the harassment by the C.O.'S is ridiculous. It's a constant problem. I used to get harassed so much by the correctional officers in Sing Sing that it was almost comical. Little petty things like, they would take your I.D. card and break it. Then you can't go anywhere for the rest of the day because you will get written up for walking around with no I.D. or an altered I.D. I mean, just constant harassment.

K.L. Do you think you were harassed more than other inmates?

N.Z. I mostly stayed to myself when I was in Sing Sing. I was a quiet dude, just staying in the law books and the bible. So I don't know who else was being harassed because I never took the time to ask them, but if anyone was being harassed more than me I feel sorry for them.

K.L. Why do you think you were harassed, were you doing anything to instigate it?

N.Z. Nah. It's just that this is the place where an officer can come and be the gangsta' that he couldn't be in the streets. He couldn't pass the test that the streets gave him to be a gangsta', he failed miserably. So he comes here and plays a tough guy to the inmate that can't defend himself without risking solitary confinement. So he has the upper hand, and he feels that that makes him a gangsta'.

44

K.L. What is a real gangsta'?

N.Z. I don't know. I'm not a real gangsta' so I can't define it. Maybe a gangsta' could answer that question for you.

K.L. What is an average day like for you in prison?

N.Z. You mean now or when I was in Sing Sing?

K.L. Well, I know you're on lock down now, so when you were in Sing Sing?

N.Z. I went on the visit a lot when I was in Sing Sing, almost everyday. So my day was pretty much wake up, take a shower, go on the visit, leave the visit at 3:00 p.m. and come back to a cell that look like a tornado hit it.

K.L What do you mean?

N.Z. Like I said, I was constantly harassed at Sing Sing so that was some of the petty things the Correctional Officer's did. They would search my cell as soon as I leave to go on the visit, so when I came back I would have to clean up the mess. Clothes, sneakers, food, just everywhere.

K.L. Why didn't you complain to the administration?

N.Z. The administration was the ones telling them to do it.

K.L. Oh.

N.Z. I don't want to come across like I'm bashing every officer in the Department of Corrections. I'm not. You have some officers that come to work just to do their eight hours and go home. They are not here to "torture" the inmates. They are here to provide for their families, to make a decent living and

45

possibly milk the system. I have no problem with these kinds of officers and they won't have any problems with me. But the officer that comes to work to be the gangsta' and the tough guy messes it up for the officer that just wants to do his job, because now you have the inmate that is going to rebel against both the bad and the good officer because he can't differentiate between the two. They look the same to the misinformed inmate, and now you've got problems.

K.L. Now that's a good point.

N.Z. Thank you.

K.L. What about the gangs in prison, can we talk about that for a minute?

N.Z. Um, yeah. To a certain extent.

K.L. Alright, I know there are the bloods and the crips in prison. Has anyone ever tried to force you to be in a gang or have they tried to force anyone else to be in their gang?

N.Z. Nah, no one has ever tried to force me to be in a gang and I don't think they try to force anyone else to be in their gangs. Your decision to be in a gang (I think) is voluntary. Now the way you leave that gang is a different story, but to join is up to you.

K.L. Would you ever join a gang?

N.Z. Nah, they tried to put me in a rap group once with two other members and

46

that definitely didn't work, so I know a gang with (200) members ain't going to happen for me. (laughs)

K.L.   (laughs)

N.Z.   Actually though, I have a lot of respect for the Bloods, Crips, Latin Kings, Neta, etc. ... I more so respect their strength and power and the way they unite as one. There is strength in numbers and they definitely have the numbers. But their strength needs to be channeled in a more positive direction.

K.L.   What would you do differently if you were the head of a gang of 200 members?

N.Z.   Um ... (thinks for a second). Well for a rough idea, currently there is seventy thousand inmates in N.Y. State prisons, probably half of that number belongs to some sort of organization or gang, so that is 35,000 inmates. 35,000 inmates that would, for the most part, come together and unite for another gang member, whether it be for violence or whatever. Just imagine if I could get $10.00 from each of those gang members. Now me being the head or the boss of that gang they would have to listen to me and give me their $10.00 right, sort of like a membership fee.

K.L.   O.K.

N.Z.   No now I'm working with $350,000 that fast. With this amount of money you can start to make small, but progressive changes in the Criminal Injustice System. Changes that definitely need to happen. I would channel that money to the streets, perhaps maybe recruit ten to fifteen law students that are still in college, that have a new found love for the law and really want to protect a person's constitutional rights. Then, I would set up an organization with these law students and also with the families of the inmates that really want to see a change, and have the students and the families start to investigate some of the inmates cases, as far as the innocent and the wrongfully convicted. With the law students in on the project they can actually train the families of the inmates in as far as what to look for when investigating a case. This way it won't be so much work on the students, the families will become trained lawyers as well. With an organization like this, students working with and training families members of the innocent or wrongfully convicted inmates, you will see an enormous amount of progress, at a much faster rate. It is one thing to hire a lawyer to investigate your case; he or she is only going to do so much for you because they don't love you and what they do for you is only business and win or lose they still get paid. On the other hand, what your family will do for you is completely different. They will go that extra mile for you, make that one extra phone call for you, stay on top of other people that are supposed to do things for your case and make sure things go right. This is because they love you and they want you

48

home but they first have to have some knowledge of the law and this is actually where my organization would help them.

K.L.   You know, that is a really good idea.

N.Z.   Yeah, but it would all have to start with the brothers in prison, unless they truly want to see a change, it will not happen.

K.L.   Well, maybe you should advise the gang members in prison, you know, be a consultant to the Bloods and Crips or something (laughs).

N.Z.   (laughs) I don't know if gangs have secretaries that I could submit my resume to, but I'll see (smile).

Chapter 4

C.E.O. Sean Williams

(an underground success)

After serving fourteen months for his 1997 conviction of possession of a forgery device, Sean was released in June of 1998 to a work release program in Queens, N.Y. under the agreement that he would maintain work and stay out of trouble. Ironically, he took up employment at a (credit reporting agency) and remained there for the next four months without any problems. Sean eventually left the agency (on his own) and started what would eventually be a modest, but successful independent record label.

Less than a year later, Sean's company, Alleyway Entertainment would move on to do business with major music distributors such as Universal Music Group, RCA, Interscope, Def Jam and Columbia just to name a few. The label would blossom even more in 2000 by signing and releasing the compilation album of five of New York City's hottest underground Hip Hop and R&B groups, but not before hosting more than ten major music industry events in the N.Y.-N.J. Tri-State area. The company would eventually fold in 2001 after it's C.E.O. is convicted of a crime he obviously didn't commit.

I questioned him about the rise and fall of the company, the ups and downs of the music industry and what it takes to maintain an edge in such a competitive business. In asking my questions I found out a lot from "Mr. C.E.O." including that

he has a new album coming out that he Executive Produced, from prison? Here is
what he had to say:

(Interview Open)

K.L.   So you are released in 1998 after the forgery conviction and you start your
        record company; what is it like to be the C.E.O. of your own company soon
        after being released from prison?

N.Z.   I think running any company requires hard work and dedication but running
        a record company, in my view, is a little more competitive than other
        businesses. The music industry is constantly changing and you have to
        learn how to change with it to be successful. New artist and new music is
        constantly being released, so you have to know how to find your edge in the
        business and keep your artist, or yourself for that matter, new and fresh. If
        you can do that then you will be all right.

K.L.   What would you say was your very first introduction into the music business,
        where did you get your start?

N.Z.   Actually my very first project in the music business was kind of unplanned.
        It was so low budget that I didn't think anyone would take us serious. I met
        these two young ladies at a talent show in Brooklyn, and they had performed
        Lauryn Hill's remake of (Killing Me Softly). I remember I was late to the
        show but the part of their performance that I was able to catch, I liked. So I

approached them after the show and we exchanged numbers and we worked together from there. We started going to the studio, working on songs together and putting together little ideas for the group.

K.L.   What was the group's name?

N.Z.   Latashe (pronounced La-ta-shay).

K.L.   Was it two girls in the group?

N.Z.   Yeah, they were sisters.

K.L.   O.K. Now, on the album it says you wrote and produced their first song. What was that like?

N.Z.   Well, I kind of knew what I wanted to hear from them and the direction I wanted the group to go in. I wrote a song called (I Will) and I sampled the beat from Special Ed's song that he had back in the days called (I got it made) and we put it together in the studio.

K.L.   Was the record successful?

N.Z.   Absolutely not. (laughs)

K.L.   (laughs) What happened?

N.Z.   Well, like I said, that was my first project and I had absolutely no idea what I was doing. All I knew is that I wanted to do what Puffy was doing. Puff was all over the place in '98. I mean everywhere you turn there was Puff Daddy so I wanted to do what he was doing. I didn't know how he was doing it but I knew I wasn't going to stop until I found out. (smile) So by making moves in the industry with this Latashe project, I was able to gather information, make contacts, get into industry parties, etc...

K.L. You shot a video to Latashe's song (I Will) and it got air play on all the local television stations in New York. What was that like?

N.Z. I contacted Fatima Robinson, who used to play Malik Yoba's baby's mother on New York Undercover and she was in the process of getting her film company off the ground so she agreed to do the video for almost nothing. So we put that together in less than a day and it came out better than a lot of people expected it to.

K.L. So now you are able to get most of the local New York stations to play the video. How did you do that?

N.Z. Now that was the unplanned part. (smiles) I had intended on mailing a copy of the video and CD to a record company with the hopes of getting a record deal, but like I said back then all my contacts was screwed up so I mistakenly mailed the video to a television station. A couple of days after I mailed the video (to the wrong address) the girls (Latashe) called me up and said that the principal of their school had sent them home early because their presence in the school was "creating a disturbance." So I asked them how were they creating a disturbance and they said all the kids in their school had seen the video on T.V. and now they are chasing them all around the school. So of course I'm saying to myself "what video on T.V."? (laughs)

K.L.   (laughs)

N.Z.   So I had to track down the station that was playing the video and find out how they got the video. I remember I spent the next day flipping through the channels trying to see if I could catch the video on a station. I turned to this one station and there is this guy hosting a video show. He's introducing the next video he is going to play, but the way he is talking about this video you would think that Biggie or Tupac's video is about to come on. (laughs)

K.L.   (laughs)

N.Z.   I mean this guy was going crazy with the introduction. He was like "All right you'll, I'm getting a lot of requests for this song. It's Hot! It's about to blow up! You'll keep calling in for it so I'm going to keep playing it!" So from the way he is talking, I'm expecting something from Jay-Z or somebody but then the beat drops and I'm like "wait a minute, that beat sounds familiar." (laughs). And then the song drops and I'm like "that song sounds familiar" and then the video drops and I'm saying "those girls in the video look familiar."

K.L.   (laughs)

N.Z.   (laughs)

K.L.   So when you finally realize that the video playing was your video how did you feel?

N.Z.   I mean I was still, at that point, asking myself three questions. How did he get the video, why was he playing it and why was he talking about us like that? I love the fact that he was playing it but I wanted to know how and why all of this was happening. So I call up the video station and I tell them that the video they are playing is ours and that I wanted to know how they got it. So they put me through to the host of the show and I ask him and he's like "man, yall got a hot record right here, everybody is requesting yall song. We need to get yall up on the show." And as I'm listening to him I'm saying to myself "does this guy know that we are nobodies". (laughs) But we eventually did appear on his show and he turned out to be a real good brother and that appearance lead to a lot of other things.

K.L. And who was the host of the show?

N.Z. Bobby Simmons. He has a local show in New York City called Flava Videos. He actually turned out to be a good friend of mine. We worked together on a few projects after that.

NOTE: (Bobby Simmons' Show, Flava Videos airs Monday-Friday 3:00 PM to 6:00 PM (Public Broadcast) 7 Channel 27

K.L. Well, if the stations in New York were playing your video why didn't the record do well in stores?

N.Z. At that point I had not mastered the structure of distribution as far as how to get your music in stores so people can actually buy it. Distribution can be complicated and you should learn it before starting a record company. So we had a video playing on at least three or four video stations, in a major market,

55

New York City, but no product in the stores. So that was a learning experience for me. It was time for me to really get serious and learn every aspect of the business.

K.L.   Now you move on from that and you start doing promotion in 1999 until 2000. What exactly were you promoting and what artist did you work with?

N.Z.   I was promoting industry events around that time such as performances, fashion shows, new music and movie releases, etc... I worked with a lot of artists such as Canibus, Lost Boys, Trina, Soul for Real, Boot Camp Click, etc... just a lot of people.

K.L.   What would you say your biggest event was in New York City?

N.Z.   I don't know if I would say my biggest, but my most noticeable and craziest event was with Tyrese at Club Large in Brooklyn.

K.L.   What happened?

N.Z.   I don't know. It was just a lot of wires crossed with that event.

K.L.   Care to explain?

N.Z.   I had received a call from Tyrese's A&R at RCA asking us to throw a big event for him in New York City because the album wasn't doing as well as they expected it to and they needed to make some noise in New York City with the album.

K.L.   This is when his single (Sweet Lady) was out?

N.Z.   Yeah. So we agreed to do it and the agreement was for a very low price

56

because it was a favor for a favor kind of thing. So I booked the Club for the event, which was Club Large, and I start to strategize a plan for the promotions because I needed this event to be really big. His label needed this event to be real big and they was relying on me to make this happen. So I'm calling every connection I had to make this a huge event. I got the D.J.'s at Hot 97 to talk about it. I had some commercials on B.E.T. 25,000 flyers was floating around New York City, and of course Bobby Simmons is constantly plugging it on his show. So everything is going good and the event is going to be big until I get a call from another promoter in Dallas, Texas. He told me that he heard about the event we was having for Tyrese in New York but he also had Tyrese booked for a super-bowl party in Miami on the same day as our event.

K.L. Um. Someone's not communicating.

N.Z. Yeah.

K.L. Did you ever call Tyrese?

N.Z. Not at this point, I'm only dealing with his label at this point.

K.L. O.K.

N.Z. So I call up the label and ask them what's going on with this promoter in Texas claiming Tyrese is booked for his event, and they told me that they had heard the same thing but that they took care of it and Tyrese would definitely be in New York to do the event. So, since they assured me that he would be there I continued with the promotion for the party. About a week later I get a hundred phone calls from people telling me to turn on M.T.V. because Tyrese is on there talking about our event, so I turn on the T.V. and Tyrese is talking about the event, but he ain't saying what I want to hear.

K.L.   What is he saying?

N.Z.   I mean, he is just literally destroying my company on National T.V. He is calling me a fraud, and that he doesn't know who I am, and that he won't be in New York City to do the event, and that we are falsely advertising his name in relation to this party that we are throwing. And not only is he saying my company name but he is calling Bobby (Simmons) a liar and a fraud and Club Large too. I mean, I just couldn't believe it.

K.L.   So what did you do?

N.Z.   After that happened I finally got through to him and his management team, which also turned out to be some cool guys, and we sat down and talked about the situation and it came to light that Tyrese didn't even know that he was supposed to be performing for me in New York, no one ever told him. So we basically wanted to find out who was at fault with the situation and why his management team was not told about the date.

K.L.   Did you ever find out?

N.Z.   Yeah, we found out.

K.L.   Who was it?

N.Z.   Some people at Famous Artist Management.

K.L.   Any names? (laughs)

N.Z.   Nah, I don't know who. It was so long ago I forget but I'm sure it's listed in some paperwork somewhere.

K.L.   So did Tyrese ever perform?

N.Z.   Nah, we was trying to fly him to New York after the Miami performance but that show started late and so he wasn't able to catch the flight that we booked for him.

K.L.   So I guess everyone was upset?

N.Z.   Actually, there was so much controversy with that event, with the fact that Tyrese actually went on M.T.V. and said that he was not going to be there, that everybody showed up just to see if he was really going to back out of the show. Twelve hundred people showed up to that party, we were going way over the fire code limits. (smile)   So I had to do something.   When we announced to the crowed that he wasn't going to be there nobody really got upset or booed or anything, I guess they kind of expected it.   But I had contacted (Canibus) a few weeks before the show and I told him that just in case Tyrese didn't show up, I would need him to come out as a surprise guest.

K.L.   And so he performed?

N.Z.   You know, when I brought him out the crowd completely went crazy.   That

59

was back when he had the conflict with LL Cool J and Wyclef so I guess everybody wanted to hear his side of the story in person. He did all his songs that night, the crowd loved him. I even heard that he made a song about that performance, so I guess he had a good time also. As a promoter, I was really satisfied with his performance.

K.L.   What other shows have you done?

N.Z.   Umm... I did events with Trina, Jadakiss, Boot Camp Click, Joe, Soul for Real, Lost Boyz. Actually, I think I may have been the last person to work with the Lost Boyz as a collective group. A day after they did Club Large for me we got the call that Freaky Tah had been murdered in Queens. I remember just sitting there for hours thinking to myself, "damn I was just with him last night." I still can't believe it.

K.L.   Yeah, I couldn't believe that either. He was a fun person to be around.

N.Z.   Yes he was.

K.L.   So now you move on from that and you start to do the New York's Illest Compilation in 2001 and you pretty much take over New York City with promotions on that album, I mean, I must have seen an advertisement for that CD everywhere. (laughs)

N.Z.   (laughs) Yeah, that was my man (General) on the promotions. I don't think that guy ever sleeps. If you got a product and you want it promoted right I would advise anyone and everyone to see him, he's probably the best in New

60

York. He was promoting the new album so much that we actually received a lawsuit from the government. True story.

K.L. For what?

N.Z. Well, it's certain places in New York City that you are not allowed to post flyers, stickers, poster boards, advertisements,etc... and the city was getting complaints that our poster boards was seen hanging on stoplights (laughs). Don't ask me who climbed all the way up there to put up a poster, but that's crazy.

K.L. Well why did they sue you? You didn't do it.

N.Z. Well, me and my girl was the owners of the company so we were responsible. So we paid a small fine and promised to stop the promotion.

K.L. Did you stop? (laughs)

N.Z. Yeah we did. You know, I can understand the government's argument with respect to the poster boards and stickers in New York City. New York is a great city, the greatest in the world, and if companies start going crazy with posters and stickers in New York, you will have garbage and debris everywhere so I can understand. But on the other hand they also have to fine the politicians because when they run for office they put up their advertisements too, so they must also follow the same laws as us.

K.L. Good point. So you Executive Produced the New York Illest compilation album. What was that like?

N.Z.   I don't think I will ever enjoy producing another album like I enjoyed producing that one. I didn't realize I had so much talent around me until we started to work on the CD. When we started recording, I was just blown back by what was actually coming out of that studio. If I had known that my peoples were that talented we would have done that project a long time ago.

K.L.   Who was involved in that project?

N.Z.   We kept everything in the family when it came to production, we didn't go outside for no help. Sidiq did a lot of the R&B tracks and one or two tracks for me and Terror I.Q. did the rest of my music. Bobby Simmons also did some tracks for me. Wit and Sidiq did most of Boe & Villa's production. Kira Scott's production was already tight before it got to us and Pepci and Thilai's production was also done by Sidiq.

K.L.   Now, how were you able to get all of these artists on one CD?

N.Z.   Actually, everyone on the compilation was cool with me before we started recording. I knew Pepci for a long time before we started the album but she never told me she could sing or even write music. I think she is very shy when it comes to that so I never knew she was that talented. The first time I heard her sing I knew I had to make it happen with her. It was just no way I was gonna sit by and just let that voice go unheard so I got her to do the album. Boe & Villa are incredible also. I would go as far as to say that they are probably one of the best rap duo's in the game. I would definitely invest

62

money in their career. I also believe Kira has a tremendous future ahead of her. I think she has the potential to be a huge pop singer, her vocal range is just that incredible. And with Thilai, I don't think there is any limit we can put on her talent. I think she can conquer Broadway, film, and music. From the start, I've always compared her to the likes of Beyoncé, I think she would give Beyoncé a run for her money.

K.L. And what about you?

N.Z. Oh, I do O.K. too.

K.L. That's it? (laughs)

N.Z. Yeah, I think I'm O.K. (laughs)

K.L. You're not going to talk about how good you are? (laughs)

N.Z. Nah, I think I would look really arrogant if I was to sit here and endorse myself to a public that doesn't really know me. I leave that up to the people when my album drops.

K.L. You have an album coming out?

N.Z. Yeah, we haven't set an approximate released date yet but it should be out sometime in 2007. We're still working out all of the intricacies so it's going to take a little while.

K.L. Any name for the album?

N.Z. Nah, not yet. I'm still throwing around a few ideas, but nothing definite.

K.L. How do you think the CD will do?

N.Z. Yeah, I think it's going to be big. The way the distributors are talking about it I think it's going to be big.

K.L. You don't sound too excited about it?

N.Z. Yeah, a lot of people tell me that. It's just that these are songs I did before I was thrown into prison and before I learned how these corrupt District Attorneys and judges are railroading my innocent brothers and sisters just so they can move up a notch on the political ladder. So some of the things I said in my music in the past, I wouldn't say now. I know how these politicians, judges and District Attorneys must laugh at us when we use the N. word or call the females B's and hoes. They actually get a kick out of that and I'm only helping them destroy us by using those words in my music, I'm only giving those words more recognition than they deserve, so I would refrain from using them now.

K.L. So why are you releasing this album if you don't feel that way anymore?

N.Z. I was contracted to a few distributors with the New York's Illest CD before I was arrested so I have to fulfill my end of the bargain with them, which is to release an album. They feel that with all the media coverage surrounding my name, now is the best time to put it out. I guess it's a good thing though, I can show people the old me with this album and then the new me when I get out. So it's all good.

K.L. What about the rest of the artists that was on the New York's Illest album, what are they doing?

N.Z. Oh, I don't know. I haven't spoken to anyone.

K.L. They don't come to see you?

N.Z. Nah.

K.L. How do you feel about that?

N.Z. The main goal of the Criminal Injustice System and the Department of Corruption is to disrupt and disconnect the Black family and all its ties. So when you come to prison you are pretty much out of sight, out of mind. I understand that now more than ever before. So it's not that I'm upset with anyone for not staying in contact with me. It's just that I know how to pick and choose associates a lot wiser now. So I will use this time to my advantage and learn from my mistakes. But I will never make the same mistakes again.

(Interview Closed)

Our conversation about the music industry continued for about another hour or so and I was actually able to learn a lot about distribution, marketing and promotion, management, etc... I started to wonder why the government would want to get rid of such a smart, intelligent young brother. I mean, this guy could pretty much educate you on various issues. We spoke about the war in Iraq, the United States Constitution, the history of the Black Panther Party, and less interesting topics such as who would win the World Series this year. In all, he was able to provide knowledge on current, and not so current events.

I asked him what he planned to do when he is released from prison. He said he wanted to continue to do music "but on a different level this time around." "I want to shy away from the hardcore hip-hop and try to focus more on R&B and Gospel music," he said. He also stated he wanted to funnel most of the proceeds generated by his new record company into a string of community centers with educational classes teaching the young about their constitutional rights, self employment, and family structure. His goals and ideas were so motivating that he suggested to me, right on the spot, that I start my own publishing company instead of battling with book publishers over royalty rates and budgets and before I knew it he was schooling me on the publishing business. It was becoming more and more obvious why Assistant District Attorney Leigh Bishop set him up the way she did, this young man was well on his way to becoming "the next Puff Daddy" and she apparently didn't want that (more on Assistant District Attorney Leigh Bishop in the next chapter).

Chapter 5

How I Was Wrongfully Convicted

(A Nightmare I Never Woke-Up From)

To the readers that have spent the money and the time to inquire more into Sean's case by purchasing this book, I thank you graciously. For the next two chapters I discuss with Sean the reasons for his instant conviction (Chapter 5) and how he subsequently became the accused of planning one of the biggest escape attempts in New York State history (Chapter 6).

His story is truly a heart-wrenching one, and because of the corruption involved, it continues to be just that. After conversing with him about his situation, I wept several times before falling asleep in the van that transported me back to the city. I remember wondering how a young man in a situation like his can withstand so much without completely going crazy.

I admired and complimented him on his fortitude and his will to continue to fight his oppressors. I informed him that the book we were preparing may be able to bring some much needed attention to his case and that the "Criminal Injustice System" may see things a little bit differently once we are able to get the community and the public's attention. He frowned at the suggestion, only responding with the "Criminal Injustice System doesn't care about public scrutiny, they only care about convictions. That's it, no more, no less". His response to my idea made me want to fight for him even more just to show him that there are people that will come together for him if he truly is being wronged by the system. This is why I thought it would be important to dedicate this part of the book to his wrongful conviction and to question him in detail about his whereabouts on September 19, 1998. In preparing this chapter of the book I investigated his case by reading the transcripts to his trial, affidavits, notes, etc. ... I spoke to witnesses, listen to audio tapes,, watched video tapes, spoke with lawyers, investigators, and went to the crime scene. In doing all of this I came to only one conclusion, a conclusion even a person who totally disliked Sean would come to. The conclusion that he is truly innocent. Here is a brief synopsis of my investigation:

Jatanya Belnavis was Sean's girlfriend on September 19, 1998, and she had been for three years prior to this date. Jatanya also had a friend named Nakia Stubbs who she was an acquaintance with for several years prior to this date. Nakia owned a Jeep Grand Cherokee in '98 that she wasn't able to make payments on anymore so she agreed to lease it to Jatanya at a price of $400 a month, and so on September 12th 1998 (one week before the 19th) Jatanya (and Sean) went to Nakia's house to pick up the Jeep and to pay her the $400 for the rental agreement. Jatanya retained the Jeep for one week, but then on September 18, 1998 Nakia called Jatanya and demanded that her Jeep be returned immediately because she felt she should have gotten more money for the rental agreement. Even though she had already

68

given Jatanya the Jeep, Jatanya had given her the money, and the 30 day deal had not expired.

After a brief dispute between the two ladies, Jatanya told Nakia that she was not in possession of the Jeep anymore and that she had given it to Sean, and that if she wanted the Jeep back she would have to contact him to get it, and so Jatanya provided Nakia with Sean's cell phone number.

Nakia contacted Sean on his cell phone around 11:00 pm on the 18th and told him to bring the Jeep to her immediately. Sean told her he was "at Exit 19 on the Southern State Parkway and that he would be there shortly with the Jeep." Hours passed, and Sean never showed up with the Jeep and so Nakia, her best friend Kariesha and her boy-friend Wilson traveled to Jatanya's house in Rosedale Queens, at 3:00 am, on September 19, 1998, (the next morning) to get the Jeep back.

Nakia and Kariesha both testified that when they arrived at Jatanya's house the Jeep was not present; that they had searched Jatanya's street by "looking up and down the street for the Jeep but it was no where to be found". The two ladies, (and Wilson) later rang Jatanya's bell to find out where the Jeep was and to have her contact Sean and tell him to bring the Jeep to her house immediately.

69

Jatanya testified that Nakia threatened her by stating "she was not going to leave her house until she got her Jeep back" and that Jatanya "did not know who she was f*cking with". Jatanya also testified that Wilson stated "that he was going to shoot up her house if she didn't get the Jeep back." Because of the commotion, several neighbors were summoned to their windows to see what the noise was about. These witnesses included Mr. and Mrs. Belnavis (Jatanya's parents), Natascha Dockery (who lives across the street from Jatanya) and Julia Hosien (Jatanya's neighbor).

Jatanya further testified that at Nakia's request, she attempted to contact Sean several times on his cell phone but was not able to get through to him. Nakia also testified that she attempted to contact Sean again while in front of Jatanya's house but could not.

Jatanya went on to testify that because she wasn't able to reach Sean, Nakia and her friends became more upset and the threats got worse. She said she contacted a friend of her's named Nandi Cooper that lived around the corner from her and told him she was being threatened by Nakia and her boyfriend in relation to the Jeep.

Several minutes after this phone call was placed by Jatanya to Nandi, three men emerged from the backyard of a nearby house and attacked Nakia by pulling her out of her car at gunpoint and dragging

70

her onto a nearby sidewalk. (It is important to note that Nakia, Kariesha and Wilson drove a second car to Jatanya's house, this is the car she states she is attacked in).

Nakia further states that the men searched her for weapons and asked her "what are you doing here" and "threatened to kill her" while she laid on the ground crying, and in fear of her life. Nakia said that subsequently, the man that was holding the gun in his hand fired it in the air eight or nine times before all three men left the scene of the crime in the same Jeep that she had loaned to Sean and Jatanya a week earlier. (Note: I know you are asking yourself, when did the Jeep get there? I will let Sean explain that part of the story.)

Needless to say, Nakia identified Sean at trial as the man that was in possession of the gun and he was convicted and sentenced to an amazing (eighteen years) in prison even though no gun was ever recovered, no one was hurt and Nakia's credibility was repeatedly impeached throughout the trial. The other two men Nakia alleged to be involved in the crime was never arrested or even looked for. Several other witnesses that was present at the scene of the crime and more than twenty alibi witnesses that could have verified Sean's whereabouts on the night in question were never interviewed or even investigated.

Because Nakia's testimony was the only evidence linking Sean to the crime, and no other evidence was ever recovered by the Queen's District Attorney's office (the same office that was responsible for placing that suspicious bag in Sean's trunk in 1997), the case got the attention of Private Investigator Kevin W. Hinkson, a thirty-year veteran of the N.Y.P.D. What he was able to uncover about Sean's case would bring tears to the eyes of a person who truly believed in the integrity and trustworthiness of law enforcement.

On a warm summer day in March of 2003, Nakia agreed to meet with Mr. Hinkson at a New York City restaurant in Manhattan's Chelsea Piers. What Nakia confessed to Mr. Hinkson was what mostly everyone who was involved in the case already knew, that Sean was not the man that attacked her with a gun in 1998.

During the conversation, Nakia told Mr. Hinkson that she wasn't sure that Sean was the person who committed the crime and that she did not want to testify against him, but was told by the D.A. "If she refused to cooperate she would be arrested on a material witness order and held in jail until she testified".

It would also emerge during the conversation that Nakia never (positively identified) Sean as the person who committed the crime in 1998, but when confronted with his picture she only told the police "that looks like him". Because of the corruption and discrepancies involved in his case, and all the evidence the was uncovered that proves his innocence, I wondered why the system that was alleged to have "20/20 vision" would turn a blind eye to something so obvious. I figured Sean would have the answer to that question and so I asked him:

72

(Interview Opens)

K.L. In reading the transcript to your trial I noticed that there were so many inconsistencies in Nakia's story, and she was impeached several times throughout her testimony. It made me wonder how could a jury of twelve reasonable people believe her? Do you think the jury was fair in your case?.

N.Z. Even though the jury members in my case convicted me, I still think they were a fair jury, as crazy as that may sound. I don't think it was the jury's fault at all. They were pretty much put in a position where they had no other choice but to convict me. My trial was set up for me to be convicted before it even started. The judge and the Assistant District Attorney that was assigned to my case put my trial together so nicely that the average layman to the law would never truly see that I was railroaded, and continued to be railroaded. Every shred of evidence that I had that would have displayed my innocence was not allowed to come into the trial. Therefore, with the jury never knowing that I could have shown them that I wasn't at the scene of the crime, they convicted me. The jury never heard (my side of the story) and never seen any of my evidence, and so, with them only hearing Nakia's testimony, and nothing from me, they found me guilty. Still to this day the jury doesn't know that they convicted an innocent man, but it's not their fault.

K.L. Well, they will know now.

N.Z. Yeah, I guess they will.

K.L. You mentioned the judge and the Assistant District Attorney that was assigned to your case, what was their names?

N.Z. The Judge in my case is (Roger R. Rosengarten) and the A.D.A. name is (Leigh Bishop.) My trial was in Queens Criminal Court, so it was assigned to them.

5A. More than (7) alibi witnesses

account for Sean's whereabouts

on September 19, 1998 @ 3:00 am.

K.L. Now, you said something about the A.D.A. and the Judge setting your trial up so that you wouldn't be allowed to call witnesses and present your evidence that proves your innocence, you do understand how hard it would be for you to convince a society that does not believe that Judges and A.D.A.'s do things like that. That is pretty hard to believe that they would do something like that to you.

N.Z. To be honest with you I still don't believe it, I might need a little convincing myself. It's like (I am living in a nightmare that I never woke up from.) But for those of you who don't believe it, I would direct everyone to read pages 29 -37 of the trial transcript.

Note: The actual and exact trial transcripts to Sean's case can be found in the appendix Chapter of this book.

N.Z. (cont'd) Just from the way he responds to my 1997 case when the A.D.A.

started to go into it in depth you can tell that there was no way I was going

to get a fair trial in accordance with the law:

EXCERPTS FROM SEAN'S TRIAL

TRANSCRIPTS: Pages 29 - 38

THE COURT: As to both indictments at the present time.

Let's do Sandoval

Miss Bishop, I will hear you on Sandoval

MS. BISHOP: Yes, Judge. Judge, I have an up-dated copy of the

defendant's rap sheet. I don't know –

THE COURT: Just tell me what your application is.

MS. BISHOP: I'll start with the first entry on the rap sheet, which is as to

YO disposition. I won't be seeking to inquire about the facts, just that this

defendant, using the name Nicholas Willis, which is different than what he's charged

with in this case, that he used that name and that he warranted during the course

of that proceeding after he had pled guilty.

Do you just want me to continue?

THE COURT: Continue.

MS. BISHOP: As for the arrest on September the 9, 1993 for

forgery, your Honor. The defendant pled guilty to criminal possession of stolen property in the fifth degree. He warranted three times during the course of this case. He used a different name, that of Nicholas Willis.

And the facts of that case I would seek to inquire about if he testified. The defendant used a credit card that did not belong to him to purchase a computer that cost in excess of $3,000 through the mail. The company notified the police and a controlled discovery was set up. And the defendant signed the Federal Express receipt using the name of the individual whose credit card he used.

And furthermore he also used that same credit card to buy three airline tickets.

Additionally, Judge, moving on to the May 31, 1994 arrest, the defendant pled guilty to criminal possession of stolen property in the fifth degree on November the 2nd. He warranted during that case. He used the name of Nicholas Willis.

And so the Court is aware, the facts of that case involve the following. The detectives executed a bench warrant that related to the YO case and the previous forgery case. And then when they got to the defendant's house they went to his room and found a semi-automatic handgun lying out on his dresser.

THE COURT: What date is this one?

MS. BISHOP: This is -- the arrest date was 5/31/94. They found this handgun out on the dresser. They also recovered four spent shell casings and an empty clip. They did some investigation on this gun and

76

learned it had been stolen five months earlier from the true owner who lived in Brooklyn. The detectives also recovered a 357 Magnum handgun from the couch in the living room.

And just so the Court knows, the defendant indicated that he was living at home with his mother at the time. These items were recovered from his household.

Moving on to January the 27, 1997, the arrest for possession of a forged instrument. The defendant pled guilty. This is a Manhattan case to the E felony of grand larceny. He received a year of incarceration for that. In that case he used the name Nicholas Zimmerman.

And the facts of that case are as follows.

He went into the, one of the Wiz locations in Manhattan and attempted to purchase a computer valued at $3,000 using a stolen credit card.

Judge, this brings me to the Queens arrest in March of 1997. And I have a rather lengthy application to make with regard to this particular arrest, if you will bear with me.

THE COURT: Uh-huh.

MS. BISHOP: The defendant was charged with possessing a forged instrument. He ultimately pled guilty to the D felony. Went to jail for 18 months to 54 months. He used the name Nicholas Willis and Nicholas Zimmerman. And the name Sean was associated with this case as well.

77

Your Honor, this case involved an investigation with the New York City Police Department, the Postal Inspector, as well as the United States Secret Service. They executed search warrants on the defendant's house and recovered the following: The defendant possessed an excess of 25 credit cards in the names of other individuals. He possessed plastic cards purporting to be credit cards in various stages of completion. He possessed blank plastics, two encoding machines, personal and company checks in the names of other individuals, documents purporting to be business checks in various stages of completion, reams of blank basketweave check paper, documents bearing the names and personal and financial information, including social security numbers, of over 200 people, convenience and personal checks of individuals other than that of the defendant, merchant receipts and names other than that of defendant bearing the credit card numbers and signatures of numerous credit card holders, computer disks bearing personal and financial information of individuals other than the defendant, a check endorsement stamp, credit card financial and personal mail addressed to other people other than the defendant.

They also recovered a 32 caliber semiautomatic firearm with a loaded magazine and in excess of 40 rounds of ammunition.

The defendant was listed as the secondary user on at least 10 accounts at Bank One that were opened by the request of an individual named Nicholas Zimmerman, and the total losses the bank suffered in connection with these accounts was $25,000. These cards were also recovered during the search of the defendant's house.

And by the way, additional cards related to the Bank 1 part of this case were recovered on the defendant during his Manhattan arrest in January of '97.

In addition, the defendant opened two credit cards in the names of George Lewis (ph) and Michael Allen (ph) that resulted in over $7500 of loss to a company named Household Credit Services. The police recovered a list bearing the personal information of these two individuals during the execution of the search warrant.

In addition, the defendant opened AT&T credit card accounts in his name, and AT&T suffered losses in excess of $21,000. This credit card was also recovered during the search. He also possessed seven other credit cards in others' names that resulted in a loss to the Wiz and the Wiz Company Credit Card Corporation in excess of $35,000.

He possessed one of the personal encoders to encode several American Express cards, and he used his home address, where he was living at the time where this search warrant was executed, in his application to apply for some of these American Express cards. The police, when they executed this warrant, tell me the defendant possessed credit cards with an aggregate value of in excess of $100,000. He possessed eight counterfeit Visa cards with the Visa access codes.

Since May 1st of 1995 the police have recovered counterfeit checks

79

resulting in excess of $60,000 lost to legitimate companies, all of which were associated -- evidence of which was recovered during the search of his house. He possessed an encoder capable of encoding amounts on payroll checks to various companies around the state and country. He possessed mail belonging to other residents on the block that he had no permission or authority to possess. And he possessed counterfeit business checks from a company in Brooklyn.

And by the way, some of the checks that he printed were actually signed, endorsed, and deposited into other accounts.

In addition to these facts I will also be seeking to introduce his plea allocution in that case, Judge.

THE COURT: You have a copy of that plea allocution? Can I see it?

MS. BISHOP: The copy is -- I should have it later today or first thing in the morning, Judge. The minutes have been requested. I'm also seeking to cross examine on the name Sean Zimmerman, which he gave to law enforcement on July 19th of 2001. And as this Court has already heard, and as his rap sheet indicates, the defendant has used at least four different social security numbers, and he's used them on multiple occasions.

The social security number 104-**-3147 belongs to a Jung Jao (ph). Social security number 104-**-3148 belongs to a Miss Sheri Fletcher. Social security number ending in 3149 belongs to a Ladonna Silvers (ph).

80

THE COURT: 3149?

MS. BISHOP: 3149. And the number ending in 3169 belongs to a
Michael Martinez (ph).

Judge, each of the actions that -- each of these cases -including the
warrants, the use of different names, the use of different social security numbers --
each of these actions indicates a willingness of the defendant to put his own
interests above that of anyone else in society. And I would submit to this Court
that's specifically with regard to the charges involving forgery, that bears directly on
his credibility. And I ask that, Judge, you allow me to examine the defendant should
he testify.

THE COURT: Miss Bishop, am I correct in stating that on June 10,
1997 he pled guilty to 170.40, possession of forgery device, a D felony, for which he
was sentenced to 18 to 54 months. Is that correct?

Ms. Bishop: Judge –

The Court: At least that's the date of sentence.

MS. BISHOP: I think he pled guilty on 5/8 of '97. You're referring
to the Queens case?

THE COURT: Yes.

MS. BISHOP: He was then sentenced in June. That's the big case.

THE COURT: Anything else?

Ms. Bishop: No, judge.

81

N.Z. (Cont'd) So after he heard about that case in '97 he started to make a lot of bad decisions, he started to deny me a lot of things that I would normally be entitled to under the law. The biggest denial came when he wouldn't allow me to present my evidence to the jury. I couldn't believe he did that.

K.L. Yeah, I actually remember reading that part of the trial and it's like they were more focused on everything you did in 1997 than what actually happened in this case. Do you feel like you are really serving time for that case instead of the weapons possession case, sort of like a double jeopardy?

N.Z. I don't think there is any question to the fact that although I have already paid my debt to society with that previous case, that I am being resentenced all over again. I don't think there is a prisoner in the State of New York that has been sentenced to as much time as I have for a case such as mine. There were witnesses at the scene of the crime that say I didn't fire a gun and that I wasn't there, there are witnesses that place me clear across town at the time of the crime, there is no gun recovered with my fingerprints on it, and we later find out that the D.A.'s only witness never positively identified me to the police the night that this happened but I somehow wind up with eighteen years in prison. I don't think people need to be convinced any further that something is very wrong with my case.

K.L.   I don't even think Shyne got as much time as you did, didn't he get less time

than you?

N.Z.   Let's compare his case to mine. He was arrested with a gun, shots were fired

from his gun, about 10 witnesses said they saw him with a gun, he admitted

he had the gun and someone is actually shot with a gun in his case and he

is sentence to (ten) years in prison.

K.L.   And you are sentenced to almost double that, I agree that things are totally

wrong in your situation. Now you say after the Judge was told about your

1997 conviction he made a lot of "bad decisions", what are some of the bad

decisions he made?

N.Z.   He made a lot of bad decisions but I will give you a couple just for the reader's

information. If you notice, almost immediately after he hears about the things

that went on in 1997, my lawyer asks for an adjournment so that my alibi

witnesses can make it to the Courthouse. Usually, when lawyers ask for

adjournments, and the adjournments have anything to do with the need to

obtain witness testimony, it gets approved because the right to call witnesses

is too important to a trial and the courts have to make sure that the defendant

is allowed to call his witnesses because these are the witnesses who can

verify what actually happened in the case. My Judge didn't want anybody

testifying on my behalf, especially anyone who could clear my name of

everything. So he denied the request for the adjournment and everything pretty much went downhill from there.

EXCERPTS FROM SEAN'S TRIAL

TRANSCRIPTS: Pages 18-19

MR. O'MEARA: Your Honor, one last time I would request an

adjournment in relation to the alibi witnesses

THE COURT: No, sir. You entered into a stipulation that these

witnesses would be produced by Monday in the district attorney's office. That has

not happened. We are going to take a couple of days possibly to pick the jury. In

the meantime if you can get these witnesses in with enough time for her to speak

with them, they may testify.   But if they are not produced in the People's Office

before we have openings, then they're going to be precluded. That's my ruling.

End of Transcript

K.L.   The Judge is saying that your lawyer agreed to take the witnesses to the

D.A.'s office and that he subsequently failed to do that, what is going on

there?

N.Z.   To fully understand that situation you would first have to understand the

incompetence of the lawyer I had. The lawyer that represented me at the trial

made a lot of decisions that would eventually ruin my life. There is no law

84

that says that in order for a defendant to be allowed to call witnesses they must first take the witnesses to the D.A.'s office to be interviewed. The burden of proof is on the D.A., not the defendant. Therefore, I would not have had to force my witnesses to go to the D.A.'s office if he wouldn't have entered into that agreement with the D.A. But for the sake of argument, I was willing to have the witnesses go to the D.A.'s office to be interview before the trial. That was the purpose of the adjournment we requested. We were waiting on the witnesses to return to New York so they can be interviewed, but my previous case pushed the Judge to make a lot of bad decisions, and that was one of them.

K.L. Are there any rules of law that says he can not deny you an adjournment for something like that?

N.Z. Actually, there is 30 years of established caselaw that says he can not do what he did. There are thousands of cases out there, but the leading case is People v. Foy (346 N.Y.S.2D, 245), the highest court in the State of New York said: "Refusal to grant adjournment to permit the accused to secure the attendance of two alibi witnesses was an abuse of discretion requiring a new trial" @ 245. So he pretty much broke that law when he denied the adjournment.

K.L. Maybe he didn't know about that law?

N.Z. That man has been handling law for more than twenty years, trust me, he

85

knew about that law, he just didn't care about it.

K.L. Now, you're asking for adjournment for your witnesses to get to the Courthouse, who were these witnesses?

N.Z. They were the four brothers of the Rhythm and Blues group Soul for Real, my lawyer had already informed the Judge and the A.D.A. that they were going to testify on my behalf in so far as they performed at Club Jam-Rock in Long Island on September 19, 1998 at 3:00 am (See Exhibit A) and that I performed immediately before them at 2:30 am. My lawyer had contacted one of the group's members and they told him that they were out of town on a tour, but that they would be back in New York in four days, in time for the trial. So that was the purpose of the adjournment, to wait until they got back to New York.

K.L. So these witnesses' testimony would have cleared your name of any wrongdoing. If Nakia says you attacked her at 3:00 a.m., and they're saying that you performed with them at 3:00 a.m., then the jury would have obviously picked up on the fact that this was a case of mistaken identity.

N.Z. Mistaken identity? Nah, this is not a case of mistaken identity. This is a case of an A.D.A. abusing her authority as such and threatening, manipulating and coercing a young black sister into helping them get rid of a young black man. That's what this case is about.

K.L. I'm pretty sure you were upset at the fact that the Judge decided to start the trial without your witnesses being present, so what happened after that?

N.Z.   After the Judge denies our request for the adjournment for these witnesses

to appear, we made another request for two other witnesses to be allowed to

testify. One witness was the promoter of the event at Club Jam-Roc and the

other was my manager. They were both present at the event and they could

have verified my presence at the Club. Once again, the Judge did not want

anyone to come forth and clear my name of these charges so he found any

excuse to deny it.

EXCERPTS FROM SEAN'S TRIAL

TRANSCRIPTS: Page 561 - 563, and 569

Exhibit 3's transcript

MR. 0'MEARA: Your Honor, as I have mentioned on Friday, the

contract that was signed by Mr. Zimmerman's manager and the promoter of the

venue where he was to perform the night of this incident. I have the contract. I have

both parties who signed the contracts as well as promotional fliers created by one

of those parties.

Your Honor, they're not going to testify that he was there that night.

They're only going to testify so far as these documents are the original documents.

They either signed them or had them created. Therefore, it should be allowed into

evidence.

THE COURT: People wish to be heard?

MS. BISHOP: Yes. As far as the witnesses go regarding this contract, they have absolutely no relevance to the charges in this case. First of all, they weren't a part of the alibi notice that defense counsel provided, and, furthermore, they're not really testifying about an alibi. They're testifying about an agreement that he made to be somewhere several hours before this happened.

So there is really no relevance to where he was before 3 o'clock in the morning. And counsel just said they're not going to be testifying that he was even there. It's just going to be they had this document and they put together some fliers about it. So I submit that this Court should not allow those witnesses to take the stand. They will only confuse the jury. They have no relevance.

THE COURT: It's not signed by the defendant either, is it?

MR. O'MEARA: Your Honor, it mentions his name, the contract. They can testify that was the stage name he went by at the time. Furthermore, the notice of alibi does state where Mr. Zimmerman was going to be. That is also within the contract and the fliers, your Honor. These witnesses should be allowed to testify. The district attorney was given notice he was, he would be at Jam Rock, a club out in Nassau County. There is no prejudice so far as it is allowing this contract and this material to be presented to the jury. If they choose to disregard or disbelieve it, so be it. That's up to the jury to decide.

THE COURT: What concerns me is the purpose of offering this is for the

88

purpose of showing an alibi in my opinion. And because you did not produce the witnesses for the defendant, for the People, that were on the notice, and because these people were not on the notice, it appears to the Court you're trying to get through the back door what you can't get through the front door. At this point we're still looking up cases in regard to this. My law secretary is still checking cases. So I'm going to reserve decision on that right now for the moment.

(After a short recess, the court returned, and made the following decision:)

Excerpt from Page 569

In regard to the evidence of the contract, it's the opinion of the Court that it is a method of seeking to get evidence relating to alibi in in an improper manner where the proper manner of presenting the alibi has not been obtained. Accordingly, that testimony will be precluded and the defendant has an exception in the record for that. Okay. That's the ruling of the Court.

End of Transcript

K.L.   There is a little confusion going on with your witnesses, the A.D.A. is saying that she doesn't want your witnesses to testify because they "will only confuse the jury"? Explain to the readers what's happening there.

N.Z.   That's just an indirect way of saying "Judge, let's hide the truth from the jury, let's deny his witnesses for absolutely no reason." In all my research of the law I have never found a case that says alibi witness testimony "confuses the jury". I think the jury is smart enough to decide the truth from a lie. The A.D.A. didn't want the truth to come out about my innocence so she asked the Judge to deny my witnesses' testimony, and he agreed. It was that simple.

K.L. The Judge is saying that he had a problem with the fact that these witnesses' names are not on the "notice of alibi". What is a notice of alibi and why is it so important?

N.Z. Under New York Law, before the defense is allowed to call alibi witnesses to a trial they must first fill out a notice of alibi, which is basically just a piece of paper with the witnesses' names, addresses, and phone numbers and what they plan to testify to. My lawyer did file a notice of alibi but he didn't add the names of my manager and promoter (Haron Wilson and Theophulas Brown). He only added the members of Soul for Real (Andre, Brian and Chriss Dalyrymple). (See Exhibit D). So because he failed to add these witnesses' names to the notice of alibi, this gave the Judge an opening to deny these witnesses an opportunity to testify as well.

K.L. But shouldn't your lawyer be penalized for that mistake, why should you be denied your right to call your witnesses because of a simple mistake like that?

N.Z. Actually, I have done some research on that issue and I've found that both my lawyer and the Judge was wrong in that instance. In cases like People v.

Morales (372 NYS2D 25, Court of Appeals 1975) the highest Court in the

State of New York stated that it is unreasonable to deny a man his right to

call witnesses because their names is not listed in the notice of alibi.

K.L.   I'm pretty sure the members of the jury realized that you were trying to prove

your innocence but the Judge and the A.D.A. is precluding you from doing

so?

N.Z.   The judge made the jury members leave the court when all this was going on,

the jury didn't know that I had witnesses in the court that could testify that I

wasn't at the scene of the crime. He made sure that they didn't hear any part

of that conversation. So without them knowing that, they convicted me.

Actually, the funny part of this story, if there is one, is that after the trial my

lawyer asked two of the jury members what did they base their reasoning on

to convict me? They both told him that they convicted me because I didn't

present any evidence or testimony that proves that I wasn't at the scene of

the crime.

K.L.   What exactly went through your mind when you heard that?

N.Z.   I just couldn't believe that this judge would do something like that to me. It's

just unbelievable.

K.L.   How many other witnesses were present at club Jam-Rock that could verify

you were there?

91

N.Z.   We've found two other witnesses, Barry Alexander and Latrina Boyd. Barry was also a promoter to the event and Latrina performed at the club on the same night that I did. We obtained affidavits from both of them, and they also state that I was at the club at 3:00 a.m. (See Exhibits E and F).

K.L.   I also read the affidavits from Samuel Belnavis and Natascha Dockery. In their statements they say that they were present when the altercation took place in front of Jatanya's house. They also state that they seen the person who fired the shots, and that the person was not you. (See Exhibits G and H). Their testimony would have definitely shed light on the situation had the jury been aware of it.

N.Z.   Samuel Belnavis is Jatanya's father and Natascha Dockery is Jatanya's neighbor. They were both at the scene of the crime when the situation took place and they know what really happened that night. But once again, thanks to the incompetence of the lawyer I had he didn't call these witnesses either. Had these witnesses testified I wouldn't be in prison today.

K.L.   What was the name of your trial lawyer?

N.Z.   Brendan O'Meara. He has an office in the Bronx, N.Y. I advise anyone that's being represented by this man to get away from him as soon as possible, he will completely ruin your case and your life and by the time you realize it, it will be too late.

92

5B. Sean's lawyer waives

the most important motion

in his case

K.L.   There is a part of your trial where your lawyer tells the judge that he wants to "waive all motions and go directly to trial". I want you to first explain to the readers what a motion is, and how did your lawyer ruin your case by waiving this motion.

N.Z.   A motion is just a legal term for a request, so when your lawyer makes a motion he is just requesting that the judge do something for him in relation to the case. Motions or (requests) can be made orally or in writing but most times they're made in writing.

K.L.   How did waiving your motions or requests ruin your case?

N.Z.   When my lawyer told the Judge that he wanted to waive "all motions" he waived the most important motion in my case. In 1967 the Supreme Court announced a landmark case in United States v. Wade (87 Sct. 1926). In that case the Supreme Court recognized that there were too many cases of mistaken identity going around. It also noticed that the police were forcing and/or encouraging witnesses to identify the wrong people in crimes. There were so many cases of mistaken identity going around that the Supreme Court decided to step in and do something about it. So what they basically did was announce a rule of law that says whenever a complaining witness

93

comes forth and alleges that they were in some way assaulted by another person, they must identify that person in a line-up, while the person stands next to five or six other people. This is to ensure that the complaining witness is 100% sure that the person they pick out at the line-up is the person that attacked them, and that there aren't any mistakes in the identification process. In my case, my lawyer waived my (Wade) motions. They're only called "Wade" motions because they were named after the landmark case of United States v. Wade. If my lawyer wouldn't have waived all my motions, I would have been entitled to a Wade hearing (before the trial started) and at this hearing we would have been able to question Nakia as to why she thinks it's me that committed this crime against her. Just the fact alone that this crime took place at 3:00 a.m. in Rosedale, Queens raises a lot of doubt to the identification. Anyone who lives in Rosedale knows that at 3:00 a.m. there's not much light out there, and more specifically the block that this crime took place on, there is almost no light on that street.

K.L.   I've actually went to that street myself a couple of weeks ago. I went there around 2:30 a.m. and you're right, there is little light out there. There is almost no light in front of the house that Nakia says she is attacked at.

N.Z.   And these are the things that needed to come out at the Wade hearing, but my lawyer waived that hearing.

K.L.   I understand now why that hearing is so important to your case, but I don't understand why your lawyer would waive this hearing if it would have helped prove your innocence.

N.Z. I really don't understand it myself.

K.L. Do you think he was working with the Judge and the A.D.A. to convict you?

N.Z. I don't think I would go as far as to say that. I haven't uncovered anything about him or my case to suggest that he was working with them. At this point, I still think his actions were based on pure mistakes and incompetence. I don't think anything he did to my case and my life was purposeful, but then again, you never know.

K.L. I've read some of your appeals to the courts and I noticed that the A.D.A. constantly argues to the Judge that your lawyer waived (all motions) because he felt that "the People couldn't find their complaining witness" and since he felt that they couldn't "find their witness" (Nakia Stubbs), his "strategy" was to waive your motions and go directly to trial, thereby doing so, the A.D.A. would have less time to find (Nakia), and if they couldn't find Nakia in time for trial, then you would have won your case. The A.D.A. claims that this was your lawyer's "strategy" and pursuant to the Supreme Court law of Strickland v. Washington (104 Sct. 2052) 1984 the fact that a lawyer's "strategy" does not work at trial and the defendant happens to get convicted because of his lawyer's mistakes doesn't automatically mean that the defendant gets his conviction overturned. What's your position on that issue?

N.Z. The only way you can label my lawyer's actions a "strategy" or a "strategic move" is if you were to say that my lawyer's "strategy" was to get me convicted from the beginning of the trial. What "strategy" could there be in not calling witnesses that would have testified that I was clear across town at the time that this crime was committed? What "strategy" could there be in not calling witnesses that would have testified that I wasn't the one that fired the gun and that I wasn't at the scene of the crime? What "strategy" could there be in waving the only hearing that would have shed light on the entire situation? His actions weren't "strategic", they were borderline stupid if you ask me.

Excerpt from Page 3

MR. O'MEARA: Acknowledge receipt and note my objection to their statement of readiness, Your Honor. If they can't even tell us where the identification witness is they certainly cannot be ready to proceed to trial.

THE COURT: I think the only way you can challenge that actually is by going to trial. If you want me to set up a trial date -

Excerpt from Page 7

THE COURT: Do you want to waive motions and go to trial right away, you said?

96

MR. O'MEARA: Your Honor, then I waive motions and we will go
directly to trial.

Excerpt Ends

K.L. After reading the transcripts to your trial it is apparently obvious that your
lawyer was calling the A.D.A.'s bluff as to whether or not they were actually
ready for trial, even the judge tells him "the only way to challenge their
readiness is by actually going directly to trial" without motions. I think even
a layman to the law can see that your lawyer got caught up in a ego battle
between himself and the A.D.A., and that battle led to him waving all your
hearings. I don't see any strategy in that.

N.Z. I fail to see any strategy myself. If you noticed in the transcripts, my lawyer
tells the judge that the A.D.A. "can't even tell us where the complaining
witness is" and so they can't be ready for trial. I seriously doubt my lawyer
was looking for Nakia. It's my understanding that Nakia has lived at the same
house for the past twenty years. All he had to do was go to her house and
talk to her, so I don't think he was really looking for her.

Interview Closed

5C. Sean's gets into a heated

discussion with Judge Rosengarten

at his sentencing court date

After Sean was convicted by the jury, Judge Rosengarten set a court date for

sentencing. At the sentencing date, Sean's family and friends showed up in record

numbers. They submitted affidavits and letters to the Judge about Sean's character

and business ventures. Family members and Ministers came from as far away as

Florida and Maryland to speak on Sean's behalf. Judge Rosengarten, disregarding

his duties in being fair and impartial, denied the ministers and family members an

opportunity to speak on Sean's behalf, and instead took a personal attack on Sean's

credibility and reputation while his family stood in disbelief. Here's what happened:

Excerpts from Pages 4 - 26

MS. BISHOP: Yes, Judge.

THE COURT: People wish to be heard?

MS. BISHOP: Yes, Judge.

THE COURT: Go ahead.

MS. BISHOP: Your Honor, I'd just like to start by asking the Court to

take note of this defendant's general disregard for the criminal justice system and

for law enforcement.

He, in the course of his criminal career, has used five aliases, and he's warranted in almost every case. And those are just sort of -- I think that reflects his general attitude towards the criminal justice system, but I'd like to specifically comment on his attitude towards the Court in this case that's presently before the Court.

First, as you know, he used an alias in this case, and more significantly, he warranted for almost three years during the course of this case. And, your Honor, I submit that the defendant's warranting in this case was intentional. In fact, in November of 1998, approximately two to three months after he actually failed to appear in Part AP6, he told another individual that he was on the run, so I submit to this Court that his actions were intentional, and that there was no confusion on his part about whether or not he had a pending felony case against him.

Secondly, this defendant, in spite of the Court's instructions to the contrary, had his girlfriend contact my complainant in this case, in violation of an Order of Protection, in an effort to dissuade her from coming to court to testify in this matter. As the Court will recall, there was also sworn testimony at the trial concerning the defendant and his girlfriend's efforts to pay off the complainant, not once but twice, also in an effort to dissuade her from moving forward with the case against him.

Your Honor, just for a moment, I'd like to comment on the witnesses that this defendant presented to you at trial, namely his girlfriend, Jatanya Belnavis,

99

who, throughout the course of this proceeding, has demonstrated to this Court a willingness to lie for the defendant. It started with her efforts to bail the defendant out of jail. It continued with her efforts to contact the complaining witness to offer her money. It was -- it continued during the course of the trial with her efforts to contact the complainant. And by the way, when the Warrant Squad went looking for this defendant, she said she had no idea where the defendant was at that time. And yet, she came in and under oath said that she had been with him for all these years.

So, you know, Judge, I -- I believe that this defendant has an ability to manipulate others, including his family and those he's close to, to aid him in his committing deceit on others and this Court, and I submit that he's done that throughout the course of this trial.

I'd like to also comment on this -- this kind of hyper-like behavior. It's a very antisocial form of behavior of this defendant putting his own interests not only above society as a whole, but above his family members and his friends. Look at the nature of his past convictions: larceny, forgery, possession of stolen property. These -- these convictions all demonstrate his -- his insidious ability to deceive those around him.

And, Judge, I submit that if you look through the package that his family has submitted to the Court, you'll see things in there -- there are statements that this man was wrongfully accused. That he's simply a businessman building a business empire. And I submit to the Court that they, too, have been blinded by this man's manipulation. And in support of this, I'd like to submit to the Court the information on his conviction from 1997: guns, credit cards, credit card encoding machines, forged --

THE COURT: I have his probation report from the prior conviction.

MS. BISHOP: These were recovered from his home where he lived with his mother and where his girlfriend frequently visited. So, you know, I submit to the Court that -- that his -- his close friends and family are simply unwilling to see what the true Nicholas Zimmerman is.

And finally, Judge, I've got two final things to say. First, that the defendant cannot be treated as a discretionary persistent felon in this case due to the fact that we -- the D.A.'s office could not get him sentenced quickly enough before he went and committed another crime, so he's been able to benefit from a loophole in the sentencing laws. He's really not going to be adequately punished for -- based on the true nature of his past, and I think the Court should take that into account in the sentencing of him on this case.

As you can tell from his rap sheet, he was arrested for a felony in January, not sentenced on that felony until May, but he committed another felony in the intervening March, and that's the only reason why I'm unable to ask for discretionary treatment today.

Furthermore, his nonviolent record really does not adequately portray his criminal actions in the past. In both the '94 Queens case and the '97 Queens case, loaded operable firearms were recovered from the defendant's home, so I submit to this Court that this is not the first instance of violence in this defendant's criminal past. I think it's appropriate for the Court to consider that in imposing sentence on the defendant today.

Your Honor, I will be asking this judge to sentence the defendant to the maximum, which is 15 years. I have case law in support of this if the Court's interested in reviewing it at this time.

THE COURT: Thank you. Mr. O'Meara.

MR. O'MEARA: Judge -

THE DEFENDANT: Judge -- I wish to be heard, Judge.

THE COURT: Well, Mr. O'Meara first, then Mr. Zimmerman, unless Mr. O'Meara doesn't want to be heard.

MR. O'MEARA: Your Honor, the first person I'd like the Court to hear from is the defendant's mother, Mrs. Willis, if she'll step up.

MS. BISHOP: I object to this, your Honor.

THE COURT: No, sir. I'll hear from you and from Mr. Zimmerman, nobody else.

MR. O'MEARA: Your Honor, the family's here to speak on the behalf of their family member.

THE COURT: I've read all the letters. There is no provision for them to speak.

MR. O'MEARA: Your Honor, he's about to be sentenced to many

years of prison. He should have at least the benefit of the Court hearing from his

family members.

THE COURT: No, sir, there's no provision in the law for that, sir.

I've read their letters.

MR. O'MEARA: Your Honor -

THE COURT: You can tell me what they were going to say.

MR. O'MEARA: Your Honor, what they're basically going to say is

that Mr. Zimmerman has been conducting himself as a productive member of

society. He has been running a business on behalf of himself and his family. Your

Honor, he has been involved with the Internet, and he has been involved in sales of

the Internet, and he has been attempting to get involved in the music industry, and

that putting him away for such an extended period of time would basically take out

his shining light insofar as he does have the ability to be a productive member of

society, your Honor.

In the past couple of years, he has shown that. Albeit he did not come

back to court in this case in 1998; nevertheless, during that time he was running a

productive business, a legitimate business, your Honor. He is a young man. He is

a very intelligent young man. He might not have been given the opportunities that

other people were given growing up; however, he has shown that he has the abilities

to take his intelligence and to use it in a productive manner and to be a productive

103

member of society.

And, your Honor, as far as his prior convictions, they are nonviolent. What the district attorney says about, well, what he really should have been considered, that's really not fair to Mr. Zimmerman. They were nonviolent offenses, your Honor, and that should also be taken into consideration.

Now, your Honor, finally, I just request that you do allow -- that you only sentence Mr. Zimmerman to the minimum amount of time under the law, which is five years. And, your Honor, Mr. Zimmerman would like to make his own statement at this time.

THE COURT: Mr. Zimmerman.

THE DEFENDANT: Your Honor, sorry about the outburst.

THE COURT: That's okay, sir.

THE DEFENDANT: I waited a long time for this day to be heard. The D.A., she's making allegations that I was rude through the trial and the things that I was saying. I sat here quietly during the trial. I didn't make one noise, one peep. I showed respect to the trial, to the jury, to my lawyer, to the D.A. I let her say things about me that's not true. I didn't say anything back. I don't know why she's saying that I was rude through the trial. I don't understand -

THE COURT: I don't recall her saying that.

THE DEFENDANT: She's saying my attitude during the criminal justice system.

104

THE COURT: Well, it wasn't during this trial. She means -- I'm sure she means your general attitude in all the things you've gotten caught and your past convictions.

THE DEFENDANT: Well, my general --

THE COURT: And the fact that you failed to come back in this case.

THE DEFENDANT: My general attitude towards this case or any other case that I've had, which, when I was guilty, I pleaded guilty to cases in the past when I was guilty. This one, I just didn't plead guilty to cause I'm not guilty. I did not do any of these things that this girl is saying I did. The D.A. failed to even ask me or have a, you know, discussion with me about this case, even though it's not procedure that she do that, but at least if you're offering me five years, at least come to me and ask me, you know, am I guilty, or what happened that night, some kind of statement.

We have no statement from what Nikia wrote to the cops that night. We have no way to know what she actually told them that night up until this day, so she could have told them she don't know who did it that night, and then today she's saying a different story as to what the D.A. may have put in her head. .

From what I understand, she didn't want to come to court. She's told us plenty of times: I don't want to go through with the trial. It was a mistake; I'm sorry. I'm not coming back to court. That was the whole reason why I didn't have her on

105

right now.

Your Honor, this individual in question who said that I'm on the run, that I admitted to them that I'm on the run, who is this individual? Who's she talking about? She's been saying this throughout the trial. Who did I tell that I'm on the run? (sic) And tell anyone that I'm on the run, cause I was not considered to be on the run at that time.

I've seen Nakia in the street during that time. We've had conversations. I didn't know anything about this case was pending. I would like to know who -- if you can ask her who was to say that I was on the run, your Honor, if you could actually ask the D.A.

THE COURT: No, sir.

THE DEFENDANT: Well, your Honor --

THE COURT: It's irrelevant to this, in any event.

THE DEFENDANT: All right. Well, what is relevant to this case is, I would like to ask the D.A., does she have any knowledge of why the bail bondsman came back and took back my bail when I posted a $35,000 bond. Does she know any reason why they would do that, your Honor. I think that has relevancy to this case, your Honor.

THE COURT: It's irrelevant, sir. He felt you were evidently a flight risk.

THE DEFENDANT: No, your Honor, that's not the truth, your

106

Honor. I have reason to believe that that's not the truth. If you would just ask her the question, your Honor. I have reason to believe that's not the truth.

THE COURT: What else do you want to say, sir; go ahead. Anything else?

THE DEFENDANT: You're not going to ask her the question, your Honor?

THE COURT: No, sir.

THE DEFENDANT: Your Honor, I'd like to raise a prejudicial issue at this time.

THE COURT: Go ahead, sir.

THE DEFENDANT: First, I'd like to read a 30.30 motion.

Any time the rendition of a verdict of guilty before the sentence of the Court made upon a defendant to set aside or modify a verdict or any part thereof upon the following grounds: Any ground appearing in the record which if raised upon appeal of the respective judgment of conviction for a crime reversal or modification of the judgment as a matter of law by an appellate court.

Your Honor, I feel it's a prejudicial issue for the D.A. to question Detective Khenil (phonetics) about me being on parole and about where he arrested me at, and that he contacted my parole officer two weeks before I was arrested and asked him what day I was coming in so -- so he could have a meeting with me, or things of that nature.

107

If you remember, your Honor, when the – when the D.A. came -- when the jury asked the questions, they specifically asked that question, where was I arrested at? That mean they based their decision on that matter just alone. That they -- they realized that I was on parole. They asked two questions, and that was one of them.

Your Honor, I didn't take the stand, so why would my parole issue be a part of the testimony? I don't -- I don't know why that was raised.

THE COURT: Go ahead, sir.

THE DEFENDANT: Another thing, your Honor. I never had a chance for my preliminary hearings.

THE COURT: What --

THE DEFENDANT: My pretrial hearings, preliminary trials. I never had those hearings.

THE COURT: You waived motions.

THE DEFENDANT: Your Honor, I didn't waive motion.

THE COURT: Well, motions were waived in your behalf. I'm sure that was not done without your knowledge and consent.

THE DEFENDANT: The -- the conversation we had, your Honor, was that I was going to go to trial. The D.A. offered me five years on this matter. I said, no, I'm not taking the five years; I would like to go to trial. I didn't know anything about waiving preliminary hearings or pretrial hearings. I didn't even know the importance of them the date that they were waived. They were waived in arraignment If you could look at the record, they were waived in arraignment. I never had these hearings. Had I had these hearings, I would have known what I was dealing with, what was against me. You know, they found me guilty of possession of a weapon, and there's no weapon involved. That top charge may have been thrown out on just the preliminary hearings alone.

THE COURT: What else, sir?

THE DEFENDANT: Your Honor, one last thing I'd like to add.

THE COURT: Go ahead.

THE DEFENDANT: My alibi witness, your Honor. With all due respect, they were denied also in this case. I went to trial 11 days from the day I was arrested, your Honor, 11 days. I had 11 days to prepare a trial, your Honor. I was arrested. I was bailed out on this case on -- let me see. Your Honor, I posted bond on November 23rd on this case. I was rearrested by the D.A. Cops came to my house, rearrested me at the same address that I provided to the court. I didn't -I didn't up put any fight, any argument, nothing. I came right back in. I knew they was there. We knew the charges were going to come in. They arrested me at my house, brought me back in December 11th, your Honor. I went from December 11th to December 21st, I was found guilty at trial.

I had 11 days to prepare for a trial. I had to find people from three years ago: my manager, the club promoter, the club owner, the limo driver. I had to find

109

these people from three years ago, your Honor, to come to court and testify on my

behalf. And then when I do find them, they were denied because they said the

notice of alibi was late. How was I supposed to defend myself in 11 days?

THE COURT: First of all, sir, the Notice of Alibi, the decision

Judge Rotker made, that was -- that was abrogated by the fact that it was -- the

district attorney agreed to accept your Notice of Alibi and agreed -- and there was

an agreement that those witnesses will be produced before the D.A. for an interview

before they testified at trial. They were never produced for the district attorney to be

interviewed, as is their right.

THE DEFENDANT: And that's what I'm saying. I only had 11 days

to do this whole -- I was brought back in on December 11th. December 21st, the

trial was over. On December 19th, we tried to submit them to you and you denied

them, your Honor. With all due respect, how was I suppose to prepare in 11 days?

How was I supposed to prepare for a trial in 11 days, your Honor?

THE COURT: Well, that was your decision.

THE DEFENDANT: Yes, I understand it was my decision, but,

your Honor, the only thing I'm asking -I'm not asking for the sun, moon, and stars,

your Honor. I'm asking for at least a retrial where my alibi witnesses will be able to

testify.

THE COURT: That application is denied. You will be given a right

to appeal. If the Appellate Division feels that there was error in the trial, then that's how you're given a new trial. Is there anything else you want to say, sir?

THE DEFENDANT: There's just one last thing, your Honor.

THE COURT: Go ahead.

THE DEFENDANT: Which is -- which goes to the effect of me reserving my issues for an appeal.

I ask you one last time, your Honor, please investigate if the D.A. knows anything about why the bail bondsman -- this -- this -- if you would let me finish, you will see how it has some relevancy to the case, but only thing I'm saying, would you please investigate if she knows anything about why the bail bondsman would come here after they already knew I had a warrant from '98. They posted the bond with an indictment number from 1998. They already knew I had a warrant, so that's not an issue.

THE COURT: That's between -- that's between you and the bail bondsman. If you want to take up some action against the bail bondsman in a civil case, that's between you and him.

THE DEFENDANT: That's not what I'm saying, your Honor. The issue that I'm trying to raise here, your Honor, is, I specifically asked Judge Grosso for a bond so I can prepare my case. He granted the bond. He already knew I had a warrant on the same exact case. He granted the bond. He gave me a bail, which was at his discretion. I bailed out, and I have reason to believe that the D.A. did something with the bail bondsman towards this case. Had she not done that, my

111

alibi witness would have been on time. I would have still been on the street preparing

my case, your Honor. That's why it has some relevance to this case.

THE COURT: All right, thank you. I'm not going to direct the D.A.

to do anything. It's not my position to do so, all right. Anything else you want to

say, sir?

MR. O'MEARA: Yes, your Honor. Just that I did submit a 330

motion.

THE COURT: That's been denied. Motion's been denied. The

decision's being handed out..

MR. O'MEARA: And the last thing, your Honor, I again would ask to

at least allow for one family member to speak. One of his brothers came up from

Maryland from the Air Force, took the day off to try to have the opportunity -

THE COURT: No, sir, there is no provision in the law for that -- for

that to happen.

MR. O'MEARA: Nevertheless, your Honor, it's at your discretion to

allow him to speak on behalf of his brother.

THE COURT: I'm not going to allow it. You have an exception, all

right.

THE DEFENDANT: Thank you for your time, your Honor.

THE COURT: All right, sir.

Mr. Zimmerman or Mr. Willis, you're a very bright person. You're

112

probably bordering on genius, and your -- from your history, it's obvious your genius has been misdirected. While you may be running businesses in the past, you've run businesses of stealing. The records indicate that you've stolen somewhere in the vicinity of $200,000 in the past.

THE DEFENDANT: Your Honor, that's not true.

TE COURT: And you pled guilty on that case, and you were sentenced to a substantial period of time. Your letters and friends -- from friends and family indicate that you're a promising businessman, and it seems that in the past, your business involved the fraudulent manufacturing of credit cards, checks, and other financial instruments with a larcenous intent.

You may be, as I said, bright but your genius has been misdirected, even though it may be in the last couple of years been directed in the proper direction. But with your record, how these people can think that you can be painted as a role model for your younger relations and friends is beyond my comprehension. You presently have another felony case pending in Nassau County where you were arrested in 2001 for grand larceny, and you have a bail-jumping case pending here for which you jumped bail on this case and caused somebody $10,000 that they lost, and then you wonder why the insurance company had second thoughts about posting -- about continuing your bail in this case.

THE DEFENDANT: Your Honor --

THE COURT: It seems that your crimes have accelerated now

from those of a larcenous and fraudulent nature to ones of violence and intimidation and the carrying of weapons, loaded weapons, and firing of loaded weapons.

It's my opinion that the people of the county and the city need to be protected from predators, both financial and violent, and now you seem to have become both.

And I note that in your address to the Court, you primarily spoke about how unfair the D.A. was, how unfair the trial was, and how you were unfairly treated during the course of the trial, which I fail to see. But if an appellate court feels so, that's their -that's their province, not mine. Under the circumstances, I think that what the D.A. requests is not outrageous. In fact, it is reasonable.

Accordingly, and I want to point out that while Mr. O'Meara in his papers indicated because Miss Stubbs had a criminal record and that she could not be believable, her testimony was corroborated by somebody who was with her at the time. It was corroborated by a person who lived somewhere in that area who heard the shots and called the police. It's corroborated by the fact that the police recovered nine spent .9 millimeter shells from the area where it is alleged that you shot the gun. It was a crime of intimidation. I think you sought to instill fear and you succeeded, but you were caught and now you failed.

Under all the circumstances of your record and the facts of this case, on the first count of the indictment, you're remanded to the custody of the New York State Department of Corrections for a period of fifteen years. The second count,

114

seven years. The fourth count, one year, all to run concurrently with each other, with the statutorily required post-release supervision, and the charges will be taken from inmate funds, if available.

COURT CLERK: Very good.

THE DEFENDANT: Your Honor, may I ask one question before I leave?

THE COURT: Yes, sir.

THE DEFENDANT: I just want to -- one question. Somewhere during the trial, with all due respect, your Honor -- please, mom.

With all due respect, your Honor, somewhere during the trial, your opinion on this case was, and you said on the record to the D.A., I think you need to see your supervisor right now about throwing out this case. You're never going to get a conviction on this case, so how could you --

THE COURT: That's not what I said. I said there should be some kind of disposition in the case.

THE DEFENDANT: Yeah. You said -- because -you said -- your exact words was, disposing of this case.

THE COURT: That's right.

THE DEFENDANT: I think you need to see your supervisor.

THE COURT: Mm-hmm.

THE DEFENDANT: So if you thought then that the case was not

going to go anywhere, how could you give me 15 years now?

THE COURT: Well --

THE DEFENDANT: When the same testimony you heard then? What will be the -- what difference did you hear --

THE COURT: The jury has spoken with a decision and based upon your history --

THE DEFENDANT: But you knew my history then.

THE COURT: That's my -- that's my decision on the sentence. You have a right to appeal. The clerk is going to notify you of your right to appeal.

MS. BISHOP: Judge, I'd also just like to continue the Order of Protection in favor of the complainant.

THE COURT: The Order of Protection will be extended.

COURT CLERK: Final Order of Protection will be extended.

Sir, you're subject to a mandatory surcharge of $150, plus a $5 crime victims assistance fee, which will be taken out of inmate funds.

And in addition, sir, you have the right to appeal to the Appellate Division, Second Department, within 30 days. In addition, upon proof of your financial inability to retain counsel and pay the costs and expenses of the appeal, you have the right to apply to the Appellate Division, Second Department, for the assignment of counsel for leave to prosecute the appeal as a poor person and to dispense with printing.

116

(Continued on the next page to include the jurat.)

COURT CLERK: The Appellate Division, Second Department, is located at 45 Monroe Place, New York, and you're being handed a copy of the notice of the right to appeal. You may take him back.

CERTIFIED THAT THE FOREGOING IS A TRUE AND ACCURATE TRANSCRIPT OF THE ORIGINAL STENOGRAPHIC MINUTES IN THIS CASE.

Signed with Reporters Signature

Nora Lee, RPR

Official Court Reporter

End of Exhibit #5

(Interview Open)

K.L. Thirty days after the jury convicted you the judge ordered you back to court for sentencing, and at your sentencing court date you and him got into a pretty heated discussion. We're you upset at the way your trial was handled and that you weren't allowed to call witnesses?

N.Z. You know, after I was convicted, I was sent back to Rikers Island to wait for sentencing. So while I'm on Rikers Island, I started to do some research, and it starts to become so apparent to me that I was basically railroaded from the beginning to the end of my trial. I found so many constitutional laws that said a man should not be denied his right to call witnesses (especially alibi witnesses) just because their names are not on the "notice of alibi". (People v. Morales, 372 N.Y.S.2d, 25; Court of Appeals 1975).

I also found cases that said a lawyer can not "waive all your motions" in arraignment and announce that he is "ready for trial" in order to call the A.D.A.'s bluff as to whether or not they are actually ready for trial. (People v. Gil, 729 N.Y.S.2d 121, First Dept. 2001).

So, for the next thirty days all I did was research the law. I had this feeling that what was being done to me can not be right, and as I am researching the law I'm finding out that everything that took place at my trial was illegal and wrong. So I was preparing and making a list of all the cases that I found, and all the errors that took place at my trial, and I figured that as long as I am able to show the judge that the law says that he shouldn't have denied me my constitutional right to call witnesses, that he would respect all the laws that I found and grant me a new trial. But keep in mind, at this point, I am so naive to corruption, and the relationship that judges have with District Attorney's, and all the things that go on in the courts before you even step in the room. I was completely ignorant to the fact that District Attorney's and judges railroad innocent people and I was more for the position that what was done to me was mistakes or errors and as long as I was able to point out the judges and the A.D.A.'s mistakes, they would be fair and just and grant me a new trial in accordance with the law. So, the thirty days in between my conviction and my sentencing hearing, I pretty much spent every minute of that time in the law library.

K.L. I noticed that you are pointing out a lot of errors in your trial to the judge, and these errors are serious violations of law, but he doesn't seem to be paying you any attention. Did you ever get the feeling during that conversation that he truly doesn't care if you are innocent?

N.Z. I got that feeling during the trial, I got that feeling during that conversation, and I still get that feeling to this day. I've learned a lot from Judge Rosengarten, that man has completely convinced me that the Criminal Injustice System is in the business of putting innocent people in prison, and holding them there even when their innocence is obvious.

If you noticed, during that conversation, I'm showing him violations of state and federal law, violations of the United States Constitution, and violation of the Code of Ethics, and he is basically responding to me by saying: "yeah, um hum, whatever!" It's like he doesn't have any respect for the law.

K.L. Yeah, I see that. It's amazing how he totally ignored you.

N.Z. What's amazing is the fact that this is a judge acting like this. I just can't believe it.

119

K.L.   I think it's important that you clear some things up for the readers. A.D.A. Leigh Bishop made an extensive argument to the judge about your criminal background at your sentencing court date. She said, (and I quote), that you were "on the run from this case for three years" that you "told another individual that you were on the run" that you attempted to "pay off the complainant from testifying against you" and that you had your girlfriend (Jatanya) "contact the complainant" (Nakia), that you have "the ability to manipulate others" and that you have a "insidious ability to deceive those around you", that your family has been "blinded by your manipulation" and they are simply "unwilling to see the true Nicholas Zimmerman". What do you have to say about all of this?

N.Z.   You know what's funny about that? This is a lady who never met me before, never had any conversation with me, never laid eyes on me before the trial and doesn't even know me, but walks right into a Supreme Court and starts firing off at the mouth about "the real Nicholas Zimmerman". Isn't that something?

K.L.   What ran through your mind at that time?

N.Z.   I was thinking to myself, is this a court room or a movie theater, because there is a lot more acting going on then justice.

K.L.   (laughs) Yeah, that was a little over dramatic.

N.Z.   And lest we forget, after this lady calls me all of these names in front of my

120

family and friends and ministers, we later find out that she is the real manipulator, liar, and deceiver that she made me out to be. We found out that she threatened and coerced Nakia into identifying me at trial.

K.L.   Yes, I've read Nakia's affidavit, I know all about it . (See Exhibit I).

N.Z.   So what kind of justice can be served when you have A.D.A.'s threatening, coercing, and forcing witnesses to identify the wrong people in criminal trials? The A.D.A.'s is just as corrupt as the criminals they set up and place in prison.

K.L.   That's a good point. Leigh Bishop says you attempted to "pay off Nakia" not to testify against you, is that true?

N.Z.   Of course not. I never attempted to pay anybody. I didn't even know any money was mentioned during the case until it came out during the trial. Nobody ever asked me for any during the trial. I think they asked Jatanya, but she didn't give them anything. The readers would just have to read the transcripts to the trial to see what really happened.

K.L.   Bishop also goes on to say that you are a "manipulator" and that your "deceive those around you". What's your response to that?

N.Z.   She's right! I am a manipulator, I do deceive those around me! What do you think Al Sharpton is? Jesse Jackson? Minister Farrakhan? What do you think Martin Luther King, Malcolm X, and Marcus Garvey were? They too were labeled manipulator's and deceivers by the government and, in fact, they

121

were actually manipulators. They had to "manipulate" the black sisters and brothers to take a stand against their oppressors and fight for their civil rights, fight for a change in the laws, and fight for a change in the way things were done. Before these brothers decided to make a change and take a stand, the black sisters and brothers of America were not fighting for their constitutional rights as American citizens. There were pretty much settling for whatever the government or society gave them. And when Martin and Malcolm started to educate the brothers and sisters on their civil rights and started to show them all the things that they were entitled to under the law, the government started to label them "trouble makers" and "manipulators." They were basically trying to assassinate their character so people wouldn't believe in their movement, and their organizations as civil rights leaders. I'm pretty sure when Martin first started out, the black sisters and brothers wasn't listening to him. They probably told him "Nigger, you crazy! We ain't marching in no 100 degrees of heat down the streets of Birmingham Alabama, with picket signs. Them white police is gonna kill us." (laughs)

K.L.   (laughs)

N.Z.   So he had to use some type of trickery and some type of manipulation to get the black sisters and brothers to come together and believe in themselves and love one another. And whatever type of trickery and manipulation he used, it worked! And today, because of that man, and so many other

122

brothers and sister that followed in his footsteps, we have an enormous amount of civil rights and power as American citizens. The only problem is we never seem to exercise those rights because the brothers and sisters don't know what those rights are.

K.L.   But the white man knows what his rights are.

N.Z.   Exactly! And this is why the prison system is over populated with Blacks and Latinos and less populated with white people. They know the law and how to use it. So it works for them and not for us.

K.L.   Were you upset at the fact that the A.D.A. called you a manipulator in front of all your family?

N.Z.   You know, as she is saying these things in Court I did get a little upset, but after I was transferred upstate and I did some time in Solitary Confinement I started to look back on my life, and I started to come to the conclusion that maybe I am a manipulator. All my life, all I have ever done was to try to get my people's up off their butts and do something positive for themselves. When I was putting together the New York Illest Project, I had to single handedly motivate (and I guess "manipulate") those artist into believing in themselves. None of the artists on that CD believed that they had potential to make a hit record. They already had the talent in them, I just had to bring it out of them. We couldn't get any investors for the album so I put up my own money and once the project got off the ground the same investors that

123

denied us before now wanted to do business with us. So I guess you can say I was always the motivator for the people I had around me, and sometimes I had to manipulate or trick them into believing in themselves but It's nothing different then what Malcolm and Martin did back in the day. I'm just a younger version of them I guess.

K.L.   When I read your transcripts I got the feeling that Leigh Bishop really wanted to get rid of you before you started to get your company off the ground. Do you have the same feeling?

N.Z.   I definitely think my case is more personal and political than "a search for justice". I think it's apparent to everyone that my conviction is retaliation for my 1997 case. Bishop didn't care if Nakia was attacked in 1998, she only used her to convict me, that was it. But to answer your question, yes, I do think she wanted to get rid of me before I got my company off the ground. That's obvious.

K.L.   She also mentioned that you are "antisocial". Do you think she was upset because you didn't talk to her? Maybe she likes you? (laughs)

N.Z.   (laughs) If she likes me, setting me up with eighteen years in prison is a crazy way of showing it. (laughs)

K.L.   (laughs) Now, this crime was actually committed in 1998, but you didn't stand trial until 2001. You were arrested in 1998 for these charges, but you failed to return to Court until 2001. I need you to explain to the readers why you

124

didn't return to court for three years.

N.Z. I really wish I could be up front with the readers about my reasons for not returning to Court. My lawyers have instructed me not to talk about that part of my case because it's still pending and that's a separate charge. So I'm sorry, but I really can't speak about it.

K.L. O.K., I understand. At your sentencing date, Judge Rosengarten labeled you a "borderline genius" and said you were a "very bright person". How did that make you feel?

N.Z. I don't buy into any of that. I don't think that I am a "borderline genius". What makes me a "genius", because I committed a crime in 1997 that white people have been committing for years? We as black people are not supposed to commit crimes that white people commit. We are only supposed to commit robberies and sell drugs and when we get involved in what I was involved in, in 1997, we are labeled as geniuses because we're not supposed to know that type of stuff, but when a white person commits those types of crimes it's typical of them to do that, and they're not labeled as "geniuses" or "very bright" because it's already established that these are the types of crimes that they are supposed to commit, because they are already supposed to be smart. To call me a "genius" is to call every other black man in America an idiot. We are not supposed to know what they know and since I knew a little bit of it, I am a "genius" and I am way too smart, and I am way out of my

125

league as a black man because I am supposed to be stupid, and "society needs to be protected from me". None of that makes any sense to me.

K.L. I don't understand it myself.

N.Z. When Rosengarten sentenced me to fifteen years for this case he basically sent a loud message to every black man in America, and what that message basically said was, "If any black men in America commit the crimes that we commit, or if there are any young black men in America that are smarter than usual, the system will set them up and violate every constitutional right they have to get rid of them". I think that's one powerful message.

K.L. The system has always taught the kids of America to go to school to become smart and now they put you in prison because of it.

N.Z. Yeah, isn't that something.

K.L. I noticed when Rosengarten sentenced you he was basically sentencing you for everything in your past. Is there any rules of law that says he can not sentence you as much as he did for this case.

N.Z. When a Judge sentences a defendant, it's at his discretion what he thinks the defendant should be sentenced to. Under the law, I could have received any where from five years to fifteen years. He decided to give me the maximum which was fifteen years. Legally, he can sentence me to the fifteen years but I don't think a more reasonable Judge would have sentenced me to as much time as he did for a case like this. What's obvious is that he didn't sentence

126

me to fifteen years for the circumstances of this case, he sentenced me to fifteen years for my previous case. If you read my sentencing transcripts, he makes numerous references to my "past", my "history", my "record", and he even goes as far as to say "You may be, as I said, bright but your genius has been misdirected, even though it may be in the last couple of years been directed in the proper direction". So when he was making these statements I'm saying to myself that the Judge recognizes that I changed my life around since 1997 and that I'm "headed in the right direction" but now he wants to take me out of that "direction" by giving me fifteen years in prison. It's just not fair.

Notice to the Readers: [The sentencing transcripts can be found at pages 97-116 of this book. For the convenience of the readers, I have taken the time to underline every reference Rosengarten and Bishop make to Sean's previous case.]

K.L.   During the sentencing, you repeatedly ask Rosengarten to question Bishop as to whether or not she had any knowledge why the bailbondsman would want to revoke the bond that he posted for you, and he refused to ask her. What were you trying to show him?

N.Z.   He already knew what I was trying to point out to him, he was only trying to keep me quiet by changing the subject. During my arraignment, Judge Grosso granted me a 35,000 bail and my family hired a bail bondsman to post the bond for my release. After I got out I started to investigate my case by hiring a private investigator and we started to track down all the people that was at Club Jam-Roc on the night that I performed there. The promoter still had the mailing list to all the people he sold tickets to for the event that night, and we were basically tracking these people down to find out if any of them remembered seeing me perform at the club that night, and if they did, would they be willing to testify on my behalf. We were able to find some people that remembered the performance. Also, my investigator wanted to speak to Nakia because we couldn't understand why she still wanted to go through with this case. She had already told Jatanya and numerous other people that I wasn't the guy that attacked her and that this was all a mistake, but now when the trial starts she's back to saying I attacked her. So my investigator wanted to speak to her to see what was going on. Bishop found out that I was tracking down witnesses from the club and that my investigator was going to speak to Nakia and she didn't want that to happen because she had a lot that she wanted to hide. So when she found out about the progress I was making with my investigation she first attempted to get my bail revoked (completely) in order to take me off the street so she could stop our progress. She first went to Judge Grosso and asked him to revoke the bond but he said no because I had been doing everything I was supposed to do. I was showing up to my Court dates on time, going to my parole officer's office and

128

reporting to my bail bondsman on a daily basis, so there was no reason to revoke the bond. After Judge Grosso didn't do what she wanted him to, I remember she got very upset and I guess she figured she was going to do anything she wanted to do to revoke the bond so that I couldn't prepare my case. So she basically decided to break the law. She went to the office of the bail bondsman with two detectives and coerced him into revoking the bond. First she told him that I was from Haiti, and that I was planning to flee the country and go back to my homeland so that I wouldn't have to go to prison. But that didn't work because the bondsman did some research and realized that I was an American. She then told him I was a "flight risk" because I had warrants in the past and that he should revoke the bail before he loses the bond that he posted for me, but that didn't work because I had already explained to him that I had a warrant on this case and I explained my reasons to him for not coming back to Court and he still agreed to post the bond. So when she couldn't get him to revoke the bond for those reasons, she told him if he didn't revoke the bond she was going to launch a major investigation into his office, and that this investigation would last twelve to fifteen months, and while this investigation was pending, his office would not be able to do any business with the Courts in so far as posting bonds for any other defendants, and instead of him being precluded from doing business for that long he decided to revoke my bond and by him doing that I was placed

129

back in jail and my witnesses did not make it to Court in time.

K.L.   I understand that you have a tape recorded conversation between Jatanya and the bail bondsman?

N.Z.   Yeah, after I was convicted Jatanya called the bail bondsman and asked him why did he revoke the bond and he admitted everything to her. She was smart enough to record the conversation and so we have that on tape.

K.L.   So the bondsman basically lied to the Judge when he told him that he wanted to revoke the bond because you were a "flight risk".

N.Z.   Yeah, that was a lie. He already knew that I had a warrant because we told him that before he posted the bond.

EXCERPTS FROM SEAN'S TRIAL

TRANSCRIPTS: Page 3 - 9

MS. BISHOP: I have an attorney here from the Bail bonds company where that bail was posted. And I believe that his intention is to ask for that bail to be revoked.

Presently down in front of Judge Griffin is a second indictment, 3690 of this year. The defendant was indicted in that case for bail jumping. He was arrested and brought to court earlier this week. Judge Griffin set $5,000 bail on that case and ordered a bail sufficiency hearing.

THE COURT: On that case --

MS. BISHOP: On that case, which is -- I guess if you want to say

it's pending. No bail has been posted so far. Also the defendant has been arraigned

on that case. And just so the Court is aware, I consented to the inspection of those

Grand Jury minutes simply because I don't believe there are going to be any real

motions in terms of the usual --

THE COURT: Yes.

MS. BISHOP: -- Wade, Huntley kind of motions on that case. I

have a copy of those motions here, if that becomes an issue for you.

THE COURT: Well, I think that's properly before Judge Griffin at

the present time, along with the bail sufficiency hearing. But the surety who

placed the bail on the instant case wishes to have the bail revoked -

MS. BISHOP: He does. He can address the Court, if you would

allow that.

THE COURT: Mr. O'Meara, do you want to be heard in regard to

this?

MR. O'MEARA: The only thing I want to be heard with regard to is to

make sure he has the authority to revoke the bail. I don't know. He doesn't work for

the bail bondsman. He works for the under surety. He told me he's not an attorney

or attorney in fact. He didn't post the bail. He didn't come in here. He had nothing

to do with it until today. If he doesn't have the authority to revoke that bail, I would

like there to be an inquiry into whether he does have that authority.

131

THE COURT: Why don't we find out? Why don't you come up, sir. What is your name, sir?

MR. SIMON: First name Chad, Simon. Attorney in fact for the Safety National Casualty Corporation.

THE COURT: Chad Simon.

I don't need to see a copy of the bond. I saw in the file a copy of a bond for $10,000. That was set earlier.

MS. BISHOP: Right. That was set back in 1998.

THE COURT: That was forfeited.

MS. BISHOP: That was forfeited. It was set -- that money was put up by the same individual who has put up the money on the 35,000.

THE COURT: What is the problem with -

MR. SIMON: Your Honor, when the new arrest came to light, when the charges were brought up as far as bail jumping, it put a red flag up for our company, which we investigated. We spoke to a Detective Olsen (ph), along with the assistant, got information in the case, which we feel the defendant is now a flight risk. We no longer want to be liable on the 35,000 that was originally posted.

THE COURT: Why don't you come up with counsel.

(Sidebar off the record.)

THE COURT: What is the name up of the company?

MR. SIMON: Safety National Casualty Corporation.

132

(Sidebar off the record.)

THE COURT: What is your name again, sir?

MR. SIMON: Chad Simon, your Honor.

THE COURT: You're are attorney in fact for the --

THE WITNESS: Safety National Casualty Corporation.

THE COURT: Safety National Casualty Corporation. Your

application

MR. SIMON: The application at this time is to have the bond, $35,000

posted, exonerated.

THE COURT: For what reason, sir?

MR. SIMON: Pursuant to section 530.80 of the CPL, at this

time we do feel Mr. Zimmerman is no longer a viable risk for our insurance company.

THE COURT: You wish to be heard, counsel?

MR. O'MEARA: No, your Honor.

THE COURT: People?

MS. BISHOP: No, Judge. Only to request that if additional bail is

posted in this matter that your Honor order a bail sufficiency hearing as to that.

THE COURT: All right. The bail is exonerated. And the bail status

will remain the same. Bail will be $35,000 dollars on this case.

MR. O'MEARA: Thank you, your Honor.

THE CLERK: 35,000 A or B?

THE COURT: Yes. Until further notice.

All right. Now, Miss Bishop, you want to put something or: the record in retard to the alibi?

MS. BISHOP: I do, Judge. But I just have a question.

THE COURT: Yes.

MS. BISHOP: Would you also hear me on a bail sufficiency -

THE COURT: Yes.

MS. BISHOP: -- argument?

Can I do that first?

THE COURT: Now -

MS. BISHOP: I'm just saying to have a hearing ordered in the event that -

THE COURT: In the event bail is posted a hearing will be ordered.

MS. BISHOP: Okay. I just want to be clear.

MR. O'MEARA: Your Honor, a hearing -- she must show some sort of reasonable cause as to belief why that money wouldn't be legitimate.

THE COURT: What is your reasonable cause?

MS. BISHOP: The individual who posted the bail originally that you just revoked in this case is employed by the Transit Authority. She makes $29,000 a year. She is the fiancée of the defendant. She was able to post approximately $15,000 cash.

134

THE COURT: Uh-huh.

MS. BISHOP: I have information in the form of a Criminal Court complaint which resulted in an indictment and a conviction for this defendant, where she was involved with this defendant in a scheme where they defrauded various banks of over $100,000. They made up their own credit cards. They forged checks. And although she wasn't arrested I can present a witness to the Court to testify about her involvement in that scheme.

THE COURT: Is that Jatanya (sic) Belnavis?

MS. BISHOP: Jatanya Belnavis, that is correct.

THE CLERK: Judge, are you finished with the bail bondsman?

THE COURT: Yes.

THE CLERK: You can have a seat, sir.

MR. O'MEARA: Your Honor, there is absolutely no indication the money she is using to post the $14,000 cash comes from anything other than legitimate means. She does have a full-time job.

THE COURT: That will be the purpose of the hearing, to determine that. All right. But that's sufficient cause for a hearing to arise.

MR. O'MEARA: Your Honor, I think it should be required that at least a link be shown. Jatanya Belnavis was not arrested, not indicted. She was not indicted, not arrested. There's been no causal link shown between whatever happened in 1996 and whatever happened last week on the 21st when that 14,000

135

was posted.

THE COURT: Well, I think she's raised allegations sufficient to require a hearing. The facts you're talking about will come out on the hearing, should there be a hearing.

MR. O'MEARA: Your Honor, she should have to state whatever evidence they -

THE COURT: That's my ruling. You have an exception for the record.

5D. Sean's Private Investigator,
Kevin W. Hinkson, finds out that
Nakia was forced to identify
<u>Sean at trial</u>

After Sean was convicted in 2001, his family hired the investigating services of Kevin W. Hinkson. Mr. Hinkson, a twenty year veteran of the New York City Police Department, had investigated several other cases of mistaken identity and was successful in overturning the convictions of numerous innocent people. Because of Nakia's shaky trial testimony, Hinkson decided to contact Nakia to see if she would be willing to participate in an interview. Nakia was more than willing to speak with Mr. Hinkson, and what she revealed at that conversation would lead to Sean's immediate release, (only if the "Criminal Injustice System" was fair and just).

136

(See Exhibit I Nakia's Recantation Affidavit).

K.L.   After you were convicted your family hired Private Investigator Kevin W. Hinkson to look into your case, and he found out that Nakia never positively identified you to the police on the night that the crime took place, and you also found out that Bishop forced Nakia to identify you at trial. How did that make you feel?

N.Z.   I know this is going to sound phony to your readers but I'm going to tell you exactly how I felt. I guess I felt how Ruben "Hurricane" Carter felt when he was set up by the A.D.A. and the police in his case. I remember watching that movie (The Hurricane) when I was home and I had so many doubts about his story and about that movie. I just thought to myself could everything in that movie be true? Do the Police and District Attorneys really set up innocent people with crimes they didn't commit? And now that I am living through what he lived through I see that that movie was a very true story. I can feel what he felt during his time in prison because I'm going through exactly what he went through when he was here.

K.L.   When and where were you arrested for this case?

N.Z.   I was arrested at my parole officer's office. Nakia was attacked on September 19, 1998 and because she gave the police my nick-name and address they were able to find out that I was on parole in Jamaica Queens. So on September 28, 1998, when I made my next scheduled visit to my parole

137

officer, the police was there waiting for me, and they arrested me. It was like I was already guilty in their eyes.

K.L. At trial, Bishop made it appear to the jury and to the judge that you and Nakia were "good friends" and that this wasn't a case of "mistaken identity" because Nakia knows you "very well", and that the two of you were known to each other for a "long time" before this crime took place. I need you to explain your relationship with Nakia (before) this crime took place.

N.Z. When Nakia took the stand against me in December of 2001 that was the first time I had ever come face to face with her. I didn't even know who Nakia was when she was testifying against me, in fact, I had mistaken Nakia for another one of Jatanya's friends. So the girl that I thought was going to testify against me actually didn't testify, and when Nakia walked into the Courtroom I'm just sitting there like "who the hell is this"? I remember my lawyer even tapped me on the shoulder and asked me "Is that Nakia?" He couldn't believe it either.

K.L. What did you say when he asked you if that was Nakia?

N.Z. I don't even think I answered him. I didn't know if that was Nakia or not. It certainly wasn't who I expected it to be.

K.L. You expected it to be another one of Jatanya's friends?

N.Z. Yeah, Jatanya had another girlfriend that she had some problems with in September of 1998, so I thought this was the girl behind all of this but it

138

turned out that it wasn't.

K.L.   At trial Nakia testified that she only met you two times before September 19, 1998 but that she "did not conversate with you at these two meetings" and that the "meetings were brief." Do you remember meeting Nakia before September of 1998?

N.Z.   If Nakia Stubbs was to walk through this door right now I wouldn't be able to tell you who she is. It wasn't until I was standing trial for this case that Jatanya attempted to remind me who Nakia was. I remember me and Jatanya did rent a Jeep Cherokee from one of her friends in 1998 and I remember me and Jatanya going to one of her girlfriend's house to pick up the Jeep, but I don't remember meeting anybody or talking to anybody that day, and I know I certainly didn't meet the same Nakia that testified against me at trial, that day. I never forget a face and the girl that testified against me at trial was very tall, so I know her height would have at least stood out to me, but I just don't remember anything about ever meeting the girl that testified against me at trial.

K.L.   Since Nakia's testimony was the only evidence linking you to this crime and absolutely no one else stated that you attacked her, it is important that you explain to the readers exactly how you got mixed up in this case. Since you never testified at trial people don't know your (side of the story) and I think it's important that you explain your situation, in detail, to the readers.

139

N.Z. The way I became the accused in this case is simple and it's very easy to understand but Rosengarten and the Queens District Attorney's office likes to complicate and twist the situation so that the average layman to the law would never truly see that the A.D.A. set this thing up. So, I'm going to explain the identification process in my case so everyone can understand what's going on here.

K.L. O.K.

N.Z. After Nakia was attacked on September 19th, 1998, she went directly to the police station and she told the police that she had been attacked by a person she knew as "Sean" and she gave them "Sean's" address, but while Nakia was relaying this information to the police, the police never asked Nakia how well does she know Sean or how positive is she that Sean attacked her? They didn't follow the proper police procedures while they were interrogating Nakia. Had they done that, I never would have been arrested in 1998. So after Nakia gave the police the nick-name of Sean and Sean's address, the police did a computer search and based off of this information Nakia gave them they were able to find out that I lived at that address and that my nick-name was Sean. So I immediately became a suspect. Also, because I had been arrested before, my picture was on file with the local police station so the police were able to obtain a photograph of me. Once the police found my picture they placed it in a photographic line-up along with five or six other

140

pictures of different people and they showed the array of photos to Nakia but Nakia didn't identify me and she didn't identify anyone else.

K.L. If Nakia knows you "very well" as A.D.A. Bishop alleges, then why wasn't she able to identify your picture from the photographic line-up?

N.Z. That is the exact question that I have been asking Judge Rosengarten for the past three years of my incarceration but he seems to find anyway to dance around the subject. But to answer your question, Nakia does not "know me very well". If fact, Nakia doesn't know me at all. The only thing Nakia knew about me on September 19, 1998 was my nick-name (Sean) and my address, and the only way Nakia knew these two insignificant things about me was through conversations she had with Jatanya. Nakia was a beautician in Queens, N.Y. and Jatanya used to go to Nakia's house to get her hair done, and when Nakia was finished doing Jatanya's hair she would call a cab for Jatanya and Jatanya would always give Nakia my address in order to tell the cab driver where she was going, and after a few months of relaying my address to the cab driver it pretty much stuck in her head. So that's how she knew my address and she basically knew my name from Jatanya.

K.L. So Nakia has never been inside your house and you have never been in her house?

N.Z. Nah, Nakia has never been to my house and I've never been in hers, that's just the way the A.D.A. set the trial up. Me and Nakia are not friends. If me and

Nakia were best friends, as Bishop alleges, she would have pointed me out to the police the night that the crime took place but she couldn't point me out because she didn't know what I look like, because she had never met me before.

K.L.   If Nakia doesn't know you by face but only knows you by name and address, what would make her think that you was the one that attacked her on September 19, 1998?

N.Z.   That is the one question that Judge Rosengarten and A.D.A. Leigh Bishop does not want Nakia to answer in Court of Law. They already know the answer to that question because I have been pointing these things out to them in my appeals and motions but they are trying extremely hard to keep their mistakes quiet, and my incarceration ongoing. But since you asked that question I will answer it so the readers can see the true corruption involved in my situation, but first let me give you an example of my case so the readers can get a full understanding of what's happening here.

K.L.   O.K.

N.Z.   Let's say you had a friend and your friend is dating Michael Jordan and your friend always talks about Michael Jordan to you. I mean, every time you see your friend she is talking about Michael Jordan. She tells you that he looks good, he's 6 feet 4 inches tall, he's 200 pounds, and he has a bald head, and of course she tells you that he is black. Now keep in mind you don't know

142

who Michael Jordan is because you don't watch basketball and you are not into sports, so the only description you have of Michael Jordan is his name and the things that your friend has told you about him, but you have absolutely no information as to his facial features.

K.L.   O.K., I follow you.

N.Z.   Now, let's say, one day you and your friend get into a very, very bad argument and that argument leads to a fight between the both of you, and while the two of you are fighting your friend tells you that she is going to call "her man" and tell him to come over and finish you off. Now you see that your friend picks up her cell phone and calls somebody but you are no longer close enough to your friend to hear the conversation that she is having with the person on the other end of the phone. A few minutes after your friend places that phone call, a man fitting the same description as the one your friend gave you of Michael Jordan shows up and attacks you.

K.L.   And I automatically assume it's Michael Jordan because the guy that attacks me fits the description of the person that my friend always tells me about.

N.Z.   Exactly! Now, when you go to the police station you tell them what happened and you tell them that "Michael Jordan" attacked you, and you also give them all the information that you have of Michael Jordan, his height, his weight, etc. But the police know exactly who Michael Jordan is because they watch basketball and they know that Michael Jordan is the biggest basketball player

143

in the world, and since Michael Jordan is the biggest basketball player in the

world the police automatically assume that you know who Michael Jordan is

and that you wouldn't mistake him with anyone else.

K.L.   And because they assume that I know exactly what Michael Jordan looks like

they never really question me as to how positive I am that he attacked me.

N.Z.   Right, because they figure everybody in the world knows who Michael Jordan

is and they figure you do too.

K.L.   Um hum.

N.Z.   But when they find Michael Jordan's picture and they place his photo in a

array of other photos and they ask you to identify him ...

K.L.   I can't because I don't know what he looks like because I never met him

before.

N.Z.   Now you see how I got involved in this case.

K.L.   So there were two things that gave Nakia the impression that you attacked

her; Jatanya attempted to call someone that night and Nakia figured it was

you, and the person that attacked her fit the description that Jatanya gave her

of you.

N.Z.   Yeah, and because of those two things she went to the police station and

gave them my name and address. There are two other discrepancies that I

want to point out to your readers. If you notice, in Nakia's affidavit she states

that she wasn't able to identify me to the police on September 19, 1998, but almost four years later on November 21st, 2001, my trial date, she is incredibly able to walk right into a courtroom and positively identify me as the person that attacked her. Now, Nakia says when she was assaulted, the person that attacked her reached into her car and opened the door and suddenly the overhead light came on in her car and she was able to get a face to face view of the person that attacked her, and she says that person was me, this is exactly what she testified to at trial on November 21, 2001. My question was, if she came "face to face" with me on September 19, 1998, and if she was able to see me under "good lighting" because the "overhead light" came on in her car, and if she drove directly to police station within twenty minutes of her attack, and if the police showed her pictures of me within a _ hour of her arriving to their station, then why wouldn't she be able to immediately identify me to the police when she was confronted with my picture? According to Nakia, I had just attacked her twenty minutes ago, but twenty minutes later she can't identify me at the police station, but almost four years later, at my trial, she testifies under oath that she is certain that I am the one that attacked her.

K.L.   I am pretty sure these things are running through your mind while she was testifying against you at trial?

N.Z.   Yeah, and the whole time I'm sitting there I'm like, someone is telling the girl what to say because the story makes absolutely no sense.

145

K.L. Did you ever think it was Bishop that forced her to testify against you?

N.Z. Nah, not in my wildest dreams. I never thought A.D.A.'s do things like that,

especially the way Bishop portrayed herself in the courtroom. She acted as

if she really believed in upholding the law and the constitution but behind the

scenes she was breaking every rule in the book. It's illegal to force someone

to testify against another person in court and this is exactly what she did.

She probably believed that she scared Nakia enough that she would never tell

anyone about what she made her do, but Nakia was brave enough to come

forth and so I commend her for that.

K.L. Are you upset with Nakia for what she has done to you and your life?

N.Z. When Nakia was testifying against me at trial and when I was convicted, I

was extremely upset and like any brother from a rough neighborhood I

thought about reacting with violence, but once I was sent upstate to prison

and I started to research the history of the law and I started to read all the

cases where it shows that these type of convictions and sentences are

handed down on a daily basis. I read so many cases where A.D.A.'s have

set up innocent people that it became apparent to me that there is nothing

irregular about my situation. This is a normal occurrence in law enforcement,

and when I started to get an understanding of that, my frustration was no

longer against Nakia. She was nothing more than a pawn in Leigh Bishop's

game. She did not voluntarily contribute to my wrongful conviction, she was forced, threatened and coerced. And my research of the law teaches me that A.D.A.'s are the best manipulators in the world, when they are in the interrogating room with their witnesses they constantly threatened them by saying "if you don't do what I want you to do I'm going to put you in jail". And the average person who doesn't know any better will do anything the A.D.A. tells them to do in order to avoid jail. So in that aspect, my beef is no longer with Nakia, my beef is with the Queens District Attorney office. They are solely responsible for setting me up.

K.L.   Leigh Bishop told Nakia "if she didn't testify against you she would put her in jail". Could she (legally) place Nakia in jail for refusing to testify against you?

N.Z.   Of course not! That's just the coercement they use to trick people into testifying against other people. Nakia would not have been arrested if she refused to testify against me, but she didn't know that at the time. And this is the main reason why Bishop didn't want Jatanya or my private investigator to talk to Nakia during the trial. She was afraid that we would find out what was going on.

K.L.   If Nakia wanted to visit you in prison, would you agree to meet with her?

N.Z.   Yes, I would. I understand now that this system is designed to turn people against other people, mainly blacks against blacks. Bishop would love for me to get out of prison and try to retaliate against Nakia for what was done to me. In that aspect she would benefit three ways. I would be back in prison,

Nakia would be badly hurt or dead, and she would move up a notch for getting

another conviction. I would never give Bishop that much satisfaction. I know

Bishop would be extremely upset if me and Nakia became friends and started

a black company together or something, that would show her that her plan to

turn one black person against another didn't work. So yes, I would love to

see Nakia. Maybe we could discuss our new business or something.

(laughs)

K.L.   (laughs) [Note to myself: Must get Nakia to visit Sean].

How did you feel when you found out that Nakia was willing to come forth

about the things that Leigh Bishop made her do?

N.Z.   I felt good because I knew that her affidavit and testimony would get me out

of prison. It took a lot for Nakia to finally break her silence. From what I

understand, Bishop told Nakia if she ever talked to anybody about my case

she would have her arrested, so she was still very afraid for her freedom and

her life but Hinkson assured her that she wouldn't go to jail for coming forward

and telling the truth about the situation and so she agreed to talk. It took a

lot of courage for Nakia to take a stand against an A.D.A. and I respect and

thank her for doing that.

5E. The "Criminal Injustice

System" turns a blind eye

<u>to all of Sean's evidence.</u>

K.L.   I understand that you are having an enormous amount of problems with the

Criminal Justice System with regards to getting them to actually overturn your

conviction. I've read all of your appeals and motions where you have included

a copy of Nakia's recantation affidavit, a copy of four affidavits from alibi

witnesses Haron Wilson (See Exhibit J.), Barry Alexander, Latrina Boyd and

Theophulas Brown (See Exhibit K.) in which they all verify your presence at

Club Jam-Rock on September 19, 1998. You also included affidavits from

Natasha Dockery and Samuel Belnavis in which they stated that they

witnessed the altercation between Nakia and Jatanya and that they got a look

at the person that fired the gun that night and that it wasn't you and that you

were not at the scene of the crime. Jatanya also testified that she did <u>not</u>

call you on September 19, 1998 while she was arguing with Nakia, but that

she contacted another friend named (Nondi Cooper). I want you to fully

explain to my readers, in detail, what you have done to get your conviction

overturned and what responses have you received from Richard Brown

(Richard Brown is the Queens County District Attorney and he is also Leigh

Bishop's boss) and Judge Rosengarten when you file your appeals and

motions.

149

N.Z. I've done several motions and appeals in order to get my conviction overturned, and these motions and appeals detail all the corruption involved in my case. Basically everything I've just told you, I've been telling Rosengarten and Brown for the past three years of my incarceration. They simply find every, and any way to change the subject or twist the subject away from the truth.

K.L. What was the first motion you filed?

N.Z. The first motion I filed was a "440 Motion". The reason why it's called a 440 motion is because it can be found at section 440.10 of the Criminal Procedures Law. Pursuant to that section of the law, you can file a motion with the court alleging that your lawyer provided you with "Ineffective Assistance of Counsel" during your trial, and because of his ineffectiveness you should be entitled to a new trial. Ineffective Assistance of Counsel means your lawyer did not provide you with the most "reasonable"assistance that a lawyer should have provided his client under the standards of the law. So what this basically means is that you can not file this motion asking for a new trial because your lawyer didn't provide you with "perfect" assistance of counsel, under the law, no man is entitled to "perfect" assistance of counsel. Instead, you must be able to show and prove that had it not been for your lawyer's errors or mistakes, you would have "probably" won your case or "at least" the outcome of the trial would have been different.

150

(Strickland v. Washington 104 Sct. 2052)

K.L.   Basically, you just can't say my lawyer was an idiot and I want a new trial.

You have to prove his mistakes and his errors in a Court?

N.Z.   You are exactly right, and this is why I filed this motion with the Court. I don't

think there is any question to the fact that my lawyer provided me with

Ineffective Assistance of Counsel. I have explained my situation in detail to

at least twenty different lawyers and they all agree that my trial lawyer has

completely ruined my life. They all said that he did things at my trial that no

lawyer on earth would do, so I filed the 440 motion in Judge Rosengarten's

court detailing all the errors and mistakes that he made.

K.L.   When did you file this motion?

N.Z.   In January of 2003.

K.L.   And what exactly did you say to Rosengarten in your motion?

N.Z.   What I basically said was my lawyer was ineffective because he did not add

the names of Haron Wilson and Theophulus Brown to the notice of alibi and

because he failed to do that Rosengarten denied me my right to call these

witnesses at my trial, and had these witnesses testified there is a

"reasonable probability" that the jury would not have convicted me because

they would have heard testimony that I performed at Club Jam-Roc at the

same time it is alleged that I committed this crime. I further explained to him

that my lawyer was ineffective because he did not call Latrina Boyd and Barry

Alexander and that they also would have testified that I was at the club.

K.L.   Did you include the sworn affidavits from these four witnesses in which they verify that you were in fact at the club?

N.Z.   Yes I did, and I also included the sworn affidavits from Natasha Dockery and Samuel Belnavis.

K.L.   What happened after you filed this motion?

N.Z.   Well, after you file any motion in Court you have to give the District Attorney's office thirty days to file a response to your motion. This is so they can have an opportunity to investigate your allegations and see if what you are saying is true. So about thirty days after I filed that motion the D.A. responded.

K.L.   And what did he have to say about your evidence and the witnesses statements?

N.Z.   The D.A. basically made the argument to the Judge that my witnesses are lying and that I manipulated them to sign the affidavits for me.

K.L.   What would give the D.A. the impression that these witnesses are lying?

N.Z.   Absolutely nothing. He had to find some way to cover up the situation so that was his argument.

K.L.   Is that all the D.A. said?

N.Z.   No, he said more, but that was basically his story. He really didn't have anything else to say. He requested that Judge Rosengarten deny the motion because "there was nothing to suggest that had these witnesses testified the

152

outcome of the trial would have been different".

K.L.   Well how can the D.A. come to that conclusion? If you have (6) witnesses

that say you didn't commit the crime, and the D.A. only has (1) witness that

said you did, and then we later find out that their "one witness" was forced to

say you did it, then how can a (reasonable) person conclude that had the

members of the jury been aware of all of this evidence that they wouldn't have

convicted you?

N.Z.   You must keep in mind, we are not dealing with "reasonable"people. We are

dealing with people who must protect the interest and the integrity of the

Criminal Injustice System, as well as their own. Every time a person is

released from prison after serving years for a crime they didn't commit, it

sends sort of a shock wave through the Criminal Injustice System. It makes

the entire system look bad to the citizens that are supposed to have trust and

faith in that system. If it starts to surface that too many innocent people are

in prison for crimes they didn't commit, society as a whole will start to lose

faith in that system because it will start to show that the system makes

mistakes and that it doesn't work as perfect as a District Attorney would have

you believe. So in order to keep the system looking good and to protect their

public image, Rosengarten and Brown continuously finds ways to keep a lid

on my innocence and to continue my incarceration.

K.L.   Are you suggesting that because they don't want to look bad to the media by admitting that they put the wrong person in prison that they would rather you do fifteen years in prison for a crime you didn't commit in order to keep the situation quiet?

N.Z.   This is <u>exactly</u> what I am suggesting.   There is no excuse to the fact that Rosengarten and Brown refuse to investigate any of the evidence that I have presented to their offices. They won't send any of their investigators to the crime scene or to Club Jam-Rock to see if I performed there, they refuse to hold a hearing where these witnesses can be properly interviewed in a Court of Law and questioned as to whether or not I was at the Club, they refuse to hold a hearing where Nakia can come in and fully explain to the Court how the D.A. forced her to testify against me. And for these reasons I am completely convinced that they simply want to keep my situation quiet.

K.L.   Did Judge Rosengarten deny the motion?

N.Z.   Yes, he did.

K.L.   And when he denied the motion what was his reasoning?

N.Z.   Actually, when he denied the motion he contradicted himself and that was surprising to me because Judges usually try not to do that. When he denied the motion, Rosengarten said he <u>didn't</u> preclude me from calling my witnesses because my lawyer failed to add them to the notice of alibi, but that he didn't allow me to call these witnesses because their testimony wasn't "the nature of a true alibi" .....

K.L. But that's not what he said at trial, I've read your transcripts several times and he specifically said, and I quote "What concerns me is the purpose of offering this (the alibi testimony) is for the purpose of showing an alibi in my opinion - and because these people were not on the notice (of alibi) - that testimony will be precluded and the defendant has an exception for the record". Now based on what he said at the trial, and what he is saying now, it is apparently obvious that he is making some very big mistakes with your case.

N.Z. "Mistakes"? There are no mistakes happening here. These errors are blatantly and purposely done. It's just their way of keeping the situation quiet, that's all.

K.L. What else have you done to get your conviction overturned?

N.Z. After Rosengarten denied that motion, I filed another motion with his Court and this motion concerned Nakia's recantation affidavit. I basically argued to the Court that Nakia was forced by Bishop to identify me at trial, and had she not been forced to do so, she would have testified truthfully about the entire situation and I would not have been convicted.

K.L. And what did Rosengarten have to say about Nakia's recantation affidavit?

N.Z. I was very shocked and disappointed in the way Rosengarten responded to that motion and Nakia's affidavit. I mean, here is a young lady that is trying desperately to undo something that a corrupt A.D.A. made her do and he just "criticizes" and humiliates her even more.

K.L.   Explain to the readers what he said.

N.Z.   He said, and I quote, that our papers (motion) are "rambling, disjointed, confusing, and repetitious" and that it is "burdensome and a waste of resources for his Court as well as the D.A. to have to be compelled to deal with my continuous submissions", and that my "multiple and repetitive motions are becoming burdensome and an impediment to the efficient functioning of the Court". He referred to Nakia's affidavit as a "recent revelation", he also said that he was "providing me with a courtesy" by even addressing the affidavit and the motion. Lastly, he said, "the law does not provide me with the opportunity to submit unlimited motions to the Court at the taxpayers expense" and if I submit any other evidence to the Court it will all be "swiftly and summarily denied".

K.L.   How did you feel when you got that decision?

N.Z.   Like I stated earlier, I've learned a lot from Rosengarten and my current situation. If it wasn't for him I would have never known that there are people in law enforcement who truly don't care about law enforcement. This is a learning experience for me, now I know that I have to raise my kids never to trust the people in our government. In my opinion, if a Judge or a District Attorney knows or even has the slightest idea that there may be an innocent person in prison, they should be more than willing to open up the case and investigate the situation but for some reason, in my case, they are not willing

156

to do that. I really don't understand it.

K.L. I can see that Rosengarten (ridiculed) your motion and Nakia's affidavit, but what was his basic reasoning for denying the motion?

N.Z. Actually his reasoning for denying the motion was the most "confusing" part of the proceedings. Rosengarten concluded that even if Nakia wasn't forced, coerced, and threatened to identify me at trial, and even if she didn't, in fact, identify me as the person who attacked her, the jury would have still convicted me because "they had ample evidence to conclude that the Defendant and the perpetrator were one in the same". He actually bases this reasoning on the (premise) that Nakia testified that after she was attacked she noticed that her car was parked in front of Jatanya's house, and that she also recognized the voice of the person that attacked her as being my voice.

K.L. I also had some questions for you in relation to Nakia's Jeep being at the scene of the crime. Nakia testified at trial that after she was attacked she noticed that her Jeep was parked on Jatanya's block, but immediately before the attack she had not noticed that the Jeep was parked there, even though she had "looked up and down the street for the Jeep". She says that after she was attacked she realized that the Jeep was parked on Jatanya's block was hers because she recognized the license plate. My question to you is, if Jatanya testified that she had given you possession of the Jeep on the night

157

in question, and if Nakia testified that she seen her Jeep on Jatanya's block after she was attacked, then this would place you directly at the scene of the crime, wouldn't it?

N.Z.   It would place me "directly" at the scene of the crime only if Nakia was being truthful in her trial testimony. When Nakia testified that she seen her Jeep on Jatanya's block it took a lot for me not to jump out of my chair and call her a "liar". That was the one part of Nakia's testimony that I instantly knew she was lying about. There is absolutely no way that Nakia saw her Jeep at the scene of the crime because the Jeep was with me, and I wasn't at the scene of the crime. Nakia's Jeep was parked in the parking lot of Club Jam-Roc on September 19, 1998 at 3:00 a.m. while I was performing inside, and at no time did that Jeep leave that parking lot! It was there when I went in the Club and it was still sitting there, in the very same spot, when I came out of the Club. So I knew she was lying.

K.L.   I think your lawyer knew she was lying also, he impeached her credibility so much on that issue that it's amazing that you were even convicted.

N.Z.   I want to point out a few things to your readers. Let's let the readers be the judge ....

K.L.   O.K.

N.Z.   Nakia testified at trial that she went to my house on September 18, 1998 at 2:30 a.m. to look for the Jeep, but that it wasn't there (Transcript Page 433,

158

Line 15) After she couldn't find the Jeep, she said she went to <u>Jatanya's</u> house to see if the Jeep was there, and that she had looked up and down the street for Jeep but it was no where to be found (Transcript Page 434, Line 11). Nakia then goes on to say that after she couldn't find the Jeep, she waited in front of Jatanya's house for a "half hour", waiting for me to arrive with the Jeep (Transcript Page 434, Line 21). She says that while she was waiting for me to arrive with the Jeep, that "I came up to her car, stuck my hand in her car window, put a gun to her head and dragged her out of her car (Transcript Page 394, Line 24). After Nakia was attacked she says that she suddenly realized that her Jeep was parked on Jatanya's block, just a couple of houses from Jatanya's house (Transcript Page 404, Line 5) and that me and the other two guys that attacked her left the scene of the crime in her Jeep (Transcript Page 407, Line 16). Now, there is a lot of things that doesn't sit right with me about that part of Nakia's story. If Nakia testified that when she got to Jatanya's house the Jeep wasn't there, and if she says that she looked up and down the street for the Jeep but she couldn't find it, and if she also goes on to say that she parked in front of Jatanya's house for a "half hour" awaiting my arrival and that the Jeep still was not there, then how is it that after she was attacked, the Jeep, somehow, (magically) appears? I mean, her Jeep just comes out of nowhere! It just somehow arrived there.

K.L. What's amazing is she doesn't say that you "arrived" in the Jeep and then

159

attacked her, she just says after she was attacked she opened her eyes and the Jeep was parked on the street.

N.Z.   Yeah, and if her Jeep was parked there, wouldn't she had noticed it the whole half hour that she was parked on that street?

K.L.   Yeah, I know that I would have noticed my car.

N.Z.   Nakia's friend, Kariesha Braithwaite also testified at my trial, but she says the three men that attacked Nakia ran away on foot, and not in Nakia's car (Page 305, line 18). Now if these two young ladies are both watching the same incident how could there be such inconsistent testimony about whether or not Nakia's Jeep was parked on Jatanya's street?

K.L.   It's obvious that Rosengarten neglected all the evidence that you put in your motion and that his decision was wrong, did you ever appeal his decision?

N.Z.   Yeah, I appealed it, but once again you have to keep in mind that Judges stick together. The same Judges that you appeal the decision (to), are friends with the Judges that you are appealing (from). So if Rosengarten wants to keep the situation quiet all he has to do is make a phone call to the Appellate Division (Court) and they will also find a way to dance around the subject. It's that easy.

K.L.   And so they also denied your appeal?

N.Z.   Yeah ....

K.L.   What is the name of the Judge that denied your appeal and what Court is he in?

N.Z. There are four Judges that denied my appeal. When you submit an appeal to an Appellate Court, a panel of Judges must rule on the appeal. I submitted my appeal to the Appellate Division, Second Department in Brooklyn, N.Y. The four Judges that sat on the panel for my appeal were Fred T. Santucci, Sondra Miller, Leo F. McGinity, and Robert W. Schmidt. They were also the four Judges that denied my appeal.

K.L. How could all of this evidence be presented to a total of five Judges and none of them do anything about your situation? How can they not see that you didn't commit this crime?

N.Z. Oh, they see it! Judges wear very good reading glasses, so they can see all the errors in my trial. It's just that they have taken the approach to turn a blind eye to my situation.

K.L. Where do you go from here, is there anything else you can do to get your conviction overturned?

N.Z. Well, at the present time, I'm working on a petition to the Federal Court System and this petition is called a "Federal Habeas Corpus". What I'm basically doing in this petition is showing the Federal Judge that a State Judge has violated Federal law in order to put me in prison and that I am entitled to a new trial.

K.L. Do you think that this petition will get your conviction overturned?

N.Z.   I have been told on numerous occasions that what goes on in State Courts

does not go on in Federal Courts in so far as Federal Judges follow the law

and they won't turn a blind eye to your situation if your Constitutional Rights

have been violated. At this point, I am only asking that these Judges follow

the law. All of the law that I found is in my favor. I'm only asking that the

Judge follow the law and let it work for me as it works for everyone else. I've

heard that Federal Judges truly take pride in their position as Justices of the

Court, and they will not allow an innocent man to sit in prison. I only hope

and pray that this is true.

Chapter 6

The Escape Attempt

Sean plans one of the biggest escape

attempts in New York State history,

or did he?

Two guns, two Correctional Officers' uniforms, three cellular phones, about

thirty thousand dollars in cash and a team of loving females was the ingredients to

Sean's May, 2003 escape plan. The intricate plot would capture the attention of

more than sixteen news publications worldwide (seven (7) of them being major news

outlets). The Westchester County District Attorney's Office (Jeanine Pirro) alleged

that Sean was, once again, "the Mastermind to what would have been a catastrophe

if the plan was a success." Pirro, and numerous media sources that covered the

story, alleged that "Zimmerman's three (3) escape attempts were only unsuccessful

because of minor mishaps." To give you a more precise outlook of the situation

(and to let you know that this is a very true story), I decided to include a rather

detailed news article about Sean's situation. The author, Lydia Polgreen writing for

the New York Times, articulated certain aspects of the escape plot that no other

writer seem to be able to do, but keep in mind, all the information she received

originated in the Westchester County District Attorney's Office. Here is her story:

163

2 of 5 DOCUMENTS

Copyright 2004 The New York Times Company
The New York Times

February 4, 2004, Wednesday, Late Edition - Final

SECTION: Section B; Page 1; Column 2; Metropolitan Desk

LENGTH: 1020 words

HEADLINE: Escape From Sing Sing: How Plans Failed

BYLINE: By LYDIA POLGREEN

DATELINE: WHITE PLAINS, Feb. 3

BODY:

It seemed like the perfect breakout plan: armed with fake guard uniforms, two handguns and a dog-eared copy of an acclaimed book about life as a prison guard at Sing Sing, two convicted violent felons would walk out of prison. They had friends on the outside willing to smuggle in supplies, and an ally on the inside, a prison guard, who gave them crucial logistical information about the inner workings of Sing Sing.

Instead, Nicholas Zimmerman, 27, who is serving a 15-year sentence on a weapons charge, and his jailhouse friend Steven Finley, 26, could now face at least four years more prison time on top of their current sentences after being charged on Tuesday. Westchester County investigators told of an elaborate plan to free the two men last spring involving at least seven people, including three of Mr. Zimmerman's girl-friends, one of whom was a guard at Sing Sing, and two men the women hired to help free Mr. Zimmerman and Mr. Finley.

The two men were charged with attempting to escape and their confederates have been charged with various crimes such as accepting bribes and attempting to aid the escape. "You've got an orchestrated, professional attempt to get two chronic felons out of Sing Sing," the Westchester district attorney, Jeanine F. Pirro, said at a news conference.

But a series of mishaps -- a panic attack, a suspicious-looking badge and a run-in with an astute police officer -- derailed three attempts and ultimately led investigators to unravel the elaborate plot, Ms. Pirro said.

Mr. Zimmerman, a rapper from Queens who recorded songs under the name Puzz Pacino, hatched the plan to escape last year with a guard he met in Sing Sing named Quangtrice Wilson, according to investigators.

The two struck up a friendship that blossomed into romance, investigators said, and Ms. Wilson agreed to give one of Mr. Zimmerman's girlfriends on the outside extensive information about the prison, including the layout of its buildings, its security procedures and most important, a digital copy of her identification card.

She also gave Mr. Zimmerman a cellphone to make calls to arrange the escape plan, Ms. Pirro said.

Ms. Wilson passed along logistical information to another of Mr. Zimmerman's girlfriends, Jatanya Belnavis, investigators said, and was paid several thousand dollars in bribes over several months. Ms. Belnavis in turn hired two men, Barry Alexander and Tony Dubose, both of Brooklyn, to help with the breakout, Ms. Pirro said. The two men were to receive $5,000 to start and $15,000 if the breakout was successful, she said.

Armed with digital copies of Ms. Wilson's identification card on which they superimposed new pictures, the plotters bought prison guard badges at a supply store and official-looking uniforms. Everyone involved was assigned to read the book, "New Jack," a first-person account of life as a prison guard at Sing Sing written by Ted Conover, a journalist who worked undercover as a guard for a year, Ms. Pirro said.

On April 24, Ms. Belnavis and a man whom investigators did not identify put on wigs and fake uniforms and walked into Sing Sing with a bag stuffed

The New York Times, February 4, 2004

with two uniforms, badges and identification cards, Ms. Pirro said. They also carried two loaded weapons: 9-millimeter and .38-caliber handguns, Ms. Pirro said. But they aborted the plan when Ms. Belnavis started hyperventilating after they reached the second floor.

On May 6, the plotters tried again, Ms. Pirro said, planning to arrive at shift change dressed as guards, using the swarm of hundreds of officers going in and out of the prison as cover. But Ms. Belnavis, Mr. Alexander and perhaps other accomplices arrived too late and again canceled their plans.

The next day, Mr. Alexander and Mr. Dubose went back to the prison in Ossining, N.Y., planning to try again. Mr. Dubose tried to enter with his fake ID card, but an officer at the gate noticed that the blue seal on his badge was raised, not flat like those of most officers, investigators said. Mr. Dubose told the officer that he was a transfer from another prison, but the officer was skeptical and sent him to the warden's office, Ms. Pirro said.

The warden demanded to see his transfer papers. Mr. Dubose asked to use the restroom. He slipped past the guard who had first stopped him by telling her he was going to get his transfer papers, then fled the prison, Ms. Pirro said. But he had left behind his fake ID card, issued under the name Anthony White, in the warden's office, an oversight that would unravel the plot.

Officials at Sing Sing immediately put the prison on lockdown and counted the inmates, but no one was missing. The State Police began an investigation, trying to determine who Anthony White was and why he had disappeared.

The crucial clue came the next day. On May 7, before Mr. Dubose tried to get into Sing Sing, an Ossining police officer, Donald Farrell, had stopped Mr. Dubose and Mr. Alexander as they moved a motorcycle that investigators said they planned to leave for the escaping prisoners near the prison. Because they were acting strangely near the prison, Officer Farrell had questioned them and looked up their driving records.

The next day, when Officer Farrell heard about the incident at Sing Sing, he told the State Police about the two men he had encountered the previous morning. Armed with the picture on the fake prison ID, investigators discovered that the Anthony White on the guard ID and the Tony Dubose whom Officer Farrell had stopped were the same person.

Mr. Zimmerman and Mr. Finley were transferred to different prisons upstate, Ms. Pirro said, and have been charged with attempted escape. The district attorney said their alleged helpers, including Ms. Wilson, 31, the guard, face a variety of felony charges, and more people could be charged when the case is presented to a grand jury.

Ron Kuby, the lawyer who represented Mr. Zimmerman in an unsuccessful attempt to appeal his weapons conviction, said: "Mr. Zimmerman would not seek to escape from prison. That is why he has lawyers."

GRAPHIC: Photo: A guard offered an inmate inside information about the Sing Sing prison. (Photo by William C. Lopez for The New York Times)

LOAD-DATE: February 4, 2004

(Interview Open)

K.L.   I want to focus the remaining part of our conversation towards the allegations

of the escape attempt at Sing Sing Correctional Facility in Ossining, New

York.

N.Z.   O.K.

K.L.   As you already know, several newspapers across the Country has covered

stories about you and the escape allegations, and it seems as if the media

was infatuated by the story. Despite the enormous amount of evidence that

Jeanine Pirro alleges to have against you, I noticed that your attorney, Ron

L. Kuby, Esq. has went on record to deny the allegations on your behalf, but

you personally have never made any statements to the media in relation to

your guilt or innocence, (until now). I would like to start off the interview by

asking you; why have you been so quiet about the situation if you know that

"you are being set up"?

N.Z.   Well, there are several reasons why I've been "quiet" about the allegations,

but those reasons has nothing to do with guilt. Simply put, I am not guilty of

attempting to escape from Sing Sing. There are so many governmental

agencies involved in this alleged "investigation", and so many high ranking

officials' jobs are on the line, that they have been doing almost anything to

keep me quiet. I don't know what other tricks these people have up their sleeves but whatever they are, it won't surprise me. I know now that they will go to any extent to keep me quiet.

K.L. When you say "these people", who are you referring to?

N.Z. I'm referring to the people that are responsible for forming the conspiracy against me, my family, and my friends.

K.L. And who are these people, can you give me some names?

N.Z. There are several people involved, and each of them represent a different government office and this is the main reason why this situation has erupted into what it is today. The people directly involved in the situation are: Deputy Inspector General, George Seyfertt, Detective Darren Daughtry, Assistant District Attorney Mike Hughes, District Attorney Jeanine Pirro, Superintendent Joe Smith, Commissioner Glen Goord, and Governor George Pataki.

K.L. I assume that all of these people somehow play a part in your case?

N.Z. Yeah, everyone is pretty much following a chain of command and the commands that were given was to go out and violate all of my family and friends' constitutional rights. There is so much corruption going on in this case that it is disgusting.

K.L. Why don't we start from the top of the story. Jeanine Pirro alleges that you attempted to escape on three separate occasions, April 24th, May 6th and May 7th of 2003. Let's start with April 24th, what exactly happened on that

165

day?

N.Z. Absolutely nothing.

K.L. Nothing?

N.Z. Yeah. Nothing.

K.L. Are you <u>sure</u> "nothing" happened?

N.Z. Yeah, I'm positive.

K.L. Well, according to Jeanine Pirro, your girlfriend or "ex-girlfriend" Jatanya Belnavis dressed up in a Correctional Officer's uniform, and a wig, and carried two loaded handguns into Sing Sing Correctional Facility. Pirro alleges that Jatanya did this with the intentions of meeting up with you somewhere in the prison and that she was suppose to give the guns and extra uniforms she had in her bag to you, so you could escape with her. Are you telling me that none of that happened?

K.L. Isn't that a great story?

N.Z. What?

K.L. This whole "James Bond style" escape plan.

K.L. So are you telling me that Jatanya didn't do the things that Pirro is alleging she did?

N.Z. I haven't answered your question yet, I only said "Isn't that a great story"?

K.L. But you are saying, "great story" as if this isn't true.

N.Z. What do you believe?

166

K.L.   I don't know, that's why I am here asking you. Only you know what happened in Sing Sing on these days. Only you were there.

N.Z.   Well, if we let Ms. Pirro tell it, I definitely tried to escape, and she wasn't "there".

K.L.   Well, the world has already heard Jeanine Pirro's side of the story, now this is your chance to explain what really happened in Sing Sing. So if Jatanya didn't do all the things that Pirro is saying she did, here is your chance to clear her name. So what happened?

N.Z.   What Pirro alleges to have taken place on April 24, May 6 and May 7 is not realistically possible. Pirro believes the information and story that was strategically and intricately fed to her. She was looking for an answer to her question as to why would a strange man walk into Sing Sing dressed as a Corrections Officer and then leave? And when this story was presented to her, she fell for it.

K.L.   So you're implying that Jatanya didn't break into Sing Sing to find you and to help you escape, and that none of this is true?

N.Z.   I will be really, really, surprised to find out that Jatanya did something like that for me.

K.L.   She was your girlfriend at the time of the alleged escape attempts, wasn't she?

N.Z.   At that time, me and Jatanya had more of a business relationship than a personal one.

K.L. Business relationship?

N.Z. Yes, we mostly stayed in contact because of the relations she had with my record company. She was still running my business for me while I was away. So our relationship focused more or less on business.

K.L. So you two weren't in love anymore.

N.Z. Nah, I don't think, at that point, she was in love with me anymore. And I know that she definitely didn't love me enough to do anything like this.

K.L. Did you still love her around that time?

N.Z. Yeah, I did.

K.L. If you're saying that Jatanya didn't break into Sing Sing on April 24th, then why would Pirro release a story like this?

N.Z. I'm not saying that Jatanya did or didn't break into Sing Sing. I can't possibly tell you what's going on on the (outside) of Sing Sing's walls because I'm on the (inside) of Sing Sing's walls and simply put, I can't see through walls. So I don't know what happened out there, but I know one thing, I damn sure ain't gonna take Jeanine Pirro's word for it.

K.L. I take it that you and Ms. Pirro do not see eye to eye?

N.Z. That lady's credibility is shot with me. She's focused too much on the media's attention. She loves to be before the cameras and to have her name in headlines, so whether or not a story is true, or even (believable) she'll call

168

up the media and have a press conference just so she can have her name in the newspapers. That lady is not prosecuting people in the pursuit of justice, she's using her position to make a name for herself, while ruining other people's lives. If she loves the cameras so much she should become an actor and leave the Criminal Injustice System alone, she's in the wrong profession.

K.L.   You sound pretty firm on your position that this story isn't true, so I want to ask you, what evidence does Pirro have against you that corroborates her allegations of the escape attempt?

N.Z.   What evidence does she have against "me"?

K.L.   Yeah ---

N.Z.   Pirro doesn't have any evidence against "me".

K.L.   She is alleging that you were the "mastermind" behind this escape attempt.

N.Z.   This is a free country, she can "allege" what she wants. She is well known for alleging things that she later can not prove (fairly) in a Court of Law. None of us were surprised when Pirro held a big press conference about this situation. I mean, give her good story and she'll run with it, that's how she works.

K.L.   So you are saying or suggesting that Pirro has absolutely no evidence against you?

N.Z.   Maybe I should lay out the (facts) for you so you can have a better

169

understanding of what's going on here, and I emphasize the words (facts) because what I give you are the facts, what the government gives you is what they want you to have and that is not facts, that is half truths, but you can't rely on that because you will never know the whole story, and therefore you can't rely on the government. So I am now prepared to give you the facts about what happened at Sing Sing.

K.L. O.K.

N.Z. On May 7th, 2003, a man who is alleged (not) to be a Correctional Officer, dressed up in a Correctional Officer uniform and attempted to walk into Sing Sing Correctional Facility. He is successful in making it into the prison but there was some type of discrepancy with his identification and so he was directed to go to the Deputy of Security's office. While the Deputy of Security was attempting to verify this young man's identification by calling another facility, the guy excuses himself and goes to the bathroom. Instead of the mystery man returning to the Deputy's office, he took a detour to the front door of the prison and was let out of the prison because he alleged that he was "only going to his car to get the rest of his paperwork."

K.L. If, at that point, the Deputy already had his suspicions about him, then why would they let him leave?

N.Z. Well, these are the questions that I am looking for answers to, and that is the point of the trial. I am almost certain they will dance around this subject, but

170

it will be interesting to hear their well prepared answers.

K.L.   Yes, that will be interesting.

N.Z.   Continuing with their allegations, when the man left the prison, he leaves behind his identification, his badge and a bag which contained two more Correctional Officers' uniforms.

K.L.   The identification and badge that were left behind, were they fake or real?

N.Z.   Pirro alleges that they were fake and that he was not a Correctional Officer.

K.L.   O.K.

N.Z.   So this man was already long gone, but like I said, he left behind his identification and so the police had a photo of him. Using the photograph, the police posted the picture on the nightly news, asking if anyone recognized him, to call in with information as to his whereabouts.

K.L.   Do you know if anyone called in?

N.Z.   I guess they did because the police tracked the man down and he was arrested on May 12th, 2003.

K.L.   Well, I guess the most obvious question is how does this man connect to you?

N.Z.   From what I have been told, and from what I understand, this guy doesn't "connect" to me at all, but there is some type of connection between him and Jatanya. The "James Bond" escape story that you read in the newspapers came from him. That was the story he gave to the police and they were

171

stupid enough to fall for it.

K.L. The guy that you are referring to, is his name Tony Dubose?

N.Z. From what I have been told so far, yes his name is Tony Dubose.

K.L. And Tony Dubose is the guy that broke into Sing Sing?

N.Z. Allegedly broke into Sing Sing, yes.

K.L. You say "allegedly" as if you don't even believe that he broke into Sing Sing?

N.Z. I believe absolutely nothing Jeanine Pirro says.

K.L. Let's back up for a minute. Pirro alleges that Jatanya broke into Sing Sing on April 24th, 2003, but that she suffered a panic attack and aborted the plans to meet up with you in the prison. Did that part of the story also come from Mr. Dubose?

N.Z. Originally, yes. That was his story.

K.L. Besides Mr. Dubose's allegations, what other evidence does Pirro have that proves that Jatanya broke into Sing Sing on April 24th? I'm sure that a prison such as Sing Sing would have video cameras at the front gates?

N.Z. There are no video tapes that shows Jatanya breaking into Sing Sing. When Mr. Dubose was arrested on May 12, 2003, he had already prepared this wonderful story of an escape plan. What the readers must keep in mind is that Mr. Dubose allegedly broke into Sing Sing on May 7th, but then he wasn't arrested until May 12th, which means he had a total of five (5) days to come up with an excuse as to why his picture was on the identification card of a

172

phony Correctional Officer. According to Pirro, Mr. Dubose already knew the police were looking for him because he mistakenly left behind his identification card in Sing Sing, and so he knew it was only a matter of time before he would be arrested, and therefore he needed a story to tell the police, and this was his story. He basically told the police that Jatanya paid him to break into Sing Sing on May 7th and not only did he agree to do this, but that he also agreed to carry two loaded handguns in the bag that he carried into the prison.

K.L. Isn't it true that when Mr. Dubose left behind his phony badge and identification in Sing Sing, he also left the bag he was carrying?

N.Z. From what I understand, yes.

K.L. Well, were there any guns found in the bag?

N.Z. No guns were found in the bag and there were never any guns found in relation to this case. Mr. Dubose is a very creative young man. He continuously adds things to his story to make it more interesting, it gets better and better as he goes along.

K.L. Pirro alleges that there was guns involved in this case but you are alleging that there were no guns recovered in this case. Do you feel that Jeanine Pirro alleged that there were guns involved in this case just to make the story more interesting?

N.Z. I think she alleged that there were guns involved because that's what she was

173

told. She didn't take the time to investigate or corroborate this man's story before making her allegations public but I think this was purposely done.

K.L. And I guess that Ms. Pirro is under the impression that Jatanya broke into the prison because Mr. Dubose told her that?

N.Z. Originally yes, he told Pirro that Jatanya broke into Sing Sing on April 24th, and that he then tried again on May 7, 2003 to get in. That was his story.

K.L. Well, you are suggesting that Jatanya didn't break into Sing Sing on April 24th, but what about May 6th, is it true that she was going to try again but that "they arrived too late to take advantage of the shift change"?

N.Z. I don't know who "arrived where" to take "advantage of what". I'm not on the outside of Sing Sing 30 foot walls, I can't tell you what goes on out there.

K.L. Pirro alleges that you told them to do this. Did anyone ever tell you that they arrived too late to get into the prison?

N.Z. Who am I, Jesus Christ? How can I possibly convince all of these people to risk their lives for me in doing something like this. I'm a 28 year old black man, remember? I don't have the power to convince people to risk their lives for me like the President does. My last name isn't Bush, it's Zimmerman.

K.L. Are you referring to the War in Iraq?

N.Z. Yes.

K.L. Well, I already know your position on that so I won't go into it, but let's move on to what happened on May 7th, 2003. Something obviously happened on

174

that day because there was a "really big commotion" at Sing Sing I am told.

6A. Did Nicholas Zimmerman and

Steven Finley know that Tony Dubose

was breaking into Sing Sing C.F.?

N.Z. That may be the only truth to the story, something did happen at Sing Sing on May 7th because I remember there was complete chaos going on in the visiting room. The prison was completely locked down for hours and the visitors weren't allowed to leave until about five or six o'clock. I remember some of the female visitors were yelling and crying because they only expected to be at Sing Sing until 2:45 pm, which is the normal time that Sing Sing's visiting room closes. But like I said, they weren't released until 6:00 pm and most of these people had children that they had to pick up from school and others had to get to work. So there was a lot of confusion on that day.

K.L. Did the officials provide any of the visitors access to a phone to contact their families and/or the jobs?

N.Z. Most times, all the police do is make a bad situation worse. There was a phone in Sing Sing's visiting room but they wouldn't let anyone use it because of "Security Concerns".

K.L. I can see how that must have caused even more problems.

N.Z.   Yeah, it was just crazy in there.

K.L.   Well, Ms. Pirro alleges that that "commotion" was because of you, and that
        you told Mr. Dubose to break into Sing Sing and meet you in Sing Sing's
        visiting room to give you and Mr. Finley the guns and Correctional Officer
        uniforms he had in his duffle bag. She says the only reason why he didn't
        make it to you is because he was stopped at the front door. She says if Mr.
        Dubose would have reached you and Mr. Finley there would have been a
        "catastrophe" at Sing Sing.

N.Z.   The only "catastrophe" here is Jeanine Pirro's long standing career in Law
        Enforcement. Ms. Pirro is no stranger to corruption herself. It wasn't too long
        ago that "Ms. Pirro" was the focus of an investigation by the Federal
        Government into her and her husband's connections to the Mafia. And let's
        not forget, she was also under investigation for tax evasion in which her
        husband plead guilty and was sentenced to two years in prison in exchange
        for her not having to go to jail. So she is no goodie two-shoes herself. (See
        Exhibit L and M).

K.L.   Oh, I didn't know that.

N.Z.   Yeah, so why should we believe her?

K.L.   Well did you or didn't you tell Mr. Dubose to break into Sing Sing?

N.Z.   I don't even know who the hell Tony Dubose is!

K.L.   You don't know a Tony Dubose?

N.Z. No.

K.L. He alleges that he broke into Sing Sing to help you and Mr. Finley escape.

N.Z. He can allege what he wants.

K.L. And you don't know who I am talking about?

N.Z. No.

K.L. Then why would he say that you told him to break into Sing Sing?

N.Z. When people are caught in the commission of a crime they will say almost anything to cover up their true intentions, so if this crazy story works for Mr. Dubose, and if he is able to conceal what really took place on May 7th by fooling everyone in Jeanine Pirro's office with this story, then this situation will go down in history as just that. I'm sure Ms. Pirro will have it no other way.

K.L. And why is that?

N.Z. Just think about it for a second. If it ever surfaces that this story isn't true, and that Mr. Dubose has fooled Ms. Pirro, a lady that has been in Law Enforcement for more than twenty years, then she is going to look like a complete idiot in the public's eye and we all know how Ms. Pirro likes to look in "the public's eye".

K.L. Umm ...

N.Z. So it's in her best interest to keep this story looking and smelling like an escape attempt, but if the truth were to ever come out, boy would a lot of people be in trouble.

K.L. You say that Mr. Dubose is "concealing what really took place" at Sing Sing on May 7th. What really did happen at Sing Sing?

N.Z. An escape attempt, right?

K.L. I don't know. Did it?

N.Z. Of course it did, the good folks in the Westchester County District Attorney's office wouldn't lie to us, now would they? (laughs)

K.L. (laughs)

N.Z. So it's an escape attempt for now, but let's see what it turns out to be at trial.

K.L. When Sing Sing was shut down on May 7th where were you and Steven?

N.Z. Mr. Finley and myself were both in Sing Sing's visiting room.

K.L. Who came to visit you on that day?

N.Z. I had a visit from my artist, Kira Scott, and her friend Tiana Payne. And Tiana brought her daughter along with her.

K.L. Who visited Steven?

N.Z. I don't know, that was two years ago.

K.L. Does the name "Kiesha Moore" ring a bell?

N.Z. According to the paperwork I received from my lawyers, Pirro alleges that Kiesha Moore visited Steven on May 7th, but once again we are talking about Pirro here.

K.L. Have you ever asked Steven who visited him on May 7th?

N.Z. Yes.

K.L. And what did he say?

N.Z. I'm sorry, but I can't discuss with you what I discuss with him. He's my co-defendant in this unfortunate situation, and so I must protect him.

K.L. How long have you known Steven?

N.Z. Uh .... I rather not answer any questions about my comrade. Other than he is a really stand-up guy. You don't come across too many people like him in these times, but he is a really good person. I have a lot of respect for that man.

K.L. Is it true that he was wrongfully convicted?

N.Z. I believe one of your colleagues is doing a story on him also . So when his book is finished he'll answer all of those questions himself. I'm not at liberty to answer them for him.

NOTE: Steven Finley's book, which is still untitled, will be released soon.

K.L. When Sing Sing was locked down on May 7th, what exactly were you thinking?

N.Z. I wasn't thinking about it too much, I just figured the count was off again.

K.L. Explain that.

N.Z. Three or four times a day, the administration at Sing Sing counts all the prisoners in the facility but it seems like no one can count past ten in Sing Sing so the count is always wrong and the prison is usually lock down until they get it right, so I thought that was the problem. But I never seen them hold the visitors in the prison like that, so that was strange.

K.L. On May 7th, while the prison was on lockdown, had anyone accused you of attempting to escape that day?

N.Z. No.

K.L. When was the first time you learned that you were accused of attempting to escape from Sing Sing?

N.Z. On May 15th, 2003, when I was transferred to Shawangunk Correctional Facility.

K.L. And that was a total of eight days after the break in?

N.Z. Right.

6B. Sean is placed in

Solitary Confinement in violation

of his Constitutional Rights

K.L. While you were being transferred to Shawangunk, from Sing Sing, did anyone accuse you of attempting to escape?

N.Z. The day I was transferred from Sing Sing, (May 15th, 2003) that was the first day I met Deputy Inspector General George Seyfertt. He asked "if I had any information that I wanted to give him" and I just basically asked him why was I being transferred and he said: "I figured you was gonna ask me that, but you will tell me everything I wanna know when I stick you in Solitary Confinement

180

for a while". After that conversation, he left, and I was transferred to Shawangunk.

K.L. What happened after you were transferred to Shawangunk?

N.Z. I was immediately placed in Solitary Confinement.

K.L. Had anyone explained to you why you were being placed in Solitary Confinement?

N.Z. No one told me anything. I repeatedly asked Sergeants, Deputies and Captains why was I being held in Solitary Confinement, but no one would tell me anything. On May 17th, I received an "Administration Segregation Report" from an officer of Shawangunk, and that was the first time I was given any information in relation to an escape attempt at Sing Sing.

K.L. Explain what an "Administration Segregation Report" is.

N.Z. An Administration Segregation Report is a document that must be given to prisoners whenever the "Administration" decides they want to "Segregate" you from general population in any prison. This report is supposed to inform the prisoner of the specific reasons why he has been placed in Solitary Confinement, and what he is accused of doing. The reason why this report is so important is because the Department of Corruption has a history of throwing prisoners in Solitary Confinement, at random, and never telling them why they were being held there. So the court has decided, in the landmark case of Hewitt v. Helms 103 Sct. 864 (1983) that this report must be issued

181

to the segregated prisoner.

K.L.   And you were given this report right?

N.Z.   Yes.

K.L.   And did the report explain why you were being placed in Solitary
Confinement?

N.Z.   The report I was given didn't really explain anything. It only said, "You are
under investigation for an attempted escape of Sing Sing CorrectionalFacility.
Your presence in general population represents a risk to the safety and
security of the facility". (see Exhibit N).

K.L.   At the time you were given this report, had anyone told you about, or did you
know anything about Jatanya or Mr. Dubose breaking into Sing Sing to help
you and Steven escape?

N.Z.   I learned about these allegations the same way you learned about these
allegations, through the media. I was placed in Solitary Confinementin May,
and the first report that came out in the media about this situation was in
June (see Exhibit O). A Corrections Officer was nice enough to give me the
article so that's how I first got any informationabout the breakin at Sing Sing.

K.L.   How did you feel when you got the first media report about the escape
attempt?

N.Z.   I was actually laughing when the Corrections Officer gave me that article. It
was kind of funny to me. My first theory was there must be another

182

"Nicholas Zimmerman" in another New York State prison and the media and the police has him mixed up with me. So I figured as soon as I speak to the Superintendent at Shawangunk or the officials involved in this situation and just explain to them that I don't know anything about any escape attempt, they would let me out of Solitary Confinement. Boy, was I wrong. I had to learn the hard way that I was the scapegoat in the situation.

K.L. You say you were transferred on May 15th. Had you been given the chance to contact your family to let them know you had been transferred?

N.Z. Nah, nobody knew where I was. My mom had tried to visit me at Sing Sing on May 19th but the Corrections Officer there told her I had been transferred, but they didn't know where to. After calling around, for a few days, my family found out that I was at Shawangunk, so they came up to see me.

K.L. I'm sure they were happy to see you?

N.Z. Jatanya and my mother came to see me on May 25th, 2003 at Shawangunk, and that was the day that I learned that Detective Darren (Daughtry) and Inspector General George (Seyfertt) were playing a sick game of cat and mouse with my family. My transfer to Shawangunk was part of Daughtry's and Seyfertt's conspiratorial plan to arrest and embarrass anyone who visited me. They knew I had a lot of family and friends, because my visiting records showed that I received visits on a daily basis, from different people, and they knew if they transferred me to another prison my family would find me and try

183

to visit me, and when they did they would be there to arrest them. So after I had the visit with my mother and Jatanya on the 25th, Daughtry was waiting in the parking lot, and he arrested them.

K.L. Daughtry arrested your mother?

N.Z. Yeah.

K.L. For what?

N.Z. Daughtry's interest in arresting my mother was for the purpose of embarrassment and abusing his authority. He had absolutely no reason to arrest my mother that day. He may have (thought) he had reason enough to arrest Jatanya, but he had no right or probable cause to arrest my mother for anything. Daughtry was, and still is, nothing more than a puppet on the strings of Inspector General George Seyfertt.

K.L. What was your mother charged with?

N.Z. She wasn't charged with anything. He had nothing to charge her with. He only wanted to make her look like a criminal to the administration of Shawangunk. He wanted to scare and embarrass anyone that visited me.

K.L. Is that why the C.O. in the processing room "warned me" that I might be arrested when I leave here? (See page 2 of this book.)

N.Z. Yeah, he probably figured what happened to them would happen to you, but he doesn't know what's going on.

K.L. You said Jatanya was also arrested. Was she charged with anything?

184

N.Z.   Jatanya was arrested and charged with "promoting prison contraband". A person is guilty of "promoting prison contraband" whenever they bring any type of contraband into a New York State prison. Based off of Mr. Dubose's allegations that Jatanya broke into Sing Sing on August 24th, Daughtry arrested her.

K.L.   I understand that you are still in Solitary Confinement?

N.Z.   Yes.

K.L.   How long have you been in Solitary Confinement?

N.Z.   It's been fourteen months now.

K.L.   Has anyone yet to explain to you why you are being held there?

N.Z.   I think it's obvious to everyone why I'm being held in Solitary. Daughtry, Seyfertt, Pirro, Hughes, and everyone else involved in this "investigation" wants me to accept the blame for what took place at Sing Sing. I have been offered the release from Solitary Confinement on numerous occasions in exchange for a plea of guilty to the charges of attempted escape and conspiracy to attempt to escape. I have repeatedly rejected the offers, and each time I was sent back to Solitary Confinement. Had I accepted their offers, I would have been released, but at the same time I would have been compromising and substituting my morals and completely throwing away my constitutional rights to a fair trial. The same constitutional rights that Malcolm and Martin died for, and I just couldn't do that.

185

K.L.   This crime took place on May 7th, 2003, but you weren't actually charged with attempting to escape until February, 2004. What took the government so long in charging you and Steven in this case?

N.Z.   The government doesn't have a case against me and/or Steven, therefore Pirro's strategy was to place us in Solitary Confinement for a year or so until we pretty much "beg for mercy" and then offer us a deal to plead guilty to attempting to escape in order for us to be released from Solitary. Her plan didn't work, there will be no deals on my behalf.

K.L.   What about Steven?

N.Z.   He has rejected the offers as well.

K.L.   Is he also in Solitary Confinement?

N.Z.   Yes.

K.L.   I need you to describe what Solitary Confinement is like for the readers.

N.Z.   Just think about the worst place on earth and there you have it?

K.L.   Explain what the punishment is like in Solitary Confinement.

N.Z.   You are locked in your cell 23 hours a day, you come out 1 hour a day for recreation (which most prisoners don't do because it's too cold outside), you get three showers a week, you're not allowed to watch television or use the phone, you're allowed one visit a week, you can't have any of your personal property in your cell, only legal work, you are not allowed to buy food from the commissary, you basically have to eat what the C.O.'s give you whenever

186

they decide they want to feed you, you can't receive any food packages from your family and the harassment by the Corrections Officers is unimaginable.

K.L. And you and Steven have been living like this for the past fourteen months because you won't plead guilty to the escape attempt charges?

N.Z. Absolutely.

K.L. Now I understand that you have filed a ten million dollar lawsuit against the Department of Corrections for what they have been doing to you for the past year or so?

N.Z. Yeah, at the present time I currently have a lawsuit pending against eighteen members of the Department of Corrections for mainly placing me in Solitary Confinement, against my constitutional rights, in order to get me to plead guilty to the escape attempt charges. The Federal Judge handling my case has agreed that my lawsuit has merit and has allowed me to proceed with the case, so I am anticipating the trial.

K.L. Can you give the readers any idea as to what it is you're alleging in your lawsuit?

N.Z. I'm suing the Department of Corrections for several reasons, deprivation of counsel, medical assistance, due process, etc... All of these issues are pretty complicated so I won't even attempt to explain them here, but there is one issue that is pretty straight forward so I'll go into that one a little bit. As I explained to you earlier, the Administration Segregation Report is the most

187

important document when placing a prisoner in Solitary Confinement. It is the starting point of the disciplinary process. The State Courts (People Ex. Rel. Vega v. Smith 495 N.Y.S.2d 332 Ct. App. 1985) and the Federal Courts Wolf v. McDonnell 94 Sct. 2963 1974 and the Department of Corrections Rules and Regulations 7NYCRR all consistently state that the Administration Segregation Report must list the "date, time and place" of the incident, and that it must also list "the names of any other inmates that were involved in the incident." If you look at the report that was given to me, it does not state anything about the "date, time and place" of the alleged escape attempt at Sing Sing Correctional Facility and it does not state that Steven Finley was involved in the incident . (see Exhibit N).

K.L.   I see that your report does not list that information, but do you really think that the Courts will award you "ten million dollars" for that?

N.Z.   To an average layman to the law this would seem like a minute thing, but to a lawyer this is like money in the bank, and I'll explain why. The Sergeant that issued this report has worked for the Department of Corruptions for over twenty years. He has written plenty of these reports during his career and he knows what information is supposed to be contained in this report. My position is that he purposely and intentionally omitted this information from the report so that I would never know what was happening to me and why I was being held in Solitary Confinement.

K.L.   Why would he do that?

N.Z.   The conspiracy that was formed by Seyfertt and Daughtry against Steven and myself was simple. Their plan was to put us in Solitary Confinement for as long as possible, and keep as much information away from us as possible, so that we would completely lose our mind while we were in Solitary Confinement. They figured that as long as they made it appear in the media that they had a "ton of evidence against us", that the word would get back to us and we would eventually plead guilty without ever investigating their allegations. So Seyfertt basically directed the Sergeant that wrote this report not to include this vital information in the report. He wanted to keep this information from us for as long as possible.

K.L.   But I still don't understand why this information is so important? Don't you already know the date, time, and place of the break in at Sing Sing?

N.Z.   Yeah, I know that information now, (a year after the alleged situation took place) but I didn't know that information on May 17th, 2003 when the report was given to me. Had I known this information on May 17th (when I was supposed to have known it) I would have been able to defend myself against these allegations at my disciplinary hearing.

K.L.   Explain what takes place at a disciplinary hearing.

N.Z.   A disciplinary hearing is like a miniature criminal trial. Mostly everything that takes place at a real trial takes place at a disciplinary hearing. You are

189

allowed to call witnesses, submit evidence and testify on your own behalf so it's pretty much the equivalent of a criminal trial, the only difference is it's conducted inside the prison and not in a courtroom.

K.L. And I take it that there is a judge there?

N.Z. Yeah, there is a judge there, but you can forget about he/she being fair and impartial. We have what is called a hearing officer at our disciplinary hearings and he/she is to act as a Judge at the proceedings. But the hearing officer is usually a Captain, Lieutenant, or a Sergeant and they work for the Department of Corruption and they are usually friends with the person that is accusing the prisoner of his wrongdoings. And so, with a disciplinary process set up so intricately as this one, there is really no way a prisoner can get a fair hearing.

K.L. You say if the date, time and place would have been contained in the report you would have been able to "defend yourself at your disciplinary hearing". Explain how this information would have helped you.

N.Z. I was given this report on May 17th, 2003 and my disciplinary hearing was held on May 23rd, 2003. When my disciplinary hearing was held at Shawangunk, I could not prove that I was innocent because I didn't know what I was accused of doing. This report wasn't alleging what I did, and this was the only information I was given in relation to this situation. So while I'm sitting at my disciplinary hearing, the hearing officer is expecting me to explain and

190

prove my innocence but I can't because I didn't know what was going on at that point and this is exactly how Seyfertt planned this thing to go down. Now if this report would have explained the date, time and place of the escape attempt, I would have been able to call some witnesses that were in Sing Sing's visiting room at the time it is alleged that I attempted to escape, and they would have been able to testify that they were in my presence at that time and that I didn't "attempt" to do anything. Seyfertt knew that I would try to call these witnesses and this is why he didn't want me to know this information.

K.L.   Did you explain all of this to the hearing officer at your disciplinary hearing?

N.Z.   Of course, but like I said they all stick together, and they are all friends, so he tried to cover it up as much as he could. He was under pressure to follow the orders that Seyfertt gave him and so he acted as if he didn't know what I was talking about. But in following Seyfertt's orders, the hearing officer broke the law and violated my constitutional rights at the same time. As I stated earlier, the Department of Corruption has a history of issuing faulty Administration Segregation Reports to prisoners in order to keep the truth and the facts about the situation away from them, and the Courts recognized this. So in 1994 the Federal Courts in Hameed v. Mann 849 F.Supp 169 announced a rule of law that says the Department of Corruption must include the date, time, and place of the incident because this information is very

191

important to the disciplinary hearing, and if they don't include it, the prisoner can sue that Department. The Courts realized how important this information was because it stated:

> "Primary reason why prison officials are required to give adequate notice to prisoner before disciplinary hearings is to give the charged party a chance to marshal the facts in his defense and to clarify what the charges are in fact; thus, notice lacking required specifics which fail to apprise the accused party of charges brought against him must be found unconstitutional because accused party cannot adequately prepare a defense" at 169

And so, because the Federal Government had already instructed the Department of Corruption to follow this law, and because they refused to follow this law, I am suing them.

K.L. I understand now how they broke the law by not including this information, and how important this information was, but do you really think you will be awarded "10 million dollars" for that?

N.Z. Actually, the failure of the Department of Corruption to list this information in the report is only the starting point of my argument to the Court. What I am basically arguing is had they listed this information in the report then I would not have been in Solitary Confinement for "fourteen months" because I would have been able to prove my innocence "fourteen months" ago at my disciplinary hearing. I'm also arguing that this was intentionally done, and was not mistakenly omitted from the report, which should make the Court penalize the Department of Corruption even more. Lastly I'm arguing all the harassment I received from the Correctional Officers during my fourteen months in Solitary Confinement, all the days I had to go without food, phone calls, showers, visits, clean linen, clean clothes, etc.. So it's a lot going on in my lawsuit.

K.L.   O.K. I think I have a better understanding of the situation now. You stated that the "Department of Corruption" has offered to release you from Solitary Confinement in exchange for a guilty plea to attempting to escape. How much extra time will be added to the sentence you are already serving if you were to accept this deal?

N.Z.   I would be pleading guilty to attempting to escape, which is an E Felony, and I have been offered one year to run "concurrent" to the sentence I am already serving.

K.L.   Explain to the readers what concurrent sentencing means?

N.Z.   When your sentence runs concurrent to another sentence, this means that the time you are doing on your first sentence also counts toward the time you are doing on your second sentence. So both sentences are running (concurrently) or at the same time. So when they allege that the one year I would get for this case, would run concurrent to the time I'm already serving, they're basically saying, in reality, that I wouldn't be doing any extra time in prison because I already served more than one year on this case.

K.L.   If they're willing to let you out of Solitary Confinement, and if you won't be doing any extra time, why don't you accept the agreement just to get out of lockdown?

N.Z.   That was Jeanine Pirro's strategy from the beginning of this ordeal and I will not give her the satisfaction of giving in to her conspiracy. There will be no plea-bargaining to anything on my behalf in relation to this case. So if they want to keep me in Solitary Confinement forever, they can do that, but I will never be a part of their corruption.

6C. How strong is Pirro's

case against Sean

K.L.   You and Steven have been charged in a twenty-one (21) count indictment by the Westchester County District Attorney's Office (See Exhibit P).   The charges include everything from conspiracy to attempted possession of a weapon. The office responsible for charging you with this indictment alleges to have "much evidence" against you and Steven. After I read the indictment myself, I started to get the impression that more people than just "Mr. Dubose" was feeding this story to Jeanine Pirro. Did you ever get the feeling, after reading these 21 count indictment, that maybe you and Steven should have accepted Pirro's offer?

N.Z. To a person who does not understand the structure of the law, they too, would start to get worried if they were to read the indictment that was handed down against me and Steven. Pirro put this indictment together, as she put every other defendants indictment together, to scare people into pleading guilty. A twenty-one count indictment seems like an awful big indictment, but when you start to apply the law to each charge in that indictment, you start to know and understand that Pirro's "allegations" will never be anything more than "allegations."

K.L. Well, why don't you "apply the law" to some of the charges for us?

N.Z. O.K., I will do that for you. But first I think it's imperative that I explain to you why "Accomplice Testimony must be Corroborated" before the case can go to trial.

K.L. O.K.

N.Z. Let's start with the definition of an Accomplice, shall we.

K.L. O.K.

N.Z. According to Webster (the dictionary) accomplice means "an assocate in a crime" and according to C.P.L. 60.22, accomplice means "a person that was in some way involved in a crime." More than three decades ago the State courts and the federal courts all agreed that accomplice testimony is the

195

most suspect evidence that could ever be offered in a criminal trial. The courts found that it was too easy for a person to be apprehended in the commission of a crime and then start to point the finger at anyone else in order to take the blame away from oneself. So the courts, in agreement with each other, started to announce rules of law that states an accomplices word must be corroborated before a trial can be held on the allegations. In layman's terms this means that whenever a person commits a crime, and get's caught, and later alleges that another person was involved in that crime, that person's word must be corroborated with evidence that tends to connect the second person to the crime **(before) the case can go to trial** (People v. Cona 424 N.Y.S.2d 146 Ct. App. 1979).

K.L. It seems like "corroboration" is the key, but what do the courts consider sufficient corroboration?

N.Z. Good question, and I guess I can best answer your question by giving you an example of what corroboration means to the courts. Let's say, for instance, me and you get together and we rob a bank one day. And when we rob this bank, you happen to get caught, but I make a clean getaway. I mean nobody else in the bank can identify me because I wore a ski mask. There are no fingerprints because I wore gloves. And no one can identify the car I was driving because all the customers were lying face down on the floor when I left the bank. But let's say you get caught because you tripped and broke your

196

leg while you were running from the bank and I leave you there, and naturally, because I left you there you get upset and tell the police that I was in on the bank robbery with you.

K.L. O.K.

N.Z. Now in this instance, the only evidence the police have against me is your word that I was involved in this bank robbery with you, and your word, at this point, is "insufficient corroboration" to arrest me and charge me with anything. There is absolutely nothing to suggest that I robbed that bank with you, but you, and that's not enough.

K.L. O.K., I have a better understanding of what corroboration is, and hopefully the readers do to, but what does any of that have to do with your case?

N.Z. Well, the problem with Pirro's case is simple? Pirro alleges that I told Mr. Dubose to break into Sing Sing, and if she is correct, that would mean Mr. Dubose is my "accomplice" because he was "in some way involved in the crime." Therefore, since Mr. Dubose is my accomplice, his word would need to be corroborated (before) this case can go to trial. Actually, his word should have been corroborated before Steven and I were arrested and charged in this case, but Daughtry decided to go ahead and break that law and that's just another reason why I'm suing him.

K.L. Well, since Jatanya was arrested for also breaking into Sing Sing on April 24th isn't that enough corroboration, she is your girlfriend.

N.Z.   Once again, the allegations that Jatanya broke into Sing Sing on April 24th come from Mr. Dubose, these allegations are based on his word, and nothing corroborates it. Even if there were any allegations that Jatanya did attempt to break into Sing Sing, that would be corroboration evidence against "Jatanya" not me. That does not show that "I" attempted to escape.

K.L.   What about the cell phone? Mr. Dubose told the police that he talked to you on a cell phone while you were at Sing Sing. Now, since Daughtry has your cell phone, isn't that corroboration?

N.Z.   What "cell phone" does Daughtry have?

K.L.   You are being charged with being in possession of a cell phone while you were at Sing Sing, right?

N.Z.   Yes, I'm being "charged" with that, but charges mean nothing.

K.L.   And you were indicted on that charge too?

N.Z.   Still means absolutely nothing.

K.L.   Well, when Daughtry testifies at your trial and they introduce that cell phone and he says that he got the cell phone from you don't you think the jury is going to convict you?

N.Z.   Daughtry won't be introducing any cell phones at my trial because he doesn't have any cell phones to introduce. The allegations of me having a cell phone while I was in Sing Sing also come from the creative mind of Mr. Dubose. From what I understand, my property and the cell I was in at Sing Sing was searched thoroughly and no mysterious cell phone was recovered. So once again, Pirro is relying on Mr. Dubose word that I had a cell phone while I was at Sing Sing, and that "word" has no corroboration.

K.L. Then why would Pirro charge you with possession of a cellular phone if she doesn't have the cellular phone that you are supposed to be in possession of?

N.Z. Pirro, as well as any District Attorney, will charged you with murdering the President of the United States if they thought you were stupid enough to plead guilty to it. If I were to plead guilty to this case tomorrow, Pirro will have no problem accepting that plea even though she knows I didn't "attempt" to escape from Sing Sing. As long as she loooks good in the media, that's all that matters.

K.L. You emphasize the word "attempt" every time you mention (escape attempt). Is there something you are trying to point out?

N.Z. Just the fact alone that Steven and I were charged with "attempting" to do anything is a joke by itself. Once again, according to Webster the word attempt means "to make an effort towards a goal" and according to C.P.L. 110.00 "a person is guilty of attempt to commit a crime when he engages in conduct which tends to effect the commission of such crime." Now, I'm no rocket scientist, but I'm smart enough to know that I didn't "engage in any conduct" or "make any effort towards any goals" on April 24, May 6 or May 7, 2003 that would suggest that I attempted to escape from Sing Sing.

K.L. I don't think Pirro is alleging that you and Steven did anything, but she is more

or less relying on the fact that had this plan worked out the way you expected

it to, and had Mr. Dubose made it to you and Steven, you would have

escaped.

N.Z. The day congress gives Jeanine Pirro the power to convict people on the mere

premise of what she thinks they "would have" done in a situation such as this

one the citizens of America can kiss their Constitutional Rights to due

process good-bye. Fortunately for Steven and myself, the courts have

repeatedly held that "the Criminal Justice System does not punish evil

thoughts" (People v. Bracey 392 N.Y.S.2d 412 Ct. of App. 1977) and what

this basically means is that Pirro wants to punish Steven and I for what she

thinks we thought about doing, and the law says she simply can not do that.

"Attempt means that a person must actually do something and since Steven

and I didn't "attempt" to walk, run, or jump out of Sing Sing than she does

not have a case."

K.L. If your allegations that Pirro doesn't have any guns or cellular phones are

correct, and if you didn't "attempt" to escape, and if Mr. Dubose word has

never been corroborated that you ever told him to break into Sing Sing, then

why would Pirro even go as far as charging you with this case and holding a

press conference?

N.Z. Well, like we discussed earlier, Pirro loves to be before the media, even if the story she is presenting has no merit. My father use to always say "how do you make yourself look good? By making someone else look bad." So the more Pirro get's out there in the media and makes it appear that she is fighting crime and bringing criminals to justice (even though they may be innocent) her position will always be solidified as the District Attorney of Westchester County. It's a dirty job but I guess somebody has got to do it. Even though Pirro's reasoning for presenting this story to the media is obvious, I think her motives run a little deeper than what we see on the surface.

6D. What was Jeanine Pirro's

true intentions in bringing this case?

K.L.   There were several people arrested in relation to this escape attempt and two of which I noticed were Barry Alexander and Latrina Boyd. I noticed that these two people were also witnesses in the case that you are currently serving time on. Barry and Latrina were actually two of the witnesses that submitted affidavits to Judge Rosengarten in Queens that state that you were in their presence on September 19th 1998, and that you didn't attack Nakia Stubbs with a gun. I can see how important they are to the case you are currently serving time on, but I don't understand why they have been arrested in relation to this escape attempt case. Maybe you can explain to me and

201

the readers their "alleged" roles in the whole thing.

N.Z. Latrina Boyd's alleged involvement in this case is a joke as well. She to was arrested just as Jatanya and my mother was. She came to visit me at Shawangunk on June 30, 2003 and Daughtry was once again waiting in the bushes of the parking lot at Shawangunk with his "S.W.A.T." team and they arrested her.

K.L. Daughtry really likes the bushes, huh? (laughs)

N.Z. Yeah, he does. (laughs)

K.L. I noticed that Daughtry arrested your mother, Jatanya, and Latrina when they all attempted to visit you at Shawangunk, but if he was really looking for them since May 7, 2003, (the date of the break-in at Sing Sing) then why didn't he just go to their house to arrest them? I'm sure he knew where they lived, that should be listed in the N.Y.S.P. computers.

N.Z. Daughtry already knew where everybody lived before he arrested them at Shawangunk. If he wanted to arrest them he could have went to their jobs or their homes and arrested them. But instead, he waited until they all visited me and then arrested them.

K.L. Do you ever get the impression that Detective Daughtry is jealous of the fact that you have a lot of girlfriends?

N.Z. I don't think there is any question to the fact that Daughtry is one jealous individual and I seriously recommend that he see a doctor about his problem

202

before he runs across a person that is not as kind and forgiving as I am. I

think the entire situation and alleged "investigation" was, and still is fueled by

more jealously and hatred then active leads. If you notice, Pirro made every

effort to announce in the media that the young ladies that were arrested was

"Zimmerman's girlfriends" ...

K.L.   Is it true that all of these girls were, in fact, your girlfriends?

N.Z.   Whether they are my girlfriends or not, what difference does it make to the

situation that allegedly took place at Sing Sing? If you are publically

presenting an alleged break-in at Sing Sing, why don't you just announce the

people that was arrested and that's it? Why is Pirro so focused on whether

or not they are my girlfriends?

K.L.   Maybe she wants you for herself? (laughs)

N.Z.   Oh great. Now I'll have two D.A.'s fighting over me, Bishop and Pirro. (laughs)

K.L.   You're sought of a ladies man aren't you? I mean, regardless if the escape

attempt story is true or not, the ladies involved in this case use to visit you on

a daily basis at Sing Sing. I have seen your visiting records, and some of

them use to visit at the same time. How did you manage all of these women,

were there ever any fights when they showed up at the same time for the

visit?

N.Z.   I'm no ladies man, that's just the way the media makes it seem. The female's

that were visiting me at Sing Sing were good friends and they knew and

203

understood my case and knew I was in prison for something I didn't do, so they supported me and visited me a lot.

K.L. You said "were visiting" you, they don't visit any more?

N.Z. Nah, nobody visits me anymore. They are all too scared that they will be arrested. That was the message that Daughtry wanted to send out to everybody that visited me. He knew if he arrested Jatanya and my mother, the word would get out that they were arrested, and people would stop coming to see me.

K.L. Did people stop visiting you?

N.S. Yeah, the feeble minded people that were foolish enough to fall for Daughtry's plans. My mother came back to visit me the day after she was arrested at Shawangunk. She was embarrassed and humiliated at the situation, but she didn't let that stop her from coming to see me. I remember her saying to me "I don't care who tell me not to visit you, I'm going to visit my son. If they wanna lock me up again, then go ahead. But I'm going to visit my son." I cried when she told me that. Knowing that my mother went through so much for me and she was still in my corner made me feel good.

K.L. What about the other females allegedly involved, have they been to visit you since this situation started?

N.Z. No.

K.L. Jatanya?

N.Z. Nope

K.L. Latrina?

N.Z. Nope

K.L. Tamara Johnson?

N.Z. Nope

K.L. Kira Scott?

N.Z. Nope

K.L. Tiana Payne?

N.Z. Nope

K.L. Quangtrice Wilson?

N.Z. Nope

K.L. Do you feel it was Daughtry's intention to stop these people from visiting you by arresting them?

N.Z. It's funny that you ask that question because I have heard that Daughtry has made personal advances to all the ladies that he has arrested in relation to this case.

K.L. Has he been successful in his advances?

N.Z. Daughtry is a cop, what would any of these ladies want to do with him?

K.L. Are you suggesting that these women don't like cops?

N.Z. I'm suggesting that I have never come across any ladies that like cops and if I did, I made it my business to stay as far away from them as I can.

K.L. You allege that you stay away from females that like cops, but you and Quangtrice Wilson had a "romantic relationship" while you were at Sing Sing, and she was a Correctional Officer. Isn't that close enough to a cop?

N.Z. I think this is a perfect time for me to clear-up my relationship with Wilson. It makes me sick to know that my name has been publically linked or even "romantically" linked as being in a relationship with anyone involved in law enforcement. I am in no way trying to appear to be (tough) by saying I don't like people that work in law enforcement. I'm only stating that when you get involved with people that are on that side of the fence (meaning law enforcement) you run an even greater risk of someone snitching on you when they get caught because these types of people do not believe in the phrases "holding it down" or "keeping it real." They live by one code and that's the "Save Yourself code." So even if I did plan an escape attempt, I certainly would not have involved a Corrections Officer.

K.L. Then where would Pirro come up with the idea of a "romantic relationship" between you and Quangtrice?

N.Z. The answer to that is simple. When the alleged break-in at Sing Sing happened, and my name was somehow thrown in the middle of it, Pirro sent her little investigator (Daughtry) to Sing Sing and they basically spoke to a lot of inmates at Sing Sing and every rat (snitch) and gossiper told him that Wilson was my girlfriend.

K.L.   What would give the inmates at Sing Sing the impression that Quangtrice was your girlfriend?

N.Z.   Behind these walls is nothing but people that constantly run their mouths and gossip about things they know absolutely nothing about. While I was at Sing Sing, the spot-light was kind of on me because of my constant visitation and the little notoriety I had from the music business so people would constantly make up rumors about me that originated only God knows where. And the on-going rumor was that me and Wilson was involved. I swear, Sing Sing is nothing but a big soap opera and my alleged "romantic relationship" with Quangtrice was like a episode that the television stations kept showing. People just always talked about it.

K.L.   Were you and Quangtrice friendlier than usual?

N.Z.   Wilson is a good person, and she has a good heart, besides the fact that she was a Correctional Officer. We used to converse sometimes and she would always smile and laugh when she was around me, and so, to jealous individuals looking on from a distance it would appear that Wilson was always blushing when I was around and inmates would perceive that as "we must be doing something." There were certain inmates that Wilson spoke to at Sing Sing more than she spoke to me and nobody ever accused her of being romantically involved with them, but as soon as I come around it was always a big issue.

207

K.L. The other inmates that Quangtrice spoke to at Sing Sing; were they handsome?

N.Z. I don't know? I don't think so.

K.L. Well there you go, that was the problem. (laughs)

N.Z. (laughs) Uhhh.... was that a compliment?

K.L. Yes.

N.Z. Thank you.

K.L. Your welcome. Do you think Quangtrice may have told someone that you and her were romantically involved and that person passed that information on to Daughtry?

N.Z. Nah, I don't think Wilson would say something like that. It's just that people would constantly watch her when she was around me and that drew a lot of suspicion. There was about a hundred cells on the tier I was on in Sing Sing, and I was in the 77th cell on the tier. So in order for Wilson to get to the cell I was in, she wold have to walk past 76 other cells and when the inmates saw Wilson walk past their cell they knew she was on her way to stop and talk to me. And as soon as she stopped at the cell I was in, everyone's mirror would come out.

K.L. "Everyone's mirror would come out?"

N.Z. Yeah, in Sing Sing, once you are locked in the cell you can only see directly in front of you. You can't see to the right or the left of you because you have

208

two cell walls blocking your view. So in order to see what's going on out on the tier, you have to stick your mirror out through the cell bars and then you will be able to see to the right and left of you.

K.L. And so "everyone's mirror would come out" to look at you and Wilson?

N.Z. Yeah.

K.L. O.K. I got it (laughs)

N.Z. Sometimes, while Wilson was standing at my cell she would say "look Sean, look how people are looking at us" and I would say "Well, since they're watching, lets make a movie". And then I would start making all kinds of stupid sex noises in my cell to give the impression that we was really doing something. (laughs)

K.L. (laughs)

N.Z. It was stupid, but it was funny back then. I regret it now because I know that it's what lead to these unfounded allegations of a romantic affair. I swear, Daughtry and Pirro will fall for anything.

K.L. So is it safe to say that you and Quangtrice never had sex?

N.Z. Nah, we never had sex. It wasn't about that. Even if we wanted to, where would we do it? Everybody was always watching us (smile).

K.L. I understand that Latrina was arrested because it is alleged that she purchased a cell phone in her name and gave it to Quangtrice. Quangtrice was arrested because it is alleged that after she picked up the phone from

209

Latrina, she snuck it into Sing Sing and gave it to you and that you had this phone while you were at Sing Sing for a total of (eight months). Contrary to these allegations, you assert that you never had a cell phone and that no cell phone was ever found in Sing Sing. My question is how can Latrina be charged with giving Quangtrice her cell phone, and then Quangtrice be charged with giving you the cell phone, and then you get charged with having (possession) of the cell phone, if there wasn't any cell phone found?

N.Z. Once again, the government will charge you with anything if they feel you are stupid enough to plead guilty to it, and accept the blame for it. My guess is they have probably managed to convince both Latrina and Wilson that there was actually a phone in Sing Sing and the only way for either of them to ever find out the truth is by going to trial and I don't think either of them have the courage to do that. To be honest with you, I wouldn't be surprised if everyone listed in the indictment was to eventually plead guilty to something in this case. The Criminal Justice System does not operate on guilt or innocence. It operates on convictions, whether or not you're guilty or innocent doesn't matter to these types of people. So they will apply as much pressure as needed to everyone in the indictment to get them to agree that there was an escape attempt at Sing Sing. I anticipate in the next couple of months you can expect some really big headlines in relation to this case.

K.L. And what would the headlines say?

210

N.Z. "Everyone Pleads Guilty Except for Zimmerman."

K.L. I understand that the girls do not visit you anymore but have you ever tried to call them to tell them the truth about the situation.

N.Z. I have no way to call them. I repeatedly ask the Superintendent to use the phone to no avail. I've written several letters to everyone in the indictment asking them to listen to (my side of the story) before they plead guilty in this case.

K.L. And what happened?

N.Z. I never got any response. This is exactly the way Pirro and her buddies (Seyfertt, Daughtry, Smith, Hughes, Lutz, etc.) planned this thing. They wanted to take me out of the picture long enough so they could railroad the rest of my friends. They knew that Steven and I was the only ones that have any understanding of the law and they did not want us explaining to everybody else what their constitutional rights were, because if we did they wouldn't be able to railroad them.

K.L. But I'm sure everyone has lawyers by now. Shouldn't they be explaining their rights to them?

N.Z. Yeah right! Lawyers work with the system, not against it. So if Pirro wants convictions in this case all she has to do is tell the lawyers to start feeding all types of lies to their clients in order to scare them and get them to plead guilty. It happens all the time.

211

K.L.   Has your lawyer tried to "scare you?"

N.Z.   I don't need a lawyer for Pirro, I can handle her myself.

K.L.   I still do not understand why Latrina was arrested for bringing her cell phone into Sing Sing if her phone was never in Sing Sing?

N.Z.   There are other motives that Pirro had in bringing these stale and false charges of an escape attempt at Sing Sing. Just ask yourself, why would a District Attorney go through all the trouble of arresting all of these people without probable cause and then hold a press conference as big as she did about their being guns, cell phones, escape attempts, lions, tigers, bears, ... (laughs).

K.L.   "Lions, Tigers Bears."

N.Z.   (laughs) Alright, forget about that, but she said everything else.

K.L.   O.K.

N.Z.   What I'm basically saying is that she is taking a big chance making up stories like this if she can't prove them in court later, she is only opening herself up, as well as everyone else involved, for a lawsuit when this thing is over. So why would she take a chance like this you say? Well the answer to that is simple, but unfortunately, since I might be standing trial for these allegations in the near future I can only explain the answer to that question briefly.

K.L.   O.K.

212

N.Z.   I want you and your readers to take a good look at Nakia Stubbs's recantation

affidavit in which she states that I wasn't the guy that attacked her with a gun

in 1998. (See Exhibit F). Look at the date in which the affidavit was signed

by Nakia. It was signed on March 24, 2003, but Pirro alleges that I was

scheduled to escape on April 24, May 6th and May 7th of 2003, which is no

more than 45 days after Nakia signed this affidavit. Now I may not be a

rocket scientist, but I am smart enough to know that prisoners usually don't

escape from prison when they uncover evidence as powerful as this that is

going to get them out of prison anyway. They usually escape when they

(don't) have any evidence to prove their innocence. As of March 24, 2003, I

had all the evidence I needed to get out of prison, so there was no reason for

me to be planning an escape attempt. I also want your readers to look at

Barry Alexanders and Latrina Boyd's affidavit. These affidavits were signed

on November 4, 2002 and October 31, 2002. Because these witnesses

statements also clear my name of any wrongdoing, the Appellate Division

was scheduled to hold a hearing on my appeal at which all of these

witnesses were to testify to what happened on September 19, 1998. Now

had this hearing taken place I would have been a free man and Leigh Bishop

would be in jail for settling me up with these charges. Richard Brown

(Bishop's boss) couldn't let this happen. So Brown put in a little phone call

213

to his friends in the Westchester County District Attorney's Office and asked them to simply place false charges on Boyd and Alexander in relation to an escape attempt at Sing Sing. In doing this, the judges in the appellate division would get word about the charges pending against us and simply sweep my appeal under the rug. And that's exactly what they did when they denied my appeal in the appellate division.

K.L. What would whatever had happened at Sing Sing have to do with whether or not they were with you at Club Jam-Roc in 1998?

N.Z. It actually had absolutely nothing to do with it but this only gives the Criminal Injustice System enough basis to keep an innocent man in prison. The courts can simply say "Why should we believe that Boyd and Alexander were really with Zimmerman at Club Jam-Roc on September 19, 1998, if they went as far as to plan an escape attempt with him, than they certainly will lie for him and say they were with him at a club on the night in question."

K.L. But that's wrong! They don't even have any evidence of an escape attempt?

N.Z. The courts don't operate on evidence, Ms. Hughes. Mere allegations are sufficient enough for a conviction in this country. I'm living proof of that.

<u>Interview Concluded.</u>

My interview with Nicholas ended pretty abruptly on this day. I had not realized that 2:00 p.m. had come so quickly. Although this was my last scheduled visit with him, I felt that he had more that he wanted to say. I also knew that I had more questions that I wanted to ask, especially about the escape allegations at Sing Sing C. F. However, I knew that I had definitely heard enough to complete my first book about his case. I read all the transcripts to the trial, affidavits, notes, etc... I watched videotapes, listen to audio tapes and visited the crime scene one last time. I was pretty clear on the evidence I had before me and I knew the only thing left to do was formulate that evidence into a book.

Approximately three weeks would pass between my last visit with him and the point I actually sat down and started to perfect this book. In between that time, Nicholas and I kept in contact through letters. My busy schedule and the writing of the book prevented me from visiting him as much as I wanted to, but I think he understood. In many of the letters he wrote me he would always include an article or literature on music, clothing or the book publishing business. It made me happy to know that someone in his predicament hasn't given up on life.

It took me approximately three months to finish the book. I made Nicholas a rough draft copy and then I made a visit with him to get his opinion on it. He was pleased with the outcome to say the least. Several publishing companies took an interest in Nicholas's story and wanted to release the book, immediately. However, a series of events would stop the release of the book dead in it's tracks.

In November 2004, Judge Barbara Zambelli ordered that Nicholas and Steven be transferred to the Westchester County jail (Valhalla) to stand trial on charges of attempted escape, bribery, attempted criminal possession of a weapon, promoting prison contraband, conspiracy, etc... Months prior, Jeanine Pirro had already held press conferences about the Zimmerman/Finley indictment in which she labeled them "two violent, chronic felons" (see exhibits N, O, P newspaper articles relating to the indictment.) State grievance committee's had warned Pirro about divulging information to the media about her cases so early in the proceedings. "Our view is these sort of comments serve no real law enforcement purpose, they serve only to increase the public opprobrium for those accused. It only makes it harder for the accused to receive a fair trial" (see exhibit Q newspaper article about Pirro's comments.) However, Ms. Pirro ignored these warnings and held numerous conferences immediately before the trial. Sadly enough, this may have been the least of Nicholas's worries. During the proceedings, Nicholas and his attorney, Kevin Griffin, Esq. had filed for "discovery" of the People's case. (discovery is the phase of the proceedings where the District Attorney must turn over to the defense all of the evidence that they plan to use at the trial -and- evidence that they do not plan to use, whether its favorable or unfavorable to the defense.) Among the several hundred pages of discovery materials were affidavits, statements and notes of witnesses who all implicated Nicholas and Steven in the escape conspiracy.

Witness testimony transcripts revealed that several people had already testified (secretly) before a grand jury and alleged that Nicholas was the ring leader of the conspiracy. Most witnesses alleged that they were "forced" by Nicholas to take part in the conspiracy even though they were in the free world and he was in prison? When Latrina Boyd was asked "If Nicholas was forcing you to plan this escape attempt, couldn't you have went to the police and told them he was forcing you to do something illegal" Ms. Boyd responded "Yeah, I guess." A further probing of the discovery

materials would show that even more friend's of Nicholas's had made

statements incriminating him, but one person in particular would

shock the entire Zimmerman family. Jatanya Belnavis (Nicholas's

girlfriend of 10 years) had signed a six page cooperation agreement

in which she agreed to testify for the government, and against

Nicholas, in exchange for a reduced jail sentence.

On March 23, 2005 Jatanya appeared in court to testify against

Nicholas. The two had not seen each other since May 25th, 2003, the

date of Jatanya's arrest at Shawangank C. F. (Jatanya's lawyer and

Jeanine Pirro had coerced Jatanya into not contacting Nicholas until

after she testified.) The prosecution team seemed very pleased with

the fact that Jatanya was working with them to prosecute Nicholas.

In my view, Ms. Belnavis seemed comfortable with the situation as

well.

After several other witnesses testified, it was Jatanya's turn. The

District Attorney banked on Jatanya's testimony to prosecute

Nicholas because of her long-standing relationship with him. She

was closer to him than the rest of his friends, and therefore she would

appear to be more credible to the jury. "Your Honor, the People call

Jatanya Belnavis to the stand" A. D. A. Neary said. Jatanya, walking

in alone, wore a white turtle neck and black suit pants. She placed an

oversized pocket book on the counter, placed her left hand on the

bible, and raised her right hand:

Court clerk: Ms. Belnavis, do you swear that the

testimony you are about to give is the

truth, the whole truth, and nothing but

the truth, so help you god?

Ms. Belnavis: I do.

The Court: You may be seated.

Mr. Neary: Ms. Belnavis, do you know the defendant

Nicholas Zimmerman?

Ms. Belnavis: Yes I do.

Mr. Neary: And how do you know the defendant?

Ms Belnavis: He was my boyfriend . . . . .

To Be Continued . . . . .

My Side of The Story-The Investigation Continues-Part II

Coming Soon!!!

TRANSCRIPTS

THE PEOPLE OF THE STATE OF NEW YORK

-against-

NICHOLAS ZIMMERMAN

1   SUPREME COURT OF THE STATE OF NEW YORK

2   COUNTY OF QUEENS : CRIMINAL TERM : PART K-20

3   -X

4   THE PEOPLE OF THE STATE OF NEW YORK   Indictment No.

5   -against-   3296-98

6   NICHOLAS ZIMMERMAN,   Sentence

7   Defendant.

8   -X

9   Supreme Courthouse
                           125-01 Queens Boulevard
10   Kew Gardens, New York 11415
                           January 17, 2002
11

12   B E F O R E:

13   HONORABLE ROGER N. ROSENGARTEN,

14   Justice

15   A P P E A R A N C E S:

16   FOR THE PEOPLE:
               RICHARD A. BROWN, ESQ.
17   District Attorney, Queens County
          BY: LEIGH BISHOP, ESQ.
18   Assistant District Attorney

19   FOR THE DEFENDANT:
               BRENDAN O'MEARA, ESQ.
20   304 Grand Concourse
               Bronx, New York
21

22

23

24   NORA LEE, RPR
                           Official Court Reporter
25

                                                    nl

1   COURT CLERK: This is calendar number one on

2   the K-20 calendar today, from the sentence calendar,

3   under Indictment 3296 of '98, People versus

4   Nicholas Zimmerman.

5   Good morning, sir. For the record, your name

6   is?

7   MR. O'MEARA: Brendan O'Meara, 304 Grand

8   Concourse, Bronx, New York.

9   COURT CLERK: Thank you. For the People?

10   MS. BISHOP: Leigh Bishop. Good morning, your

11   Honor.

12   THE COURT: Good morning.

13   COURT CLERK: And, sir, for the record, your

14   name is?

15   THE DEFENDANT: Nicholas Zimmerman.

16   THE COURT: I think he has to be arraigned on

17   the predicate felony information.

18   COURT CLERK: Yes, Judge.

19   Nicholas Zimmerman, the District Attorney of

20   the County of Queens has filed a statement saying that

21   under Indictment 1520 of '97, you, Nicholas Zimmerman,

22   were convicted on June 10th of 1997, of the statute of

23   170.40, criminal possession of a forgery device, in

24   Queens County, and you were sentenced to 18 months to 54

25   months.

1   Now, sir, you may controvert any and all

2   allegations made in this statement. If so, you must

3   specify each and every one. All uncontroverted

4   allegations in this statement shall be deemed to have

5   been admitted by you. All prior findings that you are a

6   second felony offender are binding on you in this and

7   any subsequent proceeding.

8   You may admit or you may deny that you are the

9   same person mentioned in this statement. In the event

10   that you deny or wish to controvert any of the

11   allegations set forth in this statement, it is your

12   right to be tried in a hearing before the Court without

13   a jury.

14   You are further advised that under existing

15   law, prior felony convictions may serve to increase the

16   punishment for the felony of which you now stand

17   convicted.

18   You are also advised that you have the right

19   to raise the issue of the constitutionality of such

20   prior convictions. The law provides that your failure

21   to challenge the previous conviction at this time shall

22   constitute a waiver on your part unless good cause can

23   be shown for your failure to make such a timely

24   challenge.

25   Now, sir, having been advised of your rights,

1   how say you? Are you the same person mentioned in this

2   statement?

3   * THE DEFENDANT: Yes, I am.

4   COURT CLERK: And do you further admit to your

5   prior convictions?

6   * THE DEFENDANT: Yes.

7   COURT CLERK: Defendant admits, Judge.

8   THE COURT: The defendant is adjudicated to be

9   a predicate felon, second felony offender.

10   All right, People move to sentence?

11   MS. BISHOP: Yes, Judge.

12   THE COURT: People wish to be heard?

13   MS. BISHOP: Yes, Judge.

14   THE COURT: Go ahead.

15   MS. BISHOP: Your Honor, I'd just like to

16 start by asking the Court to take note of this

17 defendant's general disregard for the criminal justice

18 system and for law enforcement.

19   He, in the course of his criminal career, has

20 used five aliases, and he's warranted in almost every

21 case. And those are just sort of -- I think that

22 reflects his general attitude towards the criminal

23 justice system, but I'd like to specifically comment on

24 his attitude towards the Court in this case that's

25 presently before the Court.

1   First, as you know, he used an alias in this

2   case, and more significantly, he warranted for almost

3   three years during the course of this case. And, your

4   Honor, I submit that the defendant's warranting in this

5   case was intentional. In fact, in November of 1998,

6   approximately two to three months after he actually

7   failed to appear in Part AP6, he told another individual

8   that he was on the run, so I submit to this Court that

9   his actions were intentional, and that there was no

10   confusion on his part about whether or not he had a

11   pending felony case against him.

12   Secondly, this defendant, in spite of the

13   Court's instructions to the contrary, had his girlfriend

14   contact my complainant in this case, in violation of an

15   Order of Protection, in an effort to dissuade her from

16   coming to court to testify in this matter. As the Court

17   will recall, there was also sworn testimony at the trial

18   concerning the defendant and his girlfriend's efforts to

19   pay off the complainant, not once but twice, also in an .

20   effort to dissuade her from moving forward with the case

21   against him.

22   Your Honor, just for a moment, I'd like to

23   comment on the witnesses that this defendant presented

24   to you at trial, namely his girlfriend, Jatanya

25   Belnavis, who, throughout the course of this proceeding,

1   has demonstrated to this Court a willingness to lie for

2   the defendant. It started with her efforts to bail the

3   defendant out of jail. It continued with her efforts to

4   contact the complaining witness to offer her money. It

5   was -- it continued during the course of the trial with

6   her efforts to contact the complainant. And by the way,

7   when the Warrant Squad went looking for this defendant,

8   she said she had no idea where the defendant was at that

9   time. And yet, she came in and under oath said that she

10   had been with him for all these years.

11   So, you know, Judge, I -- I believe that this

12   defendant has an ability to manipulate others, including

13   his family and those he's close to, to aid him in his

14   committing deceit on others and this Court, and I submit

15   that he's done that throughout the course of this

16   trial.

17   I'd like to also comment on this -- this kind

18   of hyper-like behavior. It's a very antisocial form of

19   behavior of this defendant putting his own interests not

20   only above society as a whole, but above his family

21   members and his friends. Look at the nature of his past

22   convictions: larceny, forgery, possession of stolen

23   property. These -- these convictions all demonstrate

24   his -- his insidious ability to deceive those around

25   him.

1   And, Judge, I submit that if you look through

2   the package that his family has submitted to the Court,

3   you'll see things in there -- there are statements that

4   this man was wrongfully accused. That he's simply a

5   businessman building a business empire. And I submit to

6   the Court that they, too, have been blinded by this

7   man's manipulation. And in support of this, I'd like to

8   submit to the Court the information on his conviction

9   from 1997: guns, credit cards, credit card encoding

10   machines, forged --

11   THE COURT: I have his probation report from

12   the prior conviction.

13   MS. BISHOP: These were recovered from his

14   home where he lived with his mother and where his

15   girlfriend frequently visited. So, you know, I submit

16   to the Court that -- that his -- his close friends and

17   family are simply unwilling to see what the true

18   Nicholas Zimmerman is.

19   And finally, Judge, I've got two final things

20   to say. First, that the defendant cannot be treated as

21   a discretionary persistent felon in this case due to the

22   fact that we -- the D.A.'s office could not get him

23   sentenced quickly enough before he went and committed

24   another crime, so he's been able to benefit from a

25   loophole in the sentencing laws. He's really not going

nl

1   to be adequately punished for -- based on the true

2   nature of his past, and I think the Court should take

3   that into account in the sentencing of him on this

4   case.

5   As you can tell from his rap sheet, he was

6   arrested for a felony in January, not sentenced on that

7   felony until May, but he committed another felony in the

8   intervening March, and that's the only reason why I'm

9   unable to ask for discretionary treatment today.

10   Furthermore, his nonviolent record really does

11   not adequately portray his criminal actions in the

12   past. In both the '94 Queens case and the '97 Queens

13   case, loaded operable firearms were recovered from the

14   defendant's home, so I submit to this Court that this is

15   not the first instance of violence in this defendant's

16   criminal past. I think it's appropriate for the Court

17   to consider that in imposing sentence on the defendant

18   today.

19   Your Honor, I will be asking this judge to

20   sentence the defendant to the maximum, which is 15

21   years. I have case law in support of this if the

22   Court's interested in reviewing it at this time.

23   THE COURT: Thank you. Mr. O'Meara.

24   MR. O'MEARA: Judge --

25   THE DEFENDANT: Judge -- I wish to be heard,

1   Judge.

2   THE COURT: Well, Mr. O'Meara first, then

3   Mr. Zimmerman, unless Mr. O'Meara doesn't want to be

4   heard.

5   MR. O'MEARA: Your Honor, the first person I'd

6   like the Court to hear from is the defendant's mother,

7   Mrs. Willis, if she'll step up.

8   MS. BISHOP: I object to this, your Honor.

9   THE COURT: No, sir. I'll hear from you and

10   from Mr. Zimmerman, nobody else.

11   MR. O'MEARA: Your Honor, the family's here to

12   speak on the behalf of their family member.

13   ✱ THE COURT: I've read all the letters. There

14   is no provision for them to speak.

15   MR. O'MEARA: Your Honor, he's about to be

16   sentenced to many years of prison. He should have at

17   least the benefit of the Court hearing from his family

18   members.

19   ✱ THE COURT: No, sir, there's no provision in

20   the law for that, sir. I've read their letters.

21   MR. O'MEARA: Your Honor --

22   THE COURT: You can tell me what they were

23   going to say.

24   MR. O'MEARA: Your Honor, what they're

25   basically going to say is that Mr. Zimmerman has been

1   conducting himself as a productive member of society.

2   He has been running a business on behalf of himself and

3   his family. Your Honor, he has been involved with the

4   Internet, and he has been involved in sales of the

5   Internet, and he has been attempting to get involved in

6   the music industry, and that putting him away for such

7   an extended period of time would basically take out his

8   shining light insofar as he does have the ability to be

9   a productive member of society, your Honor.

10   In the past couple of years, he has shown

11   that. Albeit he did not come back to court in this case

12   in 1998; nevertheless, during that time he was running a

13   productive business, a legitimate business, your Honor.

14   He is a young man. He is a very intelligent young man.

15   He might not have been given the opportunities that

16   other people were given growing up; however, he has

17   shown that he has the abilities to take his intelligence

18   and to use it in a productive manner and to be a

19   productive member of society.

20   And, your Honor, as far as his prior

21   convictions, they are nonviolent. What the district

22   attorney says about, well, what he really should have

23   been considered, that's really not fair to

24   Mr. Zimmerman. They were nonviolent offenses, your

25   Honor, and that should also be taken into

1   consideration.

2   Now, your Honor, finally, I just request that

3   you do allow -- that you only sentence Mr. Zimmerman to

4   the minimum amount of time under the law, which is five

5   years. And, your Honor, Mr. Zimmerman would like to

6   make his own statement at this time.

7   THE COURT: Mr. Zimmerman.

8   THE DEFENDANT: Your Honor, sorry about the

9   outburst.

10   THE COURT: That's okay, sir.

11   THE DEFENDANT: I waited a long time for this

12   day to be heard. The D.A., she's making allegations

13   that I was rude through the trial and the things that I

14   was saying. I sat here quietly during the trial. I

15   didn't make one noise, one peep. I showed respect to

16   the trial, to the jury, to my lawyer, to the D.A. I let

17   her say things about me that's not true. I didn't say

18   anything back. I don't know why she's saying that I was

19   rude through the trial. I don't understand --

20   THE COURT: I don't recall her saying that.

21   THE DEFENDANT: She's saying my attitude

22   during the criminal justice system.

23   THE COURT: Well, it wasn't during this

24   trial. She means -- I'm sure she means your general

25   attitude in all the things you've gotten caught and your

1   past convictions.

2   THE DEFENDANT: Well, my general --

3   THE COURT: And the fact that you failed to

4   come back in this case.

5   THE DEFENDANT: My general attitude towards

6   this case or any other case that I've had, which, when I

7   was guilty, I pleaded guilty to cases in the past when I

8   was guilty. This one, I just didn't plead guilty to

9   cause I'm not guilty. I did not do any of these things

10 that this girl is saying I did. The D.A. failed to even

11 ask me or have a, you know, discussion with me about

12 this case, even though it's not procedure that she did

13 do that, but at least if you're offering me five years,

14 at least come to me and ask me, you know, am I guilty,

15 or what happened that night, some kind of statement.

16   We have no statement from what Nikia wrote to

17 the cops that night. We have no way to know what she

18 actually told them that night up until this day, so she

19 could have told them she don't know who did it that

20 night, and then today she's saying a different story as

21 to what the D.A. may have put in her head.

22   From what I understand, she didn't want to

23 come to court. She's told us plenty of times: I don't

24 want to go through with the trial. It was a mistake;

25 I'm sorry. I'm not coming back to court. That was the

1   whole reason why I didn't have her on right now.

2   Your Honor, this individual in question who

3   said that I'm on the run, that I admitted to them that

4   I'm on the run, who is this individual? Who's she

5   talking about? She's been saying this throughout the

6   trial. Who did I tell that I'm on the run? And tell

7   anyone that I'm on the run, cause I was not considered

8   to be on the run at that time.

9   I've seen Nikia in the street during that

10   time. We've had conversations. I didn't know anything

11   about this case was pending. I would like to know

12   who -- if you can ask her who was to say that I was on

13   the run, your Honor, if you could actually ask the D.A.

14   THE COURT: No, sir.

15   THE DEFENDANT: Well, your Honor --

16   THE COURT: It's irrelevant to this, in any

17   event.

18   THE DEFENDANT: All right. Well, what is

19   relevant to this case is, I would like to ask the D.A.,

20   does she have any knowledge of why the bail bondsman

21   came back and took back my bail when I posted a $35,000

22   bond. Does she know any reason why they would do that,

23   your Honor. I think that has relevancy to this case,

24   your Honor.

25   THE COURT: It's irrelevant, sir. He felt you

1   were evidently a flight risk.

2   THE DEFENDANT: No, your Honor, that's not the

3   truth, your Honor. I have reason to believe that that's

4   not the truth. If you would just ask her the question,

5   your Honor. I have reason to believe that's not the

6   truth.

7   THE COURT: What else do you want to say, sir;

8   go ahead. Anything else?

9   THE DEFENDANT: You're not going to ask her

10   the question, your Honor?

11   THE COURT: No, sir.

12   THE DEFENDANT: Your Honor, I'd like to raise

13   a prejudicial issue at this time.

14   THE COURT: Go ahead, sir.

15   THE DEFENDANT: First, I'd like to read a

16   30.30 motion.

17   Any time the rendition of a verdict of guilty

18   before the sentence of the Court made upon a defendant

19   to set aside or modify a verdict or any part thereof

20   upon the following grounds: Any ground appearing in the

21   record which if raised upon appeal of the respective

22   judgment of conviction for a crime reversal or

23   modification of the judgment as a matter of law by an

24   appellate court.

25   Your Honor, I feel it's a prejudicial issue

1   for the D.A. to question Detective Kenil (phonetics)

2   about me being on parole and about where he arrested me

3   at, and that he contacted my parole officer two weeks

4   before I was arrested and asked him what day I was

5   coming in so -- so he could have a meeting with me, or

6   things of that nature.

7   If you remember, your Honor, when the -- when

8   the D.A. came -- when the jury asked the questions, they

9   specifically asked that question, where was I arrested

10   at? That mean they based their decision on that matter

11   just alone. That they -- they realized that I was on

12   parole. They asked two questions, and that was one of

13   them.

14   Your Honor, I didn't take the stand, so why

15   would my parole issue be a part of the testimony? I

16   don't -- I don't know why that was raised.

17   THE COURT: Go ahead, sir.

18   THE DEFENDANT: Another thing, your Honor. I

19   never had a chance for my preliminary hearings.

20   THE COURT: What --

21   THE DEFENDANT: My pretrial hearings,

22   preliminary trials. I never had those hearings.

23   THE COURT: You waived motions.

24   THE DEFENDANT: Your Honor, I didn't waive

25   motions.

1   THE COURT: Well, motions were waived in your

2   behalf. I'm sure that was not done without your

3   knowledge and consent.

4   THE DEFENDANT: The -- the conversation we

5   had, your Honor, was that I was going to go to trial.

6   The D.A. offered me five years on this matter. I said,

7   no, I'm not taking the five years; I would like to go to

8   trial. I didn't know anything about waiving preliminary

9   hearings or pretrial hearings. I didn't even know the

10   importance of them the date that they were waived. They

11   were waived in arraignment.* If you could look at the

12   record, they were waived in arraignment. I never had

13   these hearings. Had I had these hearings, I would have

14   known what I was dealing with, what was against me. You

15   know, they found me guilty of possession of a weapon,

16   and there's no weapon involved. That top charge may

17   have been thrown out on just the preliminary hearings

18   alone.

19   THE COURT: What else, sir?

20   THE DEFENDANT: Your Honor, one last thing I'd

21   like to add.

22   THE COURT: Go ahead.

23   THE DEFENDANT: My alibi witness, your Honor.

24   With all due respect, they were denied also in this

25   case. I went to trial 11 days from the day I was

1 arrested, your Honor, 11 days. I had 11 days to prepare

2 a trial, your Honor. I was arrested. I was bailed out

3 on this case on -- let me see. Your Honor, I posted

4 bond on November 23rd on this case. I was rearrested by

5 the D.A. Cops came to my house, rearrested me at the

6 same address that I provided to the court. I didn't --

7 I didn't up put any fight, any argument, nothing. I

8 came right back in. I knew they was there. We knew the

9 charges were going to come in. They arrested me at my

10 house, brought me back in December 11th, your Honor. I

11 went from December 11th to December 21st, I was found

12 guilty at trial.

13   I had 11 days to prepare for a trial. I had

14 to find people from three years ago: my manager, the

15 club promoter, the club owner, the limo driver. I had

16 to find these people from three years ago, your Honor,

17 to come to court and testify on my behalf. And then

18 when I do find them, they were denied because they said

19 the notice of alibi was late. How was I supposed to

20 defend myself in 11 days?

21   THE COURT: First of all, sir, the Notice of

22 Alibi, the decision Judge Rotker made, that was -- that

23 was abrogated by the fact that it was -- the district

24 attorney agreed to accept your Notice of Alibi and

25 agreed -- and there was an agreement that those

1   witnesses will be produced before the D.A. for an

2   interview before they testified at trial. They were

3   never produced for the district attorney to be

4   interviewed, as is their right.

5   THE DEFENDANT: And that's what I'm saying. I

6   only had 11 days to do this whole -- I was brought back

7   in on December 11th. December 21st, the trial was

8   over. On December 19th, we tried to submit them to you

9   and you denied them, your Honor. With all due respect,

10   how was I suppose to prepare in 11 days? How was I

11   supposed to prepare for a trial in 11 days, your Honor?

12   THE COURT: Well, that was your decision.

13   THE DEFENDANT: Yes, I understand it was my

14   decision, but, your Honor, the only thing I'm asking --

15   I'm not asking for the sun, moon, and stars, your

16   Honor. I'm asking for at least a retrial where my alibi

17   witnesses will be able to testify.

18   THE COURT: That application is denied. You ⭐ *Ruled*

19   will be given a right to appeal. If the Appellate

20   Division feels that there was error in the trial, then

21   that's how you're given a new trial. Is there anything

22   else you want to say, sir?

23   THE DEFENDANT: There's just one last thing,

24   your Honor.

25   THE COURT: Go ahead.

1   THE DEFENDANT: Which is -- which goes to the

2 effect of me reserving my issues for an appeal.

3   I ask you one last time, your Honor, please

4 investigate if the D.A. knows anything about why the

5 bail bondsman -- this -- this -- if you would let me

6 finish, you will see how it has some relevancy to the

7 case, but only thing I'm saying, would you please

8 investigate if she knows anything about why the bail

9 bondsman would come here after they already knew I had a

10 warrant from '98. They posted the bond with an

11 indictment number from 1998. They already knew I had a

12 warrant, so that's not an issue.

13   THE COURT: That's between -- that's between

14 you and the bail bondsman. If you want to take up some

15 action against the bail bondsman in a civil case,[*] that's

16 between you and him.

17   THE DEFENDANT: That's not what I'm saying,

18 your Honor. The issue that I'm trying to raise here,

19 your Honor, is, I specifically asked Judge Grosso for a

20 bond so I can prepare my case. He granted the bond. He

21 already knew I had a warrant on the same exact case. He

22 granted the bond. He gave me a bail, which was at his

23 discretion. I bailed out, and I have reason to believe

24 that the D.A. did something with the bail bondsman

25 towards this case. Had she not done that, my alibi

witness would have been on time. I would have still been on the street preparing my case, your Honor. That's why it has some relevance to this case.

THE COURT: All right, thank you. I'm not going to direct the D.A. to do anything. It's not my position to do so, all right. Anything else you want to say, sir?

MR. O'MEARA: Yes, your Honor. Just that I did submit a 330 motion.

THE COURT: That's been denied. Motion's been denied. The decision's being handed out. *

MR. O'MEARA: And the last thing, your Honor, I again would ask to at least allow for one family member to speak. One of his brothers came up from Maryland from the Air Force, took the day off to try to have the opportunity --

THE COURT: No, sir, there is no provision in the law for that -- for that to happen.

MR. O'MEARA: Nevertheless, your Honor, it's at your discretion to allow him to speak on behalf of his brother.

THE COURT: I'm not going to allow it. You have an exception,* all right.

THE DEFENDANT: Thank you for your time, your Honor.

1   THE COURT: All right, sir.

2   Mr. Zimmerman or Mr. Willis, you're a very

3   bright person. You're probably bordering on genius, and

4   your -- from your history, it's obvious your genius has

5   been misdirected. While you may be running businesses

6   in the past, you've run businesses of stealing. The

7   records indicate that you've stolen somewhere in the

8   vicinity of $200,000 in the past.

9   THE DEFENDANT: Your Honor, that's not true.

10   THE COURT: And you pled guilty on that case,

11   and you were sentenced to a substantial period of time.

12   Your letters and friends -- from friends and family

13   indicate that you're a promising businessman, and it

14   seems that in the past, your business involved the

15   fraudulent manufacturing of credit cards, checks, and

16   other financial instruments with a larcenous intent.

17   You may be, as I said, bright but your genius

18   has been misdirected, even though it may be in the last

19   couple of years been directed in the proper direction.

20   But with your record, how these people can think that

21   you can be painted as a role model for your younger

22   relations and friends is beyond my comprehension. You

23   presently have another felony case pending in Nassau

24   County where you were arrested in 2001 for grand

25   larceny, and you have a bail-jumping case pending here

nl

1   for which you jumped bail on this case and caused

2   somebody $10,000 that they lost, and then you wonder why

3   the insurance company had second thoughts about

4   posting -- about continuing your bail in this case.

5   THE DEFENDANT: Your Honor --

6   THE COURT: It seems that your crimes have

7   accelerated now from those of a larcenous and fraudulent

8   nature to ones of violence and intimidation and the

9   carrying of weapons, loaded weapons, and firing of

10   loaded weapons.

11   It's my opinion that the people of the county

12   and the city need to be protected from predators, both

13   financial and violent, and now you seem to have become

14   both.

15   And I note that in your address to the Court,

16   you primarily spoke about how unfair the D.A. was, how

17   unfair the trial was, and how you were unfairly treated

18   during the course of the trial, which I fail to see.

19   But if an appellate court feels so, that's their --

20   that's their province, not mine. Under the

21   circumstances, I think that what the D.A. requests is

22   not outrageous. In fact, it is reasonable.

23   Accordingly, and I want to point out that

24   while Mr. O'Meara in his papers indicated because

25   Miss Stubs had a criminal record, she could not be

1   believable, that her testimony was corroborated by

2   somebody who was with her at the time. It was

3   corroborated by a person who lived somewhere in that

4   area who heard the shots and called the police. It's

5   corroborated by the fact that the police recovered nine

6   spent .9 millimeter shells from the area where it is

7   alleged that you shot the gun. It was a crime of

8   intimidation. I think you sought to instill fear and

9   you succeeded, but you were caught and now you failed.

10   Under all the circumstances of your record and

11   the facts of this case, on the first count of the

12   indictment, you're remanded to the custody of the New

13   York State Department of Corrections for a period of

14   fifteen years. The second count, seven years. The

15   fourth count, one year, all to run concurrently with

16   each other, with the statutorily required postrelease

17   supervision, and the charges will be taken from inmate

18   funds, if available.

19   COURT CLERK: Very good.

20   THE DEFENDANT: Your Honor, may I ask one

21   question before I leave?

22   THE COURT: Yes, sir.

23   THE DEFENDANT: I just want to -- one

24   question. Somewhere during the trial, with all due

25   respect, your Honor -- please, mom.

1   With all due respect, your Honor, somewhere

2   during the trial, your opinion on this case was, and you

3   said on the record to the D.A., I think you need to see

4   your supervisor right now about throwing out this case.

5   You're never going to get a conviction on this case, so

6   how could you --

7   THE COURT: That's not what I said. I said

8   there should be some kind of disposition in the case.

9   THE DEFENDANT: Yeah. You said -- because --

10   you said -- your exact words was, disposing of this

11   case.

12   THE COURT: That's right.

13   THE DEFENDANT: I think you need to see your

14   supervisor.

15   THE COURT: Mm-hmm.

16   THE DEFENDANT: So if you thought then that

17   the case was not going to go anywhere, how could you

18   give me 15 years now?

19   THE COURT: Well --

20   THE DEFENDANT: When the same testimony you

21   heard then? What will be the -- what difference did you

22   hear --

23   THE COURT: The jury has spoken with a

24   decision and based upon your history --

25   THE DEFENDANT: But you knew my history then.

1   THE COURT: That's my -- that's my decision on

2   the sentence.   You have a right to appeal.   The clerk is

3   going to notify you of your right to appeal.

4   MS. BISHOP: Judge, I'd also just like to

5   continue the Order of Protection in favor of the

6   complainant.

7   THE COURT: The Order of Protection will be

8   extended.

9   COURT CLERK: Final Order of Protection will

10   be extended.

11   Sir, you're subject to a mandatory surcharge

12   of $150, plus a $5 crime victims assistance fee, which

13   will be taken out of inmate funds.

14   And in addition, sir, you have the right to

15   appeal to the Appellate Division, Second Department,

16   within 30 days.   In addition, upon proof of your

17   financial inability to retain counsel and pay the costs

18   and expenses of the appeal, you have the right to apply

19   to the Appellate Division, Second Department, for the

20   assignment of counsel for leave to prosecute the appeal

21   as a poor person and to dispense with printing.

22   (Continued on the next page to include the

23   jurat.)

24

25

Proceedings

1   COURT CLERK: The Appellate Division, Second

2   Department, is located at 45 Monroe Place, New York, and

3   you're being handed a copy of the notice of the right to

4   appeal. You may take him back.

5   **********************************
    CERTIFIED THAT THE FOREGOING IS A TRUE AND
6   ACCURATE TRANSCRIPT OF THE ORIGINAL STENOGRAPHIC
    MINUTES IN THIS CASE.

7

8   _____
                Nora Lee, RPR
9   Official Court Reporter

10

11

12

13

14

15

16

17

18

19

20

21

22

23

24

25

nl

1   irrespective of the source. So I'm going to decline

2   the bond. I'm going to revoke bail at this time. The

3   defendant is remanded for the course of the trial. The

4   defendant has an exception for the record.* The faster

5   the trial goes --

6   VOICE FROM AUDIENCE: Your Honor, I'm --

7   THE COURT: Sit down or you're going in.

8   THE CLERK: Is that as to each indictment?

9   THE COURT: As to both indictments at the

10   present time.

11   Let's do Sandoval.

12   Miss Bishop, I will hear you on Sandoval.

13   MS. BISHOP: Yes, Judge. Judge, I have an

14   updated copy of the defendant's rap sheet. I don't

15   know --

16   THE COURT: Just tell me what your

17   application is.

18   MS. BISHOP: I'll start with the first entry

19   on the rap sheet, which is as to YO disposition. I

20   won't be seeking to inquire about the facts, just that

21   this defendant, using the name Nicholas Willis, which

22   is different than what he's charged with in this case,

23   that he used that name and that he warranted during the

24   course of that proceeding after he had pled guilty.

25   Do you just want me to continue?

1   THE COURT: Continue.

2   MS. BISHOP: As for the arrest on September

3   the 9, 1993 for forgery, your Honor. The defendant

4   pled guilty to criminal possession of stolen property

5   in the fifth degree. He warranted three times during

6   the course of this case. He used a different name,

7   that of Nicholas Willis.

8   And the facts of that case I would seek to

9   inquire about if he testified. The defendant used a

10   credit card that did not belong to him to purchase a

11   computer that cost in excess of $3,000 through the

12   mail. The company notified the police and a controlled

13   discovery was set up. And the defendant signed the

14   Federal Express receipt using the name of the

15   individual whose credit card he used.

16   And furthermore he also used that same credit

17   card to buy three airline tickets.

18   Additionally, Judge, moving on to the May 31,

19   1994 arrest, the defendant pled guilty to criminal

20   possession of stolen property in the fifth degree on

21   November the 2nd. He warranted during that case. He

22   used the name of Nicholas Willis.

23   And so the Court is aware, the facts of that

24   case involve the following. The detectives executed a

25   bench warrant that related to the YO case and the

1   previous forgery case. And then when they got to the

2   defendant's house they went to his room and found a

3   semi-automatic handgun lying out on his dresser.

4   THE COURT: What date is this one?

5   MS. BISHOP: This is -- the arrest date was

6   5/31/94. They found this handgun out on the dresser.

7   They also recovered four spent shell casings and an

8   empty clip. They did some investigation on this gun

9   and learned it had been stolen five months earlier from

10   the true owner who lived in Brooklyn. The detectives

11   also recovered a 357 Magnum handgun from the couch in

12   the living room.

13   And just so the Court knows, the defendant

14   indicated that he was living at home with his mother at

15   the time. These items were recovered from his

16   household.

17   Moving on to January the 27, 1997, the arrest

18   for possession of a forged instrument. The defendant

19   pled guilty. This is a Manhattan case to the E felony

20   of grand larceny. He received a year of incarceration

21   for that. In that case he used the name Nicholas

22   Zimmerman.

23   And the facts of that case are as follows.

24   He went into the, one of the Wiz locations in Manhattan

25   and attempted to purchase a computer valued at $3,000

1   using a stolen credit card.

2   Judge, this brings me to the Queens arrest in

3   March of 1997. And I have a rather lengthy application

4   to make with regard to this particular arrest, if you

5   will bear with me.

6   THE COURT: Uh-huh.

7   MS. BISHOP: The defendant was charged with

8   possessing a forged instrument. He ultimately pled

9   guilty to the D felony. Went to jail for 18 months to

10   54 months. He used the name Nicholas Willis and

11   Nicholas Zimmerman. And the name Sean was associated

12   with this case as well.

13   Your Honor, this case involved an

14   investigation with the New York City Police Department,

15   the postal inspector, as well as the United States

16   Secret Service. They executed search warrants on the

17   defendant's house and recovered the following: The

18   defendant possessed an excess of 25 credit cards in the

19   names of other individuals. He possessed plastic cards

20   purporting to be credit cards in various stages of

21   completion. He possessed blank plastics, two encoding

22   machines, personal and company checks in the names of

23   other individuals, documents purporting to be business

24   checks in various stages of completion, reams of blank

25   basketweave check paper, documents bearing the names

1   and personal and financial information, including

2   social security numbers, of over 200 people,

3   convenience and personal checks of individuals other

4   than that of the defendant, merchant receipts and names

5   other than that of defendant bearing the credit card

6   numbers and signatures of numerous credit card holders,

7   computer disks bearing personal and financial

8   information of individuals other than the defendant, a

9   check endorsement stamp, credit card financial and

10   personal mail addressed to other people other than the

11   defendant.

12   They also recovered a 32 caliber

13   semiautomatic firearm with a loaded magazine and in

14   excess of 40 rounds of ammunition.

15   The defendant was listed as the secondary

16   user on at least 10 accounts at Bank One that were

17   opened by the request of an individual named Nicholas

18   Zimmerman, and the total losses the bank suffered in

19   connection with these accounts was $25,000. These

20   cards were also recovered during the search of the

21   defendant's house.

22   And by the way, additional cards related to

23   the Bank 1 part of this case were recovered on the

24   defendant during his Manhattan arrest in January of

25   '97.

1   In addition, the defendant opened two credit

2   cards in the names of George Lewis (ph) and Michael

3   Allen (ph) that resulted in over $7500 of loss to a

4   company named Household Credit Services. The police

5   recovered a list bearing the personal information of

6   these two individuals during the execution of the

7   search warrant.

8   In addition, the defendant opened AT&T credit

9   card accounts in his name, and AT&T suffered losses in

10   excess of $21,000. This credit card was also recovered

11   during the search. He also possessed seven other

12   credit cards in others' names that resulted in a loss

13   to the Wiz and the Wiz Company Credit Card Corporation

14   in excess of $35,000.

15   He possessed one of the personal encoders to

16   encode several American Express cards, and he used his

17   home address, where he was living at the time where

18   this search warrant was executed, in his application to

19   apply for some of these American Express cards. The

20   police, when they executed this warrant, tell me the

21   defendant possessed credit cards with an aggregate

22   value of in excess of $100,000. He possessed eight

23   counterfeit Visa cards with the Visa access codes.

24   Since May 1st of 1995 the police have

25   recovered counterfeit checks resulting in excess of

1    $60,000 lost to legitimate companies, all of which were

2   associated -- evidence of which was recovered during

3   the search of his house. He possessed an encoder

4   capable of encoding amounts on payroll checks to

5   various companies around the state and country. He

6   possessed mail belonging to other residents on the

7   block that he had no permission or authority to

8   possess. And he possessed counterfeit business checks

9   from a company in Brooklyn.

10   And by the way, some of the checks that he

11   printed were actually signed, endorsed, and deposited

12   into other accounts.

13   In addition to these facts I will also be

14   seeking to introduce his plea allocution in that case,

15   Judge.

16   THE COURT: You have a copy of that plea

17   allocution? Can I see it?

18   MS. BISHOP: The copy is -- I should have it

19   later today or first thing in the morning, Judge. The

20   minutes have been requested. I'm also seeking to cross

21   examine on the name Sean Zimmerman, which he gave to

22   law enforcement on July 19th of 2001. And as this

23   Court has already heard, and as his rap sheet

24   indicates, the defendant has used at least four

25   different social security numbers, and he's used them

1   sentence.

2   MS. BISHOP: I think he pled guilty on 5/8 of

3   '97.   You're referring to the Queens case?

4   THE COURT: Yes.

5   MS. BISHOP: He was then sentenced in June.

6   That's the big case.

7   THE COURT: Anything else?

8   MS. BISHOP: No, Judge.

9   THE COURT: Mr. O'Meara, you wish to be

10   heard?

11   MR. O'MEARA: Yes, I do wish to be heard.

12   THE COURT: Go ahead, sir.

13   MR. O'MEARA: First of all, your Honor, in

14   regards to the charges that are brought against him

15   now, which are basically violent felonies with the

16   possession of a weapon, his use of that weapon and

17   these other charges from 1993, '94 and '97 are so

18   different that allowing those prior convictions or

19   allegations thereof to be used in cross examining him

20   would be so prejudicial against Mr. Zimmerman it would

21   completely thwart the case, your Honor.   It would

22   overshadow the facts on all that.

23   He should be tried on the facts of this case,

24   whether or not he possessed that gun and whether or not

25   he put anybody into danger.   Your Honor, going back to

1   witnesses will be brought into question, and then look

2   for the evidence that brings Mr. Zimmerman to this

3   crime. With that, that's all I have for you. And I

4   thank you for your time.

5   THE COURT: Thank you.

6   You have your first witness?

7   MS. BISHOP: Yes, Judge. The People call

8   Karisha Brathwaite.

9   K A R I S H A   B R A T H W A I T E, a witness called on

10   behalf of the People, after having been first duly

11   sworn and having stated her residence as Queens County,

12   took the witness stand and testified as follows:

13   THE CLERK: Thank you. You may be seated.

14   THE COURT: Miss Brathwaite, I'm going to ask

15   you to keep your voice up. You have a small voice.

16   Get real close to that mike so everybody will be able

17   to hear you. Okay, will you do that?

18   THE WITNESS: Okay.

19   THE COURT: Okay, Miss Bishop.

20   DIRECT EXAMINATION

21   BY MS. BISHOP:

22   Q   Miss Brathwaite, just if you speak into the

23   microphone. If you'd like to take your coat off if you

24   would be more comfortable, that will be fine.

25   A   I'm fine. I'm fine.

1   Q   Miss Brathwaite, you're from Queens?

2   A   Yes.

3   Q   How long have you been a resident of Queens?

4   A   More than five years.

5   Q   You grew up here?

6   A   Yes.

7   Q   Were you educated here?

8   A   Yes.

9   Q   Are you presently in school?

10   A   Yes.

11   Q   Where do you go to school?

12   A   DeVry Institute of Technology.

13   Q   What are you studying there?

14   A   Computer information systems.

15   Q   Okay. You know I'm having a hard time hearing

16   you. So if you can speak into the microphone so everybody

17   in the room can hear you.

18   THE COURT: Get the chair in close. Okay.

19   Q   Okay. What are you studying at DeVry?

20   A   Computer information systems.

21   Q   That's for a bachelor's degree?

22   A   Yes.

23   Q   Now, are you also working?

24   A   Yes.

25   Q   In what field do you work?

1   A   I work for a staffing agency as a front desk

2   receptionist.

3   Q   How long have you held that position?

4   A   More than a year.

5   Q   Now, I want to ask you, do you know a person

6   named Nikia Stubbs?

7   A   Yes.

8   Q   How do you know her?

9   A   She is one of my best friends.

10   Q   How long have you known Miss Stubbs?

11   A   More than five years.

12   Q   You spend a lot of time with her?

13   A   On and off. We talk mostly on the phone. See

14   each other then and again cause --

15   Q   You get together socially?

16   A   Yeah. Yes.

17   Q   Now, I want to direct your attention now to

18   Saturday night, September the 18th of 1998. Do you remember

19   that day?

20   A   Yes. That's the day Nikia was attacked by

21   someone.

22   Q   And were you with her that day?

23   A   Yes.

24   Q   All right. Now, I want to start back. That was

25   a Saturday evening, early in the evening on that Saturday.

1   Where were you at that time?

2   A   Nikia and I were in her house, in her den.   We

3   were watching T.V. and talking.

4   Q   And where does Nikia live, what part of Queens?

5   A   In Elmont.

6   Q   Had you ever been to her house before?

7   A   Yes.

8   Q   Was anyone else there with you guys?

9   A   No.

10   Q   Just the two of you?

11   A   Yes.

12   Q   Now, you said you were just sort of hanging out

13   watching T.V; is that correct?

14   A   Yes.

15   Q   Did anything take Miss Stubbs away from the two

16   of you talking?

17   A   She was receiving several phone calls.

18   Q   Do you know who those calls were from?

19   A   Sean, someone that had her car --

20   MR. O'MEARA: Objection, your Honor.   How can

21   she know --

22   THE COURT: If you know.   Do you know who

23   called?

24   THE WITNESS: Yes.   She said Sean in her

25   conversation.

A-24

1   MR. O'MEARA: Objection. That's hearsay.

2   She's testifying --

3   THE COURT: Objection is overruled.

4   Q   Okay. So she was getting some calls from someone

5 named Sean.

6   A   Yes.

7   Q   Okay. And did he call just once?

8   A   He called to my knowledge three times that

9 evening.

10   Q   Okay. And after she got off the phone with him

11 for the first time, what did you guys do?

12   A   We were waiting for him to return her vehicle.

13   Q   And what vehicle was that?

14   A   Her Grand Cherokee.

15   Q   So he had that car?

16   A   Yes.

17   Q   So after he called and she talked to him, did he

18 come over to her house?

19   A   No, he never came over.

20   Q   So did she speak with him again?

21   A   The last time that he called was around 10

22 o'clock that evening.

23   Q   Okay. And after 10:00 did he ever come to her

24 house?

25   A   No, he didn't.

A-25

1   Q   Now, did anyone come to her house that evening?

2   A   Her boyfriend.

3   Q   Do you remember approximately what time he got

4   over there?

5   A   Around 11:00 or 12:00.

6   Q   Were you guys still waiting on this person named

7   Sean?

8   A   Yes.

9   Q   By about 12 o'clock that night had he gotten

10   there?

11   A   No.

12   Q   To your knowledge had Miss Stubbs made any other

13   attempts to get hold of Sean?

14   A   She called him several times on the cell phone.

15   Q   Was she able to get through to him?

16   A   No.

17   Q   Now, midnight going into that Sunday morning.

18   What, if anything, do y'all decide to do?

19   A   To go to Sean's house.

20   Q   Okay. And where does he live?

21   A   In Rosedale.

22   Q   That's in Queens?

23   A   Yes.

24   Q   Okay. And so how did you get over to Sean's

25   house?

1   A   We drove Nikia's new car to Sean's house.

2   Q   Now, who went with you to Sean's house?

3   A   It was me, Nikia, and her boyfriend Wilson.

4   Q   Wilson is the name of her boyfriend?

5   A   Yes.

6   Q   Now, tell the members of the jury where you were

7 seated as you all drove over to Sean's house.

8   A   I was seated in the back seat, Nikia was in the

9 driver's seat, and Wilson was in the passenger seat.

10   Q   And did you go to Sean's house?

11   A   Yes.

12   Q   And when you got there, what did you see?

13   A   We were mainly looking for the car, to see if the

14 car was outside of his house.

15   Q   Was it there?

16   A   No.

17   Q   So did you stay at Sean's house?

18   A   No. After not seeing the vehicle we proceeded to

19 Sean's girlfriend's house.

20   Q   Okay. What is the name of Sean's girlfriend?

21   A   Jatanya.

22   Q   Before that evening had you ever met Jatanya?

23   A   No.

24   Q   Do you recall where you went, the area of Queens

25 where you went to get to Jatanya's house?

A-27

1   A   It was in the same area because it took less than

2   five minutes to get to her house from Sean's house.

3   Q   And do you remember any of the roads that you

4   took to get there?

5   A   Her house is off of Brookville and there is a

6   fire station right up the block from her house.

7   Q   Okay. Now, you said it took less than five

8   minutes?

9   A   Yes.

10   Q   Okay. So did you -- who drove over there, by the

11   way?

12   A   Nikia.

13   Q   So did there come a time when you eventually got

14   to the front of 240-06 142nd Avenue?

15   A   Yes.

16   Q   Whose house is there?

17   A   Jatanya's house.

18   Q   Now, as you, you pull onto that street, where did

19   you put the car?

20   A   It was parked across, across the street from

21   Jatanya's house.

22   Q   And after you guys parked the car, what did you

23   do?

24   A   We proceeded to walk to Jatanya's house. We

25   entered through the gate. Nikia then went to the front

1   door, knocked on the door. Wilson stood by the front of the

2   gate and I stood at the bottom of the steps from the front

3   door.

4   Q   Okay. Now, this street where Jatanya's house

5   was, is it a commercial street?

6   A   It's a residential area.

7   Q   Okay. And so you're standing in front of

8   Jatanya's house. Are there houses on either side?

9   A   Yes.

10   Q   Are there houses across the street?

11   A   Yes.

12   Q   Okay. So you three went up to the house. How

13 far were you from Nikia as she stood at the front door of

14 Jatanya's house?

15   A   A couple of feet. Not too far.

16   Q   And then where was Wilson in relation to you?

17   A   A few meters. It's not that big of a yard, so he

18 wasn't that far from me either. I can't distinguish

19 distance.

20   Q   So is it fair to say you were standing in between

21 Nikia at the front door --

22   A   Yes.

23   Q   -- and Wilson down by the gate?

24   A   Yes.

25   Q   Okay. Now, as Nikia went to the front door,

A-29

1 after she got there what did she do?

2   A   She knocked on the door. Rang the doorbell.

3   Q   Okay.

4   A   And waited for someone to come to the door.

5   Q   Did anyone come to the door?

6   A   Jatanya came to the door.

7   Q   Okay. And when she came to the door what was she

8 wearing?

9   A   A nightgown or outfit. Sleepwear.

10   Q   Sleeping clothes?

11   A   Yeah.

12   Q   Now, after she answered the door, what happened?

13   A   Nikia began to voice her anger for Sean not

14 bringing back the vehicle when he said he was. And she

15 felt -- no, she was explaining that you know she didn't

16 understand why he was taking so long.

17   Q   Okay. And did Jatanya have a conversation back

18 with Miss Stubbs?

19   A   Not really. It was mostly Nikia doing all of the

20 talking because she was upset and she was pacing back and

21 forth and she was being -- I don't know -- like anybody

22 that's upset when something happens to you. She was just

23 voicing her opinion to Jatanya --

24   Q   Okay.

25   A   -- about the fact you know her boyfriend didn't

1   bring back her car.

2   Q   Did you say anything to Jatanya?

3   A   Me, no. Wilson said nothing. We were just

4   standing there.

5   Q   So neither you nor Wilson said a word?

6   A   No.

7   Q   Did you or Wilson move closer to the door?

8   A   No.

9   Q   Okay. So after Nikia spoke with Jatanya,

10   expressed her anger about this car, what happened?

11   A   Jatanya went into the house and we waited. And

12   when she came back out, we proceeded back to the car.

13   Q   Okay. Now, did she go with you back over to the

14   car?

15   A   No. After a few minutes she came back out in a

16   different, different clothing. She changed out of her

17   sleepwear into I believe some sweatpants or something.

18   Q   Okay. So by the time she came out in this

19   different outfit, where were the three of you?

20   A   Sitting in the car.

21   Q   Okay. Now, how did you three get back into the

22   car? Where were each of you sitting?

23   A   I was in the same position. I was in the back

24   seat. Wilson was in the passenger seat. Nikia was in the

25   driving seat.

A-31

1   Q   Okay. You said that Jatanya eventually came out

2   in a different outfit?

3   A   Yes.

4   Q   How much time passed approximately between the

5   time that you three got back in the car and then Jatanya

6   came back out?

7   A   No more than five minutes.

8   Q   Now, when Jatanya came out, where did she go?

9   A   She was standing by the driver's side of the

10   door.

11   Q   Okay. The driver's side of the car you were in?

12   A   Yes.

13   Q   Okay. And was she saying anything to y'all?

14   A   No, no. She spoke a few words, but the -- most

15   of the conversation was between us three in the car.

16   Q   And do you recall whether or not the window on

17   the driver's side was open?

18   A   Yes.

19   Q   It was.

20   A   Yes.

21   Q   Okay. And by the way, is this a 2-door car or

22   4-door car?

23   A   It's a 2-door car.

24   Q   Now, did the person named Sean come? Did he

25   arrive there?

A-32

1   A   Not to my knowledge. Until --

2   Q   While you guys were waiting.

3   A   While we were waiting someone approached, a car

4   with a gun. And as the person was reaching into the car

5   Nikia shouted out, Sean. I'm assuming --

6   MR. O'MEARA: Objection, your Honor. She is

7   directly testifying about what somebody else said.

8   THE COURT: It's part of the res gestae. At

9   this point the objection is overruled.

10   Q   Okay. Let's step back a little bit.

11   A   Uh-huh.

12   Q   You were sitting in the back seat of the car.

13   A   Uh-huh.

14   Q   What is the first thing you heard?

15   A   I heard, duck, and then I heard Jatanya go across

16   the street, move away from the car.

17   Q   At that point Jatanya was still standing by the

18   driver's side where Nikia was sitting?

19   A   Yes.

20   Q   So did you see Jatanya do anything?

21   A   She moved across the street.

22   Q   Okay. Across the street in front of her house?

23   A   Back towards her house, yes.

24   Q   So after you heard, duck, Jatanya, get out of the

25   way, what did you see next?

A-33

1   A   I saw someone come up behind the car on the

2   passenger -- on the driver's side of the car with the gun

3   pointed towards the back of the car slowly inching their way

4   up towards the driver's side of the car, towards the

5   driver's window.

6   Q   Were you able to get any kind of a look at the

7   person that had this gun?

8   A   I saw the person as being a brown-skinned

9   individual with a low haircut.

10   Q   What is a low cut?

11   A   Like not bald, but the hair is cut really low to

12   the scalp.

13   THE COURT: Closely cropped hair?

14   THE WITNESS: There you go, yeah. Thank you.

15   Q   So he was a male. I'm sorry, I didn't mean to

16   interrupt your description of him.

17   A   A brown-skinned male black with a low-cropped

18   haircut.

19   Q   Did you make any observation about his build?

20   A   He was small build. He wasn't like a heavyset or

21   very large individual.

22   Q   Okay. And did you make any observations about

23   what he was holding?

24   A   He was holding a gun in his hand.

25   Q   Do you recall which hand?

A-34

1   A   In his right hand.

2   Q   Okay. Now, as you said you saw this individual

3 with the gun come up the side of your car --

4   A   Yes.

5   Q   -- the car you were sitting in?

6   A   Yes.

7   Q   Okay. As he got to the window what happened?

8   A   As he got to my window, the little window -- it's

9 a convertible coupe, so to my window, it's a small window.

10 As the gun pointed to, toward me, I ducked forward into the

11 back of the seat. Then the person proceeded to point the

12 gun to Nikia and pointed it against her head and ordered her

13 out of the car.

14   Q   Okay. Now, how far were you from Nikia when the

15 gun was at her head?

16   A   It's a coupe, like I said. So it's a very small

17 back seat. So I was directly behind Nikia. So less than a

18 foot.

19   Q   Okay. Now, you said that the person, while he

20 had this gun to her head he ordered her out of the car.

21 What exactly did he say? These are his words.

22   A   His words were, get the F out of the car. He

23 just repeated saying it.

24   Q   Now, did Nikia just jump out of the car?

25   A   No. The person was trying to pull her out of the

A-35

1   car through the window. But she is very tall, so it didn't

2   work. So he opened the door and pulled her out of the car

3   by her collar.

4   Q   So he grabbed ahold of her clothes?

5   A   Yes.

6   Q   Okay. Now, you said there was -- Nikia's

7   boyfriend was also in the car at this time --

8   A   Uh-huh.

9   Q   -- Wilson.

10   What was he doing, if you could see?

11   A   I can say by the time the individual dragged her

12 out of the car Wilson was no longer in the car.

13   Q   So he had gotten out of the car.

14   A   Yeah, at some point. I don't know when.

15   Q   All right. So once Nikia had been dragged out of

16 the car, what did you see?

17   A   I saw the individual drag her across the street

18 onto the sidewalk and towards the back of a house.

19   Q   Okay. And was the person dragging her across the

20 street by himself?

21   A   Yes.

22   Q   Okay. And approximately how far down, down the

23 street did he drag her?

24   A   Two or three houses. Two, two houses.

25   Q   You kept your eyes on her the whole time?

A-36

1   A   Until I couldn't see her after he dragged her

2 down the driveway to the back of the house.

3   Q   So there came a point you lost sight of --

4   A   I lost sight of her, yes.

5   Q   Now, Miss Brathwaite, what was Nikia wearing at

6 that time?

7   A   A velour sweatsuit.

8   Q   Now after this man dragged her out of your sight,

9 what did you do?

10   A   I was still in the back seat. I proceeded to get

11 out of the car. And being scared and shaken and crying, I,

12 I didn't know which direction to go into. And before I

13 could even think about what I was going to do, shots rang

14 out. And at that point there were neighbors outside. And

15 when the shots ran off they ran into the house. I ran in

16 the house with them. I didn't know them, but I ran in with

17 them into their house.

18   Q   Okay. Now, you say, shots rang out. Do you

19 recall how many shots?

20   A   More than five.

21   Q   Did those shots sound close to you, far in the

22 distance --

23   A   It came in the direction where Nikia was dragged

24 by the person.

25   Q   Okay. You ran into a neighbor's house?

A-37

1   A   Yes.

2   Q   Did you know those people?

3   A   No.

4   Q   Okay. Now, what happened after that?

5   A   After a few minutes I saw three individuals run

6   from the place where Nikia, where I lost sight of Nikia.

7   And a minute or less later Nikia walked out.

8   Q   Okay. Now, you say you saw three individuals?

9   A   Yes.

10   Q   Had you seen two other individuals?

11   A   After the person dragged Nikia out of the car two

12   individuals came and were crouched down across the street

13   behind another car, which was directly across from the car I

14   was in. It was a light-skinned guy and a brown-skinned guy,

15   but I didn't really get a look at them. But I knew what

16   skin color they were. And those were the two people with

17   the other person.

18   Q   Okay. And now you said that the three of them

19   ran away. Did you see where they went?

20   A   Down the block from the direction they came.

21   Q   Okay. And as, as the man with the gun had taken

22   Nikia across the street, was that near where Jatanya was

23   standing?

24   A   No. Jatanya was standing at a house, the next --

25   the house that's next to her house, in front of that gate,

A-38

1   whatever.

2   Q   She was still out there --

3   A   Yes.

4   Q   -- while this was happening to Nikia?

5   A   Yes.

6   Q   What did Jatanya do to help Nikia?

7   A   Nothing.

8   Q   Now, you said the three men ran down the street.

9   Is that towards Brookville Boulevard or away?

10   A   Away from Brookville.

11   Q   Away from Brookville Boulevard?

12   A   Uh-huh.

13   Q   And did there come a time when you saw Nikia?

14   A   When she came back out from behind the house.

15   Q   What did she look like?

16   A   She was shaken. She was crying. Her shirt

17   collar was ripped off. Her hair was messed up because the

18   person was also pulling her by her hair. And I, I met her

19   at her car.

20   Q   Okay. So you came back out?

21   A   I came back out from the house.

22   Q   Okay. Now, when you two got back to the car,

23   what did you do?

24   A   We proceeded to try to locate her boyfriend. And

25   we came out from off Jatanya's block. We made a left going

1   down Brookville and two blocks away her truck, her Grand

2   Cherokee, met us at one of the blocks. Like it was coming

3   down one of the streets. And we were on Brookville. And so

4   as we passed that block, the person sped out behind us and

5   chased us up about six more blocks.

6   Q   Okay. Let me just make sure I understand this.

7   You pulled off of Jatanya's block --

8   A   Yes.

9   Q   -- onto Brookville.

10   A   Yes.

11   Q   And as you were going down Brookville you saw

12   Nikia's other car?

13   A   Yes.

14   Q   And is that the car that she had loaned Sean?

15   A   Yes.

16   Q   Okay. And was he actually at that point on

17   Brookville Boulevard, or was he also on a side street?

18   A   He was on the side street coming onto Brookville.

19   Q   Okay. And now you two were driving. Did he turn

20   onto Brookville behind you?

21   A   Yes.

22   Q   And what happened after he turned and got behind

23   you?

24   A   He chased us. There is -- before Brookville goes

25   into Long Island, there is a road. There is a Snake Road.

A-40

1   THE COURT: Is that the one that ended in

2   Rockaway Boulevard?

3   THE WITNESS: No -- yes, Rockaway Boulevard

4   is on the other end, Rockaway Turnpike.

5   A   So he chased us into Snake Road.

6   Q   Did he catch up with you?

7   A   He made a U-turn the block before Snake Road.

8   Q   But he was in Nikia's other car?

9   A   Yes.

10   Q   Okay. All right. Now, after he made the U-turn,

11   where did you and Nikia go?

12   A   We proceeded back to Nikia's neighborhood to her

13   precinct.

14   Q   And that's the 105 Precinct?

15   A   Yes.

16   Q   And when you got to the 105 Precinct, what did

17   you do there?

18   A   We filed a report.

19   Q   So you told the police what happened?

20   A   Yes.

21   Q   Okay. Now, Miss Brathwaite, if you saw the

22   person again that had the gun and that pulled Nikia out of

23   the car, would you be able to recognize him?

24   A   No.

25   MS. Bishop: Okay. All right. Thank you. I

1   have nothing further.

2   THE COURT: Mr. O'Meara.

3   MR. O'MEARA: Your Honor, can I just have one

4   minute?

5   THE COURT: Take your time, sir.

6   MR. O'MEARA: I just have a few questions.

7   THE COURT: Go ahead.

8   CROSS EXAMINATION

9   BY MR. O'MEARA:

10   Q   I'd just like to know where Wilson was while all

11   of this was going on.

12   A   I don't know.

13   Q   Did he run away?

14   A   I don't know.

15   Q   Did he walk back with you to the car after you

16   left Jatanya's house?

17   A   No.

18   Q   So -- just so I get this straight. You're in

19   front of Jatanya's house.

20   A   Uh-huh.

21   Q   And then you leave Jatanya's house.

22   A   Uh-huh.

23   Q   You go back to her car.

24   A   Nikia's car.

25   Q   To Nikia's car.

1   A   All three of us.

2   Q   All three of you.

3   A   Yes.

4   Q   Did Wilson go back in the car?

5   A   Yes.

6   Q   At some point Wilson left the car?

7   A   Yes.

8   Q   He ran down the block. You just didn't see where

9   he went.

10   A   I have no idea which direction he went.

11   THE COURT: When you're on Brookville

12   Boulevard afterward, was Wilson back in the car with

13   you or not?

14   THE WITNESS: We didn't see Wilson till later

15   that night.

16   THE COURT: Pardon me?

17   THE WITNESS: We didn't see Wilson till later

18   that night.

19   THE COURT: He didn't get back in the car

20   after the incident?

21   THE WITNESS: No, we couldn't find him.

22   Q   When did you finally find Wilson?

23   A   At the police station with Nikia's mother.

24   Q   Do you know what he did after?

25   MS. BISHOP: Objection.

1   THE COURT: If you know.

2   A   I have no idea. I know he ran to a phone as far

3   as I know to call Nikia's mother. As far as -- that's all

4   the information I have on where he went after he got out the

5   car.

6   Q   Nikia's boyfriend ran out of the car and left you

7   two there?

8   A   I don't know what happened.

9   Q   Now, this was at approximately 3:00 a.m. in the

10 morning?

11   A   Yes.

12   Q   Did you think it was a good idea to go banging on

13 someone's door at 3 o'clock in the morning?

14   MS. BISHOP: Objection.

15   THE COURT: Overruled. You can answer.

16   A   I was with Nikia and she wanted her vehicle back.

17 And the individual Sean said he was going to bring it.

18 Someone tells you they're going to do something, they don't

19 do it. Just because we went to that person's house, it

20 doesn't matter what time it was. That's my own opinion.

21   THE COURT: The answer is yes.

22   A   Yeah. Yes, thank you.

23   Q   Yes? It's okay?

24   A   It was okay. I felt it was, it was okay for us

25 to do that.

1   Q   Did you see the automobile outside the house at 3

2   o'clock in the morning?

3   A   No.

4   Q   Did you see it -- now, you said it's okay to go

5   to somebody's house at 3:00 a.m. in the morning if they're

6   bringing the car to get the car?

7   A   Uh-huh.

8   THE COURT: She's already answered the

9   question.

10   Q   Did Miss Belnavis borrow that car?

11   A   Who?

12   Q   Miss Jatanaya --

13   A   Not to my knowledge.

14   Q   But that's whose house you were at at 3:00 in the

15   morning, correct?

16   A   Yes.

17   Q   Thank you. And just one more question. You have

18   no idea who had the gun outside of Nikia's car?

19   A   No.

20   Q   You can't identify him now?

21   A   No.

22   Q   You couldn't identify him then?

23   A   If I saw him probably -- it was three years ago,

24   no.

25   Q   The answer is, no, you can't identify him --

1   A   No.

2   Q   -- then or now?

3   A   Probably then I would have, but now, no. It's
4   been a long time. No.

5   Q   Did anybody give you the opportunity to identify
6   him three years ago?

7   A   No, I never saw a picture or anything.

8   Q   Nobody asked you?

9   A   No. No. No one ever showed me a picture.

10   Q   They didn't show you a picture?

11   A   No.

12   Q   Didn't bring you to a lineup?

13   A   No.

14   MR. O'MEARA: No further questions, your
15   Honor.

16   THE COURT: Thank you.

17   Anything else, Miss Bishop?

18   MS. BISHOP: No, Judge.

19   THE COURT: Thank you, ma'am. You can step
20   down.

21   THE WITNESS: Thank you.

22   (The witness left the courtroom.)

23   THE COURT: Counsel.

24   (Sidebar discussion off the record.)

25   THE COURT: All right, ladies and gentlemen,

1   THE CLERK: Thank you.

2   THE COURT: Okay. Ladies and gentlemen, I

3   again apologize for the delay. It was not a very long

4   one. There were some legal issues we had to resolve

5   before proceeding with the next witness. And we're now

6   ready for the next witness.

7   People, your next witness, please.

8   MS. BISHOP: Yes, Judge. The People call

9   Miss Julia Hosein.

10   J U L I A   H O S E I N, a witness called on behalf of the

11   People, after having been first duly sworn and having

12   stated her residence as Bronx County took the witness

13   stand and testified as follows:

14   THE COURT: Miss Hosein, I'm going to ask you

15   to keep your voice up or move up in the chair all the

16   way in. Get nice and close to the mike so everybody

17   can hear you, okay.

18   THE WITNESS: Okay.

19   THE COURT: Give it a tap. See if it's

20   working.

21   Okay, Miss Bishop.

22   DIRECT EXAMINATION

23   BY MS. BISHOP:

24   Q   Good morning, Miss Hosein.

25   A   Good morning.

1   Q   You live now in the Bronx; is that right?

2   A   Yes.

3   Q   How long have you lived in the Bronx?

4   A   Approximately three years.

5   Q   Where did you live before that?

6   A   In Queens, Rosedale.

7   Q   Have you lived in New York your whole life?

8   A   No.

9   Q   Where -- are you originally from New York?

10   A   I'm from Dominican Republic.

11   Q   How old were you when you came to New York?

12   A   11, 12 years old.

13   Q   You have been here ever since?

14   A   Yes.

15   Q   Now, do you have family here, Miss Hosein?

16   A   Yes, I do.

17   Q   What family members?

18   A   My parents, my brothers, and sisters. My

19   children, niece and nephews.

20   Q   You mentioned that you lived in Rosedale, Queens

21   for a time?

22   A   Yes.

23   Q   What time period were you in Rosedale?

24   A   From '78 to '99.

25   Q   Okay. Now, were you living in Rosedale in

1   September of 1998?

2   A   Yes.

3   Q   And what was your address when you lived there?

4   A   240-32 142nd Avenue.

5   Q   What main road is that near?

6   A   Brookville Park.

7   Q   It's right near Brookville Park?

8   A   Yes.

9   Q   Is there a main street that runs right alongside

10   the park, Brookville Boulevard? Is that near Brookville

11   Boulevard?

12   A   Yes.

13   Q   Okay. All right.

14   Now, when you were living at your home in

15   Rosedale did you live there with anyone?

16   A   Yes.

17   Q   Who?

18   A   I lived there with my boyfriend and my two

19   children.

20   Q   And at the time how old were your two children?

21   A   My daughter was 15. And my son was 18.

22   Q   Okay. And at that time were you working?

23   A   Yes.

24   Q   Are you working now?

25   A   Yes.

1   Q   What area what field of work are you in?

2   A   Home care agency.

3   Q   How long have you been a home care agency?

4   A   13 years.

5   Q   What are your responsibilities there?

6   A   To send home attendants to care clients.

7   Q   And you were working in that position in 1998?

8   A   Yes.

9   Q   Now, 142nd Avenue where you were living, what

10   type of street is that?

11   A   It's a residential street.

12   Q   Okay. And would you describe for the jury the

13   types of homes that are on that street?

14   A   They're 1-family house. They detached.

15   Q   Okay. And by "detached," does each person have a

16   yard area?

17   A   Yes, they do.

18   Q   Okay. And did you know any of your neighbors

19   when you lived there?

20   A   Yes.

21   Q   Okay. Were your neighbors fairly friendly?

22   A   Yes, they were.

23   Q   You got together --

24   A   Yes.

25   Q   -- occasionally?

1   Okay. Now, I want to direct your attention to

2   Saturday night, September the 18th of 1998 going into Sunday

3   morning, September the 19th. Do you remember that day?

4   A   Yes.

5   Q   And were you at your home that evening?

6   A   Yes, I was.

7   Q   And who were you there with?

8   A   My boyfriend and my two children.

9   Q   Okay. That Saturday night there come a time when

10   you went to bed?

11   A   Yes.

12   Q   Okay. And where is your bedroom in your house?

13   Is it more towards the front or is it more towards the back?

14   A   The front.

15   Q   And do you actually have a window in your

16   bedroom?

17   A   Yes.

18   Q   And which direction does the window face?

19   A   The front of the house.

20   Q   Okay. And from that window do you see 142nd

21   Avenue?

22   A   Yes.

23   Q   Okay. Now, you went to sleep. And I direct your

24   attention to about 3 o'clock in the morning in the early

25   part of Sunday morning. What, if anything, did you hear at

1   that time?

2   A   I heard some gunshots.

3   Q   Okay. Do you recall how many gunshots you heard?

4   A   No.

5   Q   Do you know if it was more than one?

6   A   Yes.

7   Q   Okay. And did those shots awake you?

8   A   Yes.

9   Q   And after you woke up what did you do?

10   A   I called the police. I called 911.

11   Q   Okay.

12   A   I looked outside. I didn't see anything.

13   Q   Okay.

14   A   And I make sure that my children were okay. My

15   daughter, which she was still sleeping.

16   Q   Okay. And was everyone okay?

17   A   Yes.

18   Q   Okay. And after you said you looked out the

19   window and you didn't see anything --

20   A   No.

21   Q   -- aside from the gunshots that you heard, did

22   you hear anything else out there?

23   A   No.

24   Q   Okay. Now, after you looked out the window you

25   said you called 911; is that correct?

1   A   Yes.

2   Q   And did the police come just around 3 o'clock

3   that morning?

4   A   Yes.

5   Q   And did you have a brief conversation with them?

6   A   Yes, I did.

7   Q   And were you able to tell them anything about who

8   had fired these shots?

9   A   No.

10   Q   Okay. Now, after you had a brief conversation

11   with the police, what did you do?

12   A   I went back inside the house.

13   Q   And were you and your family able to get back to

14   sleep that evening?

15   A   No.

16   Q   Okay. Now, I want to direct your attention to a

17   few hours later, around 7:00 or 7:30 in the morning, you

18   know maybe three or four hours after you heard the gunshot.

19   At that time did you leave your house and go into the front

20   yard area of your house?

21   A   Yes, I did.

22   Q   And did you see other people out at that time?

23   A   Some of the neighbors were outside.

24   Q   And did you have a chance at that time to look

25   around your yard?

1   A   Yes.

2   Q   And did you see anything there that you hadn't

3   seen before?

4   A   There was some bullet shells.

5   Q   Okay.

6   A   The shells.

7   Q   What did they look like? About how big were

8   they?

9   A   They were little ones.

10   Q   Okay. And were they made out of metal?

11   A   Yes.

12   Q   And when you saw them what did you do?

13   A   I called 911 again.

14   Q   Okay. And do you recall exactly where you saw

15   the shells?

16   A   In my yard in the grass.

17   Q   And did you handle the shells in any way?

18   A   I picked them up with, with a stick.

19   Q   Okay. And did you later on pick them up with

20   your hands?

21   A   No.

22   Q   And so after you said you went back in and called

23   911 again?

24   A   Yes.

25   Q   And do you recall at that time how many shells

1   you had seen up to that point?

2   A   Maybe about three, four.

3   Q   Okay. And so did the police come?

4   A   Yes.

5   Q   And do you recall the name of the police officer

6   who came?

7   A   No, I don't remember his name.

8   Q   When he arrived did he come in, in a marked

9   police car?

10   A   Yes.

11   Q   And did you speak with him?

12   A   Yes, I did.

13   Q   And what did you tell him?

14   A   I told him that I had called before and after the

15   police left we found some shells in front of the house.

16   Q   Okay. And after -- and did you give him your

17   name?

18   A   Yes, I did.

19   Q   Now, after you spoke with the police officer did,

20   did the police and perhaps even yourself or other neighbors

21   continue to look around your yard --

22   A   Yes.

23   Q   -- if you can recall?

24   A   Yes.

25   Q   And do you recall if any additional casings were

A-46

1   found at that time?

2   A   Yes.

3   Q   Do you recall how many?

4   A   Two more.

5   Q   Now, did there come a time when the police left

6   that morning?

7   A   Yes.

8   Q   And what did they take with them?

9   A   The bullet shell that I had given them.

10   Q   And do you recall how many bullet shells that

11 they took with them when they left that morning?

12   A   I believe it was seven.

13   Q   Okay. And now later on did you see anything else

14 in your yard that didn't belong to you?

15   A   Yes.

16   Q   What?

17   A   Bullet shells again, but there were two only.

18   Q   You found two more?

19   A   Yes.

20   Q   And do you recall meeting with a police detective

21 on September the 24th at your home?

22   A   I don't remember.

23   Q   Is it possible that you did?

24   A   Yes, possible.

25   Q   And is it possible that at that time you gave

1   those two additional shell casings --

2   A   Yes.

3   Q   -- to the detective?

4   A   Yes, possible.

5   Q   Now, Miss Hosein, when you touched the shell

6   casings did you have any gloves on?

7   A   No.

8   Q   Okay. And aside from the shell casings did you

9   ever find anything else in your yard area that didn't belong

10   to you?

11   A   It was not in my yard. It was in the next house.

12   It was a hair -- it was like a Chinese stick.

13   Q   That you use --

14   A   It was holding the hair, yes.

15   Q   -- to put up --

16   A   Right.

17   Q   -- a woman might use in her hair?

18   A   Yes.

19   Q   Okay. And what did you do with those?

20   A   I threw away.

21   MS. BISHOP: I have nothing further at this

22   time, Judge.

23   THE COURT: Mr. O'Meara.

24   MR. O'MEARA: Just a few questions.

25   CROSS EXAMINATION

1   BY MR. O'MEARA:

2   Q   Do you remember speaking to the detectives when

3   they came to your house?

4   A   Yes.

5   Q   Did you ever tell them you had seen a car

6   leaving?

7   A   No.

8   Q   You never said that?

9   A   No.

10   Q   You never said there was a black car?

11   A   No.

12   Q   When you looked out the window you saw a black

13   car speeding away?

14   A   No, I did not.

15   Q   Then when you looked out the window you didn't

16   see anything?

17   A   I didn't see anything, no.

18   Q   You didn't see anybody being dragged?

19   A   No.

20   Q   You didn't see anybody shooting a gun?

21   A   No.

22   MR. O'MEARA: All right. Thank you.

23   THE COURT: Is that it? Any redirect?

24   MS. BISHOP: Just a few questions, Judge.

25   REDIRECT EXAMINATION

1   BY MS. BISHOP:

2   Q   Miss Hosein, did you ever tell the police that

3   you had seen any kind of black car driving away?

4   A   No, my neighbors -- after I call the police,

5   that's the second time the neighbors were talking about that

6   they had seen a car. But I didn't see anything.

7   Q   Okay. And to your knowledge did the police speak

8   with your neighbors; if you know?

9   A   No, I don't know.

10   Q   Okay. All right. Thank you.

11   THE COURT: Anything else?

12   MR. O'MEARA: One more question, your Honor.

13   RECROSS EXAMINATION

14   BY MR. O'MEARA:

15   Q   When the neighbors were speaking was the police

16   officer around?

17   A   No.

18   Q   So when the neighbors --

19   MS. BISHOP: Objection, Judge. She already

20   said she doesn't know.

21   THE COURT: The objection is overruled.

22   Q   When all the neighbors were speaking and talking

23   about a black car, was the police officer there?

24   A   No.

25   Q   There was no police officer around?

1   A   No.

2   MR. O'MEARA: Thank you.

3   THE WITNESS: You're welcome.

4   THE COURT: Do you know if any of your

5   neighbors spoke to the police?

6   THE WITNESS: No.

7   THE COURT: Did the police ever show you

8   anything they wrote?

9   THE WITNESS: No.

10   THE COURT: Anything else?

11   MS. BISHOP: No.

12   THE COURT: All right. Thank you, ma'am.

13   You can step down.

14   (The witness left the courtroom.)

15   THE COURT: Ready for your next witness?

16   MS. BISHOP: Judge, may we step up.

17   THE COURT: Step up for a second.

18   (Sidebar discussion off the record.)

19   THE COURT: People, your next witness,

20   please.

21   MS. BISHOP: Yes. The People call Police

22   Officer Alan Rosenberg.

23   A L A N   R O S E N B E R G, Police Officer, a witness

24   called on behalf of the People, after having been

25   first duly sworn and having stated his shield number as

1   And I'm showing that to counsel.

2   (Court Exhibit 5 marked.)

3   MS. BISHOP: And Judge --

4   THE COURT: Mr. O'Meara?

5   MR. O'MEARA: No objection.

6   THE COURT: They will be received and marked

7   as People's Exhibit 2.B. in evidence.

8   MS. BISHOP: And ask they be published to the

9   jury as well.

10   THE COURT: All right. Let's get them marked

11   first.

12   (People's Exhibit 2.B. marked in evidence.)

13   THE COURT: Just take a look at that. Just

14   pass it on to your next juror without comment, please.

15   (People's Exhibit 2.B. published to the

16   jury.)

17   THE COURT: Okay. Would you call your next

18   witness.

19   MS. BISHOP: Yes, Judge. The People call

20   Miss Nikia Stubbs.

21   N I K I A   S T U B B S, a witness called on behalf of the

22   People, after having been first duly sworn and having

23   stated her residence as Queens County took the witness

24   stand and testified as follows:

25   THE CLERK: Thank you. You may be seated.

1   THE COURT: Miss Stubbs, I'm going to ask you

2   to try to keep your voice up or move real close to that

3   mike so everybody will be able to hear you, okay?

4   THE WITNESS: Yes.

5   THE COURT: Miss Bishop.

6 DIRECT EXAMINATION

7 BY MS. BISHOP:

8   Q   Miss Stubbs, you live in Queens County?

9   A   Yes.

10   Q   How long have you lived in Queens?

11   A   About 26 years.

12   Q   Is that your whole life?

13   A   Yes.

14   Q   Now, do you have family in Queens?

15   A   Yes.

16   Q   Who?

17   A   My mother and my sister.

18   Q   Is your father still living in Queens?

19   A   No, he is not.

20   Q   Now, Miss Stubbs are you married?

21   A   No, I'm not.

22   Q   Do you have a boyfriend?

23   A   Yes, I do.

24   Q   How long have you had a boyfriend?

25   A   For about four and a half years.

1   Q   What is his name?

2   A   His name is Wilson Barnes (ph).

3   Q   Does he live in New York also?

4   A   Yes, he does.

5   Q   Now, you said you have been here for most of your

6   life. Were you educated here?

7   A   Yes, I was.

8   Q   How far did you go with your education?

9   A   I got my bachelor's degree in criminal justice

10   from St. John's University.

11   Q   When did you receive that degree?

12   A   In May of 1997.

13   Q   Since then after you graduated did you become

14   employed?

15   A   Yes, I have.

16   Q   Where did you work starting -- well, around May

17   of 1997?

18   A   I temped for several staffing agencies. And the

19   last time that I testified I was working at a -- as a

20   recruiter for a staffing agency.

21   Q   Approximately when was that?

22   A   That was in 1998.

23   Q   Okay. Do you recall what time period in 1998 you

24   were working for that staffing agency?

25   A   From the winter of 1998 to the fall of 1998.

A-53a

1   Q   So from the winter of 1998 to the following year?

2   A   Yes.

3   Q   You said you were in human resources?

4   A   Yes.

5   Q   What particularly did you do there?

6   A   I recruited candidates for my employers.

7   Q   Okay. What type of organization did you work

8   for?

9   A   I worked for a nonprofit organization.

10   Q   Okay. Is this, just so I'm clear, is this during

11   the summer of 1998?

12   A   Yes.

13   Q   Okay. So now at that time when you were employed

14   there, were you living at home?

15   A   Yes, I was employed and living with my mother.

16   Q   Now, after -- did there come a time when that job

17   through the temping agency came to an end?

18   A   Yes, it came to an end in September of 1998.

19   Q   Towards the beginning or end?

20   A   Towards the middle sometime.

21   Q   And did you continue to seek other employment

22   after that?

23   A   Yes, I did.

24   Q   And did you continue to seek further education

25   after that?

1   A   No.

2   Q   Okay. When was the next time you became

3   employed?

4   A   The summer of 1999 full time. But during that

5   time I also did hair part time.

6   Q   Now, when you say you did hair, what does that

7   mean?

8   A   I was a hair dresser before, through college, and

9   so I went back to doing hair when I lost my position.

10   Q   And then you became employed again in the summer

11 of 1999?

12   A   Yes.

13   Q   And where did you work at that time?

14   A   I worked for New Beginnings Financial Services.

15   Q   What type of company is that?

16   A   They do financial services and also real estate.

17   Q   And what division of that company did you work

18 in?

19   A   I worked in the real estate division.

20   Q   Okay. And how long did you work in that company?

21   A   For the summer of 1999.

22   Q   And then after that you didn't work for them any

23 longer?

24   A   No.

25   Q   Okay. Now, as a result of your employment at New

1 Beginnings --

2   A   Yes.

3   Q   -- did you become involved in a criminal scheme?

4   A   Yes.

5   Q   And were you eventually arrested?

6   A   Yes, I was.

7   Q   When were you arrested?

8   A   In September of 2000.

9   Q   Okay. And did the U.S. Attorney's Office

10 prosecute you as a result of that arrest?

11   A   Yes.

12   Q   And did you ultimately plead guilty to the

13 charges for -- withdrawn.

14   Did you ultimately take responsibility for your

15 actions in that case?

16   A   Yes, I did.

17   Q   And what did you specifically do?

18   A   I pled guilty to referring clients to my

19 employers, faxing loan applications to automobile

20 dealerships that contained false statements, and for having

21 possession of false documents in the trunk of my car.

22   Q   Okay. And did you actually go to court and plead

23 guilty to some kind of fraud in that case?

24   A   Yes, I did.

25   Q   Okay. Now, when did you plead guilty?

1   A   I think maybe last month.

2   Q   So this year?

3   A   This year.

4   Q   And have you been sentenced yet on this case?

5   A   No, I haven't.

6   Q   And are you aware of what range or sentence that

7   you're facing in that case?

8   A   Yes.

9   Q   What is that range?

10   A   Zero to five years.

11   Q   Okay. Now, as you just said the U.S. Attorney's

12   Office is responsible for prosecuting you in that case; is

13   that correct?

14   A   Yes.

15   Q   And did the particular federal prosecutor that's

16   prosecuting you, is he aware that you're testifying here

17   today?

18   A   Yes.

19   Q   And did he make any promises to you about your

20   testimony here today in state court?

21   A   No.

22   Q   And did he promise you any kind of a benefit or

23   any kind of deal if you showed up today for court?

24   A   No.

25   Q   Now, you have been -- has anyone in my office,

A-55

1   the Office of the District Attorney of Queens County, made

2   any promises to you about your testimony here today?

3   A   No.

4   Q   Now, since your arrest have you been employed?

5   A   Yes.

6   Q   And where have you been working?

7   A   I have been a human resources recruiter for a

8   national staffing firm.

9   Q   And how long have you been in that position?

10   A   A year.

11   Q   And you're still presently employed there?

12   A   Yes.

13   Q   All right. Now let's go back to the summer of

14   1998.

15   A   Okay.

16   Q   Where again were you working at that time?

17   A   I was working as recruiter for a nonprofit

18   organization.

19   Q   You said you were living at home?

20   A   Yes, I was.

21   Q   Okay. Now, when -- were you living with your

22   mom?

23   A   Yes.

24   Q   And did you have some sort of like rent

25   arrangement with your mother at that time?

1   A   No, I lived rent free.

2   Q   And did your mom charge you for food or utilities

3   or anything like that?

4   A   Nothing.

5   Q   Do you recall approximately how much money you

6   were making back then?

7   A   Approximately 18 dollars an hour.

8   Q   And were you also doing hair on the side?

9   A   Yes, I was.

10   Q   Okay. Now, at that time did you own any

11   vehicles?

12   A   Yes.

13   Q   What cars did you own?

14   A   I owned a 1995 Jeep Grand Cherokee and a 1998

15   Mercedes Benz CLK 320.

16   Q   Why did you need two cars?

17   A   I originally had my Grand Cherokee and I had

18   subleased it to a friend of mine. And I purchased another

19   car in the time frame that my other friend had my car.

20   Q   Now, when you say you subleased your Jeep, did

21   the person that you sublet it to actually take over the

22   payments for you?

23   A   Yes.

24   Q   Okay. And what color was that Jeep, by the way?

25   A   It was light gray or silver color.

A-57

1   Q   And a Jeep is like one of these SUV type

2   vehicles?

3   A   Yes.

4   Q   All right. Now, when did you get the Mercedes?

5   A   In June of 1998.

6   Q   And did you actually purchase that car or did you

7   make arrangements to lease it?

8   A   I leased it.

9   Q   And why don't you tell the jury a little bit how

10   you went through to get the lease?

11   A   I just applied through and got a loan for the car

12   actually through the dealership.

13   Q   Through the dealership?

14   A   Yes.

15   Q   You dealt with them directly?

16   A   Yes.

17   Q   And were you able to obtain a lease from the

18   dealership?

19   A   Yes.

20   Q   Okay. Now, how much were the payments on that

21   lease?

22   A   650.

23   Q   A month?

24   A   Yes.

25   Q   And was anyone helping you out with those

A-58

1   payments?

2   A   Yes, my boyfriend.

3   Q   So each month you two would put together the

4   money to pay for this car?

5   A   Yes.

6   Q   Now, in the meantime where was the Jeep?

7   A   My girlfriend had possession of the Jeep.

8   Q   Okay. This was a friend of yours. And they were

9   paying the notes on that Jeep as well?

10   A   Yes.

11   Q   Now, the people that you were subleasing the Jeep

12 to, you had worked out a length of time with them that they

13 were going to cover the notes for you?

14   A   Yes.

15   Q   And did there come a time when they were unable

16 to continue paying those notes?

17   A   Yes.

18   Q   And when was that?

19   A   About the end of August of 1998.

20   Q   Okay. And what happened? Did they return the

21 Jeep back to you?

22   A   Yes.

23   Q   Okay. And at that time what were you faced with?

24   A   Two car payments that I didn't know how I was

25 going to pay both of them.

1   Q   And what was -- what was that combined payment

2   amount going to wind up being for you approximately?

3   A   Over a thousand dollars a month.

4   Q   All right. Now, do you know someone named

5   Jatanya Belnavis?

6   A   Yes.

7   Q   And how do you know her?

8   A   We were friends for many years and actually I

9   used to do her hair.

10   Q   Okay. And how far back does your friendship go

11   with her?

12   A   Over ten years.

13   Q   Do you know where Miss Belnavis lives?

14   A   Yes.

15   Q   Where does she live?

16   A   In Rosedale, Queens, on like 142nd Avenue.

17   Q   Have you ever been to her house before?

18   A   Yes, several times.

19   Q   Is it fair to say that up until September you and

20   she were fairly good friends?

21   A   Yes.

22   Q   And now once you had these two cars did you speak

23   with Miss Belnavis?

24   A   Yes.

25   Q   And what was your conversation with her about?

A-60

1   A   I made an arrangement with her and her boyfriend

2   to rent the car from me, the Grand Cherokee, for

3   approximately a week.

4   Q   Okay. And do you know why they only needed the

5   car for a week?

6   A   They were purchasing a car and until they were to

7   get their car they were going to rent my car.

8   Q   So that would help you with the payments and help

9   them with the car?

10   A   Yes.

11   Q   Now, you said you spoke with Jatanya and her

12   boyfriend. What was her boyfriend's name?

13   A   Sean.

14   Q   And had you ever met Sean before?

15   A   Yes.

16   Q   When had you met him?

17   A   I met him several times before. Actually one

18   time at her house and one time at my house. He came by as I

19   did her hair.

20   Q   So you had met him a couple of times?

21   A   Yes.

22   Q   Okay. He was introduced to you as Sean?

23   A   Yes.

24   Q   Now, the person that you know as Sean do you see

25   him in the courtroom today?

A-61

1   A   Yes.

2   Q   Please point out where you see him --

3   A   He is sitting over there with the black suit.

4   MS. BISHOP: Judge, indicating the defendant.

5   THE COURT: Well, there's two people with

6   black suits. What color shirt?

7   THE WITNESS: The black man.

8   THE COURT: The black gentleman with the

9   black suit?

10   THE WITNESS: Yes.

11   Q   And you recognize him as Sean?

12   A   Yes.

13   Q   Now, did you later learn the defendant to go by a

14   different name?

15   A   Yes.

16   Q   What name is that?

17   A   Nicholas Zimmerman.

18   Q   Now, let's go back to the middle of September. I

19   want you to tell the jury a little bit about this agreement

20   with your car that you worked out with the defendant and his

21   girlfriend Jatanya Belnavis?

22   A   Okay. I had made an arrangement for them to rent

23   the car, and they were supposed to pay me day by day on how

24   long they had the car. And subsequently they gave me about

25   $200 for the time they did have the car.

A-62

1   Q   And were they eventually supposed to give you

2   money in addition to that?

3   A   Yes.

4   Q   Okay. And that was -- if the, the time period

5   they had the car extended, they were going to give you more

6   money?

7   A   Yes.

8   Q   Okay. Now, do you recall when you gave them your

9   Jeep?

10   A   A week prior to the 18th.

11   Q   Okay. And do you recall where that transaction

12   took place?

13   A   Yes.

14   Q   Where was that?

15   A   At my house.

16   Q   Okay. And who came to get the Jeep?

17   A   I remember Jatanya and Sean coming to get the

18   car.

19   Q   So they came to your house. Did you give them

20   the keys to your Jeep?

21   A   Yes, I did.

22   Q   Did they give you anything in return?

23   A   Yes.

24   Q   What did they give you?

25   A   About $200.

1   Q   Okay. And you say this was the week leading up

2   to the 18th?

3   A   Yes.

4   Q   This was during that time period. Okay.

5   Now, did you put this agreement, this rental

6   agreement, in writing?

7   A   No, it was verbal.

8   Q   Okay. Now, I want, I want to direct your

9   attention to a few days later. And this is before Saturday

10   the 18th, so this is a little later in the week. Did you

11   have a conversation with your boyfriend Wilson about this

12   agreement that you had with the defendant and Jatanya?

13   A   Yes.

14   Q   And what was his reaction to the fact that you

15   had, you had this agreement?

16   A   He was very annoyed that I gave the car to

17   another set of people.

18   Q   Okay. And, and did you as a result of talking

19   with him become concerned about the defendant having this

20   car?

21   A   Yes.

22   Q   And why did you become concerned?

23   A   Because I was in a situation before in which the

24   car was returned to me because the people couldn't make the

25   payments any more. And then I felt like I didn't want to

1   get into that situation again. So I was basically wanted

2   the car back just to ease him because he was a little

3   annoyed and felt like, you know, sell the car instead of

4   renting the car to someone else.

5   Q   So you wanted the car back so you could sell it

6   and relieve yourself of the responsibility?

7   A   Yes.

8   Q   Okay. And just by the way, both of your cars,

9   the Jeep and the Mercedes, did you have these, the license

10   plates, and were all the papers in order with the Department

11   of Motor Vehicles as they should have been?

12   A   Yes, they were.

13   Q   Okay. Now, after you decided that you wanted the

14   car back, did you make any phone calls?

15   A   Yes.

16   Q   Who did you call?

17   A   I called Jatanya.

18   Q   All right. What day did you call her on?

19   A   I called her on the, September 18th.

20   Q   Okay. That was a Saturday?

21   A   Yes.

22   Q   All right. And you had a conversation with her?

23   A   Yes, I did.

24   Q   Okay. What did you ask her to do?

25   A   I asked her if she could return the car to me.

1   Q   Okay. And do you recall about what time of the

2 day it was? Was it daytime, nighttime?

3   A   I would say it was daytime but getting towards

4 the evening.

5   Q   Okay. And after your conversation with her, did

6 you expect to see your jeep later on that evening?

7   A   Yes.

8   Q   Okay. Now I want to direct your attention to the

9 early part of the evening on September the 18th. Where were

10 you at that time?

11   A   I was home.

12   Q   All right. And when you say, home, where is your

13 home?

14   A   In Queens Village.

15   Q   All right. And what specifically is your

16 address?

17   A   221-42 112th Avenue.

18   Q   And where in Queens Village is that?

19   A   It's -- kind of borders Nassau County, Elmont.

20   Q   Okay. But it's definitely on the Queens side of

21 that border?

22   A   Yes.

23   Q   And you said you were at home that evening. Was

24 anyone with you?

25   A   Yes, Kharisha was there and my mother, and I'm

A-66

1   not sure if my sister was there.

2   Q   But you remember Kharisha.

3   A   Yes.

4   Q   Is Kharisha is friend of yours?

5   A   Yes.

6   Q   How long have you known her?

7   A   Almost about four or five years.

8   Q   How would you describe your relationship with

9   her?

10   A   She is one of my best friends.

11   Q   Okay. You guys were home. Do you remember what

12 you had on?

13   A   Yes.

14   Q   What was that?

15   A   I had on gray jogging pants and a gray long

16 sleeved T-shirt and some sneakers.

17   Q   Okay. And what were you two doing that evening?

18   A   Just hanging out. Talking.

19   Q   Okay. Where were you specifically? Were you in

20 the house?

21   A   We were in the house and we also went outside and

22 sat on my porch.

23   Q   Okay. Now, during the course of this evening, at

24 least up to this point during the early part of this

25 evening, did the defendant return your car to you?

1   A   No.

2   Q   And when you waited for a little bit and he

3   didn't arrive, did you try to contact him?

4   A   Yes.

5   Q   How did you do that?

6   A   I called him on his cellular phone.

7   Q   Did you get ahold of him?

8   A   Yes.

9   Q   Did you talk to him?

10   A   Yes, I did.

11   Q   What did you say?

12   A   I asked him how long would it take him to get to

13   my house. He told me he was on his way. That he was on the

14   Southern State, exit 19, and he would be at my house

15   shortly.

16   Q   With the Jeep?

17   A   Yes.

18   Q   Okay. And so you hung up. And did he come?

19   A   No.

20   Q   All right. So you gave him a little bit -- a

21   little bit of time passed?

22   A   Yes.

23   Q   And did you try to call him again?

24   A   I kept trying to call him multiple times.

25   Q   This was on the cell phone?

1   A   Yes.

2   Q   Were you able to speak with him again?

3   A   No.

4   Q   Were you able to speak with anybody once you put

5   the call through?

6   A   No.

7   Q   Now I want to direct your attention to about 11

8   o'clock in the evening. Did anyone arrive at your house

9   around that time?

10   A   Yes.

11   Q   Who was that?

12   A   My boyfriend Wilson.

13   Q   Okay. And did you tell him what was going on

14   with your car and this defendant?

15   A   Yes.

16   Q   And after that did the three of you continue to

17   wait for this defendant to show up to your house?

18   A   No.

19   Q   Okay. What did you decide to do?

20   A   We got into my Mercedes and we drove to Rosedale.

21   And we actually went to go search to see if we can see the

22   other car in the vicinity, and we drove to the defendant's

23   house.

24   MS. BISHOP: Okay. Now, Judge, actually if I

25   can get that map?

A-69

1   THE COURT: Sure. Put the map up.

2   Q   All right. Miss Stubbs, you said you lived in

3   Middle Village?

4   A   Queens Village.

5   Q   I'm sorry, Queens Village. And you went to the

6   defendant's house in Rosedale?

7   A   Yes.

8   Q   Would you take a look at that map and just point

9   out to the jury where the defendant's residence was back at

10   that time.

11   A   (Pointing.)

12   MS. BISHOP: Judge, let the record reflect

13   the witness is indicating --

14   THE COURT: 148th Street, 148th Avenue?

15   THE WITNESS: 148th Road.

16   THE COURT: 148th Road.

17   Q   And what specific address is that?

18   A   243-40 --

19   Q   What is it again?

20   A   243-40 148th Road.

21   Q   253-40?

22   A   Yes.

23   Q   All right. Now, Miss Stubbs, you said the three

24   of you got into your car and drove to this location in

25   Rosedale.

1   A   Yes.

2   Q   Who drove?

3   A   I drove.

4   Q   Okay. And where did Wilson and Kharisha sit?

5   A   Wilson was in the passenger seat and Kharisha was

6   behind him.

7   Q   Okay. And when you drove up to where the

8   defendant lived, did you actually get out of your car?

9   A   Not at all.

10   Q   Did anyone get out of your car?

11   A   No.

12   Q   Okay. When, when you got there, what were you

13   looking for?

14   A   I was looking for the Grand Cherokee.

15   Q   Did you see it there?

16   A   No.

17   Q   Okay. So did you make any decisions after you

18   didn't see the Jeep there?

19   A   Yes.

20   Q   What did you decide to do?

21   A   I decided to drive to Jatanya Belnavis's house.

22   Q   Where does Jatanya Belnavis live?

23   A   She lives on 142nd Avenue by the park.

24   Q   Okay. And if you can point out on that map where

25   her house is.

1   A   Yes.

2   Q   And the position of your car was facing

3   Brookville Boulevard?

4   A   Yes.

5   Q   All right. Now, once you got there what did you

6   do?

7   A   I honked the horn several times. Then no one

8   came to the door. So what I did, I got out and I rang her

9   bell several times.

10   Q   Okay. Now, you said you got out of the car. Did

11   Kharisha or Wilson get out of the car?

12   A   Yes.

13   Q   All right. And did the three of you go all the

14   way to the door?

15   A   No.

16   Q   All right. Where was Wilson standing?

17   A   They were standing in actually the walkway.

18   Q   Okay. And so they were a few feet back from

19   where you were at the door?

20   A   Yes.

21   Q   Now, when you got up to the door, what did you

22   do?

23   A   I rang her bell several times.

24   Q   Did someone eventually come to the door?

25   A   Yes.

1   Q   Who came?

2   A   Jatanya came to the door.

3   Q   And what was she wearing?

4   A   She had on pajamas and a nightgown and she had a

5   scarf on her head.

6   Q   Okay. And what did you say to her?

7   A   I asked her could she call her boyfriend. Can

8   she return my car. I wanted my car right now. And that I

9   was not leaving until they brought my car to me.

10   Q   Were you upset?

11   A   Extremely.

12   Q   And what did Jatanya do in response to your

13   demand?

14   A   She went and picked up the telephone and then she

15   closed the front door.

16   Q   So did you just stay, standing there at the front

17   door?

18   A   For a moment. I walked down the stairs. I stood

19   in the walkway. But it was a little cold, so I decided to

20   go sit back in my car.

21   Q   What about Wilson and Kharisha? Where did they

22   go?

23   A   They got back in the car with me.

24   Q   All right. Now, when the three of you returned

25   to the car, where were each of you sitting?

A-71

1   A   Same position. I got back in the driver's seat,

2   Kharisha in the back seat behind Wilson in the passenger

3   seat. She sat behind Wilson.

4   Q   Now, your car is like a sports car, right?

5   A   Yes.

6   Q   And is it -- does it have a regular-sized back

7   seat?

8   A   Little smaller than average.

9   Q   Okay. So Kharisha got in the back?

10   A   Yes.

11   Q   Now, do you recall whether or not your windows in

12   the car were rolled up or rolled down?

13   A   They were rolled down.

14   Q   Okay. And do you recall at that time when you

15   went back out to the car whether or not there were any

16   street lights or house lights that were on on 142nd Avenue?

17   A   There were street lights and there were house

18   lights on.

19   Q   Okay. So you didn't have any problem seeing

20   Wilson and Kharisha and things that were within a fairly

21   close range?

22   A   Not at all.

23   Q   Okay. Now, did there come a time a little bit

24   later when you saw Jatanya again?

25   A   Yes.

A-72

1   Q   And was she coming out of her house?

2   A   Yes.

3   Q   And was she still wearing her nightgown and her

4   hair scarf?

5   A   No, she changed her clothes and put on like a

6   sweatsuit.

7   Q   Okay. And by the way, how did you have your hair

8   that evening?

9   A   I had my hair up in a pony tail and I had some

10   Chinese sticks in like a bun.

11   Q   And those sticks were still in when you came back

12   out to your car?

13   A   Yes.

14   Q   All right. Now, after you saw Jatanya come out

15   of her house, where did she go?

16   A   She walked over to the car where I was sitting.

17   Q   And when you say she walked over to the car,

18   where specifically did she stand?

19   A   She stood next to me. And she faced me.

20   Q   Okay. And you were sitting in the driver's seat?

21   A   Yes.

22   Q   Okay. And when you say that she stood next to

23   you, if you're sitting in the driver's seat with the

24   steering wheel right here, and there is a rear-view mirror

25   right to your left, was she on this side of the mirror or on

1   that side of the mirror?

2   A   She was on behind the rear-view mirror.

3   Q   On this side?

4   A   Yes.

5   Q   On the side that's closest to the handle to the

6   door?

7   A   Yes.

8   Q   And when she, when she came out and was facing

9   you, did you and she have a conversation?

10   A   Yes.

11   Q   What was that conversation about?

12   A   About my day. How it was. You know, if I went

13   to work that day.

14   Q   Okay. And did you respond to her?

15   A   Yes.

16   Q   Okay. And did you continue to talk with her?

17   A   No.

18   Q   What did you do?

19   A   I was having a conversation with Wilson and

20   Kharisha, laughing.

21   Q   So you were just waiting?

22   A   Waiting.

23   Q   Okay, on the defendant?

24   A   Yes.

25   Q   All right. Now, did there come a time a few

1   minutes later when Jatanya no longer was facing into the car

2   but she was facing a different direction?

3   A   Yes.

4   Q   And what direction was she facing?

5   A   The street going back towards 243rd Street.

6   Q   Okay. So if she was standing next to your car,

7   was she looking in the direction of the back of your car or

8   the front of your car?

9   A   The back of my car.

10   Q   Okay. And after she started looking in that

11 direction what, if anything, did you hear?

12   A   I heard, Jatanya move. Duck down.

13   Q   And did you recognize that voice?

14   A   Yes.

15   Q   Whose voice was that?

16   A   The defendant.

17   Q   Okay. And after you heard that, did Jatanya

18 move?

19   A   Yes.

20   Q   Do you know where she went?

21   A   No.

22   Q   Okay. And after that what, if anything, did you

23 see?

24   A   I saw the defendant and another man come up to

25 the car, stick their hand in the car, put a gun to my head,

1   and tell me to get the fuck out the car and pulled me out

2   the car.

3   Q   Now let's back up a little bit. You said you saw

4   the defendant --

5   A   Yes.

6   Q   -- and you saw another person?

7   A   Yes.

8   Q   Did you recognize that second person?

9   A   No.

10   Q   And did you see what direction the defendant and

11   the other guy came from?

12   A   No.

13   Q   Okay. As you were sitting in your car facing

14   forward, had you seen them come from that direction?

15   A   I saw them come from the side the same way

16   Jatanya approached the car. They walked straight towards

17   me.

18   Q   You had not seen them come from the Brookville

19   Boulevard direction?

20   A   No, not at all.

21   Q   Now, you said somebody had a gun?

22   A   Yes.

23   Q   Who had the gun?

24   A   The defendant.

25   Q   And what did he do with the gun?

1   A   He put the gun to my head.

2   Q   All right. He was holding it in his hand when he

3   did that?

4   A   Yes.

5   Q   Now, please describe for the jury what the gun

6   looked like?

7   A   It was a silver gun. I would say an automatic

8   type of gun.

9   Q   Now, have you ever seen a gun before September

10   the 19th?

11   A   Yes, my father was a cop, so I saw guns before.

12   Q   So you're familiar with the difference between a

13   revolver type gun and a semi-automatic type of gun?

14   A   Yes.

15   Q   And what did you recognize this gun to be, what

16   type?

17   A   It was an automatic semi-automatic type of gun.   .

18   Q   So it didn't have the revolver on it?

19   A   No, not at all.

20   Q   All right. Now, so he puts the gun to your head

21   and says what to you?

22   A   Get the fuck out the car, bitch. What the fuck

23   are you doing here. I should kill you. I'm going to kill

24   your boyfriend. Just kept repeating it over and over and

25   over. What the fuck you doing here. I should kill you now.

1   And basically pulled me across the street from where my car

2   was parked.

3   Q   All right. Now, before he got you out of the

4   car, did anyone else touch you?

5   A   Yes.

6   Q   Who was that?

7   A   Wilson. At one point when I heard, Jatanya,

8   move, duck down, he grabbed me first and tried to pull me

9   onto his side of the car to try to pull me out. But he kind

10 of lost the struggle, because the defendant had the gun and

11 there was another man with the defendant trying to pull me

12 the other direction.

13   Q   And Wilson was sitting in the front passenger

14 side; is that right?

15   A   Yes.

16   Q   And as far as you knew Kharisha was still in the

17 back seat?

18   A   Yes.

19   Q   Okay. Now, how did they get you out of that car?

20   A   My door wasn't locked, but he reached inside and

21 pulled the latch, the door handle, and pulled it. And then

22 I stepped out.

23   Q   Okay. And the gun is still on you at this point?

24   A   Yes. And actually the gun as he was opening the

25 door was just pointed towards me.

A-78

1   Q   So it wasn't touching your head like it had been

2   earlier?

3   A   No.

4   Q   All right. Now, when that door opened, did the

5   light that's in the ceiling, the roof of the car, come on?

6   A   Yes.

7   Q   And at that point did you have a really clear

8   view of the person holding the gun?

9   A   Yes.

10   Q   And who was it?

11   A   It was the defendant.

12   Q   Now, when you got out of the car were you aware

13   of what was happening to Wilson and Kharisha?

14   A   No.

15   Q   Okay. Did you become aware that there was

16   possibly someone else near the car?

17   A   Yes. There was a third man actually and he was

18   at the rear of the car on the passenger side.

19   Q   And did he appear to be with the defendant and

20   the second man?

21   A   Yes.

22   Q   And did you know him?

23   A   No, I didn't.

24   Q   Do you recall what he looked like?

25   A   I remember him being shorter and being of dark

1   complexion, black --

2   Q   So he was black?

3   A   Yes, he was.

4   Q   Okay. All right. So now you're outside of your

5   car. And does the defendant still have the gun?

6   A   Yes.

7   Q   And where is the gun at this point?

8   A   It's just pointed to me. And actually he is kind

9   of grabbing me and yelling in my ear.

10   Q   And the person that was with him, that male, what

11 did he look like?

12   A   He was a black male, light complexion.

13   Q   And what was he doing?

14   A   They basically felt my body and they asked me if

15 I had any weapons on me. And they threw me on the ground

16 and felt my breasts and my legs and tried to search me for

17 weapons.

18   Q   Okay. Now, that happened across the street?

19   A   Yes.

20   Q   Okay. Now, prior to getting across the street,

21 tell the members of the jury a little bit about how you got

22 from outside of your car to this different location down the

23 street.

24   A   Well, they kind of pulled me and dragged me, but

25 I was cooperative in which I walked with them. But they

1   were tugging on me.

2   Q   Were they touching your hair at that time?

3   A   No.

4   Q   Okay. Now, were they saying anything to you as

5   you, as you were being taken across the street?

6   A   Yes.

7   Q   What were they saying?

8   A   What the fuck are you doing here, bitch. I

9   should kill you. When I see your man I'm going to kill him.

10   What the fuck you doing here. Just over and over. I'm

11   going to kill you. I should kill you. That's basically

12   over and over.

13   Q   It was the two of them saying this?

14   A   Just Sean, the defendant.

15   Q   Okay. And now you went across the street?

16   A   Yes.

17   Q   And from where your Mercedes was, did you go in

18   the direction towards Brookville or did you go in the

19   direction towards 243rd --

20   A   What do you mean --

21   Q   As you crossed the street did you stay directly

22   across the street from your car?

23   A   Kind -- more so towards 243rd Street.

24   Q   So you were down some feet?

25   A   Yes.

1   Q   And did you actually stay on the sidewalk for the

2   entire time?

3   A   I stayed on the sidewalk for when they searched

4   me. Then I went -- they picked me up and then I was

5   actually dragged into someone's driveway.

6   Q   Okay. Let's talk a little bit about this search.

7   Where did that take place?

8   A   It happened on the sidewalk, maybe between

9   Jatanya's house and another house. Like further down from

10   her house. Maybe her, next door to her house.

11   Q   Okay. And speaking of Jatanya, did you see

12   Jatanya at all during this?

13   A   Not at all.

14   Q   Were you looking for her?

15   A   No.

16   Q   What were you looking at?

17   A   I was looking at the defendant and the other man

18   with him. I was more so concerned about myself at that

19   point.

20   Q   Okay. Now, all right. Now, when the defendant

21   and his friend searched you, you were standing up?

22   A   At first, yes. But I fell. I think they pushed

23   me to the ground.

24   Q   Okay. And were you on your back or on your

25   stomach at that point?

1   A   I was on my back.

2   Q   What exactly did they do to search you?

3   A   They grabbed at my breasts. They patted me down.

4   And they patted down my ankles, my legs everything.

5   Q   Did you have any weapons with you?

6   A   No.

7   Q   Okay. Now, after they finished searching you,

8   did you get up?

9   A   Yes.

10   Q   And were they continuing to talk to you?

11 . A   Yes.

12   Q   Was the defendant continuing to say stuff to you?

13   A   Yes.

14   Q   What was he saying?

15   A   I should let you go. You need to run for your

16   life.

17   Q   All right. And you said there came a time when

18   he dragged you into a driveway?

19   A   Yes.

20   Q   All right. Do you recall approximately how many

21   houses down this driveway was from where your car was

22   parked?.

23   A   From which car?

24   Q   Your Mercedes.

25   A   Maybe one or two houses. I'm not sure.

1   Q   Okay. And at that point you say you went off the

2   sidewalk and to a little further back on a driveway.

3   A   Yes.

4   Q   Okay. And now when you did that who was with you

5   at that time?

6   A   The defendant.

7   Q   Okay. And was that other person there also?

8   A   He stood out on the sidewalk.

9   Q   So about how far was he from where you and the

10   defendant were?

11   A   Maybe five, six feet. Not that far. I didn't go

12   that far into that driveway.

13   Q   So you were just set back a little off the

14   sidewalk?

15   A   Yes.

16   Q   Now, how did they drag you to that point?

17   A   To the driveway?

18   Q   Uh-huh.

19   A   They just pulled me. Pulled me. Just kind of

20   forcefully pulled me toward the driveway.

21   Q   And when you got into the driveway what, if

22   anything, did the defendant say to you?

23   A   He told me to run for my life.

24   Q   And where was the gun?

25   A   He still had the gun just pointed.

1   Q   It was pointed at you?

2   A   Yes.

3   Q   And did the guy that was with him say anything?

4   A   No.

5   Q   Now, at that point did you see anything else in

6   that general area that you recognized?

7   A   Yes.

8   Q   What did you see?

9   A   My Jeep.

10   Q   And how did you know it was your Jeep?

11 . A   I knew the license plate. It was parked. It was

12   parked actually in front of the driveway that I was at. In

13   front of that house actually.

14   Q   So you were standing in the driveway. The Jeep

15   was right there?

16   A   Yes.

17   Q   Was it parked in the driveway or parked like on

18   the street?

19   A   It was parked on the street.

20   Q   Okay. After the defendant held the gun on you

21   and said run for your life, did you run for your life?

22   A.   No.

23   Q   What did you do?

24   A   I stood there and I looked at him. I was

25   shaking.

A-81

1   Q   Why didn't you run?

2   A   Because I feel that if I was to run I don't know

3 if he was to shoot me in my back, in my head --

4   MR. O'MEARA: Objection, your Honor.

5   THE COURT: Overruled.

6   Q   Go ahead.

7   A   So in my fear I just stood there in like a panic.

8   Q   Okay. And what happened after that?

9   A   He then fired the gun in the air.

10   Q   Okay. And when you say, in the air, could you

11 demonstrate how he held the gun when he fired it?

12   A   In the upward angle like that.

13   Q   So at an angle?

14   A   Yes.

15   Q   And do you recall actually seeing him fire the

16 gun?

17   A   Yes.

18   Q   What did you see?

19   A   I saw like sparks or something from the gun.

20   Q   Okay. As it was discharging?

21   A   Yes.

22   Q . And do you recall how many times he fired the

23 gun?

24   A   No. I would say until it finished because I

25 heard the gun click.

1   Q   Okay. And did he continue to pull the trigger

2   after it was clicking?

3   A   Yes.

4   Q   And you said you don't know how many times

5   exactly that he fired the weapon. Can you say if it was

6   more than once?

7   A   Yes.

8   Q   It was more than five times?

9   A   Yes.

10   Q   And beyond that you're not really sure?

11. A   No, I don't remember.

12   Q   Now, as he was firing this weapon, was his friend

13   saying or doing anything?

14   A   They looked a little surprised. I wouldn't say

15   they looked at him like he was crazy in a sense.

16   Q   By that time had the third person that you had

17   seen at the back of your car originally, had he come over to

18   where you and the defendant were?

19   A   Yes.

20   Q   Okay. So by the time he was finished firing the

21   gun, the other two that he had come with were within a few

22   feet of you also?

23   A   Yes.

24   Q   And as he was firing the gun did he say anything

25   to you?

1   A   No.

2   Q   And after he fired the gun did he say anything to

3   you?

4   A   No.

5   Q   All right.   Now, he's fired this gun several

6   times.   And then you hear the clicking?

7   A   Yes.

8   Q   What happens next?

9   A   I run for my other car that I came over in

10   originally.

11 .   Q   All right.   And so you're running in the

12   direction of Brookville Boulevard?

13   A   Yes.

14   Q   Back towards your car?

15   A   Yes.

16   Q   And do you see where the defendant and his two

17   friends go?

18   A   Yes.

19   Q   Where do they go?

20   A   They got into my other car, my Jeep.

21   Q   And could you see who got into the driver's seat

22   of the Jeep?

23   A   The defendant got into the driver's side.

24   Q   And by the time you got back to your car now did

25   you have your Chinese sticks?

A-84

1   A   No.

2   Q   Okay. So how would you describe your appearance

3   by the time you got back to the car?

4   A   I looked like I was attacked. My hair was all

5   over my head. My hair was up in a bun. My hair came down

6   actually and my clothes were ripped.

7   Q   Okay. And how did you feel at that time?

8   A   Oh, I felt scared. I was like crying.

9   Q   Okay. Now, when you got back to your car, did

10 you see Wilson or Kharisha?

11   A   I only saw Kharisha.

12   Q   And where was she coming from?

13   A   She was coming from the side of the street where

14 I parked the car and got in someone's yard.

15   Q   So you didn't really see where she came from.

16 You just saw her general direction?

17   A   Yes.

18   Q   Now, at that point do you see Wilson?

19   A   No.

20   Q   And what do you and Kharisha do?

21   A   We pull off. I actually in my confusion, in

22 being scared I actually drove to Brookville Boulevard and I

23 made a left instead of making a right.

24   Q   Okay. Now, before you got to the point where you

25 drove off, did you do anything to try to find Wilson?

1   A   Yes.

2   Q   What did you do?

3   A   I just -- I actually I drove back and I just was

4   like looking down streets, but I actually didn't know what

5   to do at that point.

6   Q   Did you see him?

7   A   No.

8   Q   So he's gone. So now you're in the car with

9   Kharisha?

10   A   Yes.

11   Q   Okay. Now, if you want, using that map, why

12   don't you indicate where you went when you decided to leave

13   142nd Avenue.

14   A   Okay. Okay. I pulled off of 142nd and I made a

15   left down Brookville Boulevard.   .

16   Q   Okay. Why a left?

17   A   I don't even know why I made a left. I was

18   just -- I just was so scared, I just pulled out and turned.

19   Q   And you proceeded down Brookville Boulevard; is

20   that correct?

21   A   Yes.

22   Q   Now what, if anything, happened as you were

23   driving down Brookville?

24   A   As I got to maybe over here, I saw my Jeep again.

25   Q   You did. And from what direction was your Jeep

1   coming at that point?

2   A   Down one of these streets.   It came onto

3   Brookville Boulevard.

4   Q   So you saw your Jeep coming up one of the side

5   streets there?

6   A   Yes.

7   Q   And do you recall which one it was specifically?

8   A   No.

9   Q   Okay.   And how did you know it was your Jeep?

10   A   I knew the color.   I knew the license plate.   It

11   was close enough for me to see everything about the car.

12   Q   Could you see who was driving?

13   A   Yes.

14   Q   Who was driving?

15   A   The defendant was driving.

16   Q   As he came up one of these side streets toward

17   Brookville Boulevard what, if anything, did he do?

18   A   He turned and followed me.

19   Q   Okay.   And you continued down Brookville?

20   A   Yes.

21   Q   And about how far, if you can recall, did he wind

22   up following you?

23   A   I know I ended up turning off by 147th Avenue.

24   So I didn't see him any more after I got to about that

25   point.

1   Q   Okay. And when you say he was following you, was

2   he you know behind you at a normal distance that any other

3   driver would be, or was he doing something different?

4   A   He was driving at a normal distance, but I mean I

5   was going fast, so he was kind of going fast too.

6   Q   So he was keeping up with you?

7   A   Yes.

8   Q   And how fast would you say you were going at that

9   point?

10   A   Oh, 120 or so. I was --

11   Q   100 miles per hour?

12   A   There were no cars out. I just took off.

13   Q   And he was right behind you?

14   A   Yes.

15   Q   Now, you said --

16   A   Should I stand?

17   Q   You can have a seat.

18   You said eventually you got away from him?

19   A   Yes.

20   Q   And you turned off of Brookville?

21   A   Yes.

22   Q   And where did you go immediately after that?

23   A   I went home.

24   Q   Okay. And who was at your house?

25   A   My mother.

1   Q   And you spoke with your mother?

2   A   I spoke with my mother.

3   Q   What did you tell her?

4   A   I told her what happened. Apparently she knew.

5   Q   Okay. And you had a conversation with her?

6   A   Yes.

7   Q   And it became clear she had spoken with Wilson?

8   A   Yes.

9   Q   Okay. And did you and she continue to talk about

10   what you would do next?

11   A   Yes.

12   Q   And did you arrive at any decisions?

13   A   Yes.

14   Q   Okay. What was the plan?

15   A   I told her to go back to Rosedale to see if she

16   could find Wilson, because I was afraid for his life. And I

17   went to the 105th Precinct.

18   Q   And who did you go with?

19   A   I went with Kharisha.

20   Q   And you knew at that point that your mother had

21   actually spoken with Wilson?

22   A   Yes.

23   Q   So she was going to go get him?

24   A   Yes.

25   Q   And then after she got him, what were you guys

1   going to do?

2   A   Meet at the 105th Precinct.

3   Q   So now, from where you turned off and lost the

4   defendant from chasing you, from that point until you got

5   home, approximately how many minutes passed?

6   A   About 10, if that many.

7   Q   Took you about 10 minutes to get home?

8   A   Yes.

9   Q   And then once you got home about how long did you

10   stay there before you went onto the 105th Precinct?

11   A   Less than five minutes.

12   Q   So is it fair to say you went to the precinct

13   within 15 or 20 minutes of this happening?

14   A   Yes, because I never went inside the house

15   actually. When I pulled up my mother came to the door.

16   Q   Okay. Now, tell the jury what happened when you

17   got to the 105th Precinct.

18   A   The whole precinct pretty much ran over to me as

19   in, oh, my God. What happened. You okay. And actually

20   after that I took a police report.

21   Q   Had you changed clothes while you were at home?

22   A   No.

23   Q   Had you fixed your hair?

24   A   No.

25   Q   So you pretty well walked into the precinct in

1   the same condition as when you left Jatanya's neighborhood?

2   A   Yes.

3   Q   Now, you said you made a report with the police?

4   A   Yes.

5   Q   What did you tell them?

6   A   I gave them -- I told them what happened. I also

7   gave them a description of the defendant and basically gave

8   them his address and his name.

9   Q   Okay. Now, after you provided that information

10   to the police that evening, were you able to go back to your

11   house and sleep that night?

12   A   No, my mother wouldn't let me. I went to

13   Kharisha's house.

14   Q   Your mother didn't want you there?

15   A   No.

16   Q   She was fearful?

17   A   Yes.

18   Q   Now, I want to direct your attention to September

19   the 23rd, a few days after this happened.

20   A   Yes.

21   Q   Actually I will withdraw that.

22   In between the 19th and the 23rd did you actually

23   get your Jeep back?

24   A   Yes, I did.

25   Q   Okay. Now, can you just tell us briefly how that

1 happened?

2   A   I spoke to one of my friends who she made

3 arrangements and got the Jeep back for me.

4   Q   Who did she make arrangements with?

5   A   She made arrangements with Jatanya.

6   Q   And so she made arrangements with Jatanya and

7 then Jatanya got your Jeep back to this friend and she got

8 it back to you?

9   A   Yes.

10   Q   And that was in between the 19th and the 23rd?

11 .   A   Yes.

12   Q   Okay. Now, on the 23rd did you have an occasion

13 to speak with the police again?

14   A   Yes.

15   Q   And who did you speak with?

16   A   I spoke with Detective Kanehl.

17   Q   Is he the detective that's assigned to this case?

18   A   Yes.

19   Q   Okay. When you spoke with the detective, what

20 did you tell him?

21   A   I told him what happened to me and I gave him a

22 description and I gave him the name and the address of the

23 defendant.

24   Q   Okay. And he took that information?

25   A   Yes, he did.

A-86

1   Q   Okay. Now, did you speak with him again during

2   that day?

3   A   Yes.

4   Q   Where did that second conversation take place?

5   A   At the 105th Precinct.

6   Q   And so you went to the 105th Precinct and stayed

7   there for a while?

8   A   Yes.

9   Q   And after that did you go back to your house?

10   A   Yes.

11   Q   And then a little bit later on in that afternoon

12   did you speak with Detective Kanehl again?

13   A   Yes.

14   Q   Okay. And that was on the 23rd?

15   A   Yes.

16   Q   Okay. Now, some days after that did you become

17   aware of -- did you become aware at any time that the

18   defendant had been arrested?

19   A   Yes.

20   Q   And after you became aware of that, did you ever

21   go to the district attorney's office with relation to this

22   case?

23   A   Yes, I did.

24   Q   And for what purpose did you go to the D.A.'s

25   office?

1   A   To testify in front of the grand jury.

2   Q   Okay. And that happened at some point near the

3   end of the September, the beginning of October?

4   A   Yes.

5   Q   Okay. And now the night before you went, the

6   night before you came to the D.A.'s office for the purpose

7   of testifying, did you receive any telephone calls?

8   A   Yes, I did.

9   Q   Who were those telephone calls from?

10   A   Jatanya Belnavis.

11   Q   Okay. And had you heard from her directly since

12   this incident?

13   A   No.

14   Q   Okay. Now, did you in fact the following day go

15   on and testify at the grand jury?

16   A   Yes, I did.

17   Q   Okay. Now, after you did that did there come a

18   time later on that fall when you saw the defendant and had a

19   conversation with him?

20   A   Yes, I did.

21   Q   And what day was that?

22   A   It was the day before Thanksgiving, November of

23   that year.

24   Q   Okay. And please tell the jury the circumstances

25   of that conversation.

1   A   Basically I saw him in Hollis, Queens, and he

2   told me -- he apologized to me for what had happened.

3   MR. O'MEARA: Objection, your Honor. It's

4   hearsay.

5   THE COURT: Overruled.

6   Q   Okay. You were in Hollis, Queens?

7   A   Yes, on 217th Street.

8   Q   Were you on foot?

9   A   No, I was in my car.

10   Q   Okay. Were you by yourself?

11   A   No, I was with my boyfriend.

12   Q   And you two were driving on 217th Street?

13   A   Yes.

14   Q   And what caught your attention that morning?

15   A   I saw the defendant in a black Tahoe Jeep.

16   Q   A Tahoe is like an SUV --

17   A   Yes.

18   Q   -- type of car?

19   How did you recognize that particular vehicle?

20   A   I recognized it because it was parked in front of

21   a person that I went to school with's house.

22   Q   And did you know whether or not that person and

23   the defendant were friendly with each other?

24   A   Yes.

25   Q   Were they friendly?

1   A   Yes.

2   Q   In fact, was it one of his girlfriends?

3   A   Yes.

4   Q   You saw him sitting in this black Tahoe?

5   A   Yes.

6   Q   What did you and Wilson do when you saw him

7   sitting there?

8   A   We drove past. And I had asked Wilson if that

9   was a car he had recognized before. And we made a U-turn

10   and we came back down the street. And we approached the

11   defendant and basically made another U-turn and went to the

12   corner. And actually he pulled up aside of us and we had a

13   conversation where he apologized.

14   Q   Now, you said that, that this black Tahoe, this

15   wasn't the first time you had heard about this black Tahoe?

16   A   Not at all.

17   Q   And did you know of this defendant being in this

18   black Tahoe before, the day before Thanksgiving?

19   A   No.

20   Q   Did Wilson?

21   A   No.

22   Q   Okay. Now, you said you U-turned a couple of

23   times?

24   A   Yes.

25   Q   What position was your car in when you ultimately

1 had this conversation with the defendant?

2   A   I was parked and he pulled up aside me.

3   Q   So you're in your car and he is in his car?

4   A   Yes.

5   Q   And who is driving your car?

6   A   Wilson.

7   Q   And are the two cars facing in the same

8 direction?

9   A   Yes.

10   Q   Okay. Now, were your windows down?

11   A   Yes.

12   Q   And was everyone in the car?

13   A   What do you mean, my car?

14   Q   Were you and Wilson still in the car?

15   A   I was in the car. Wilson got out of the car.

16   Q   After he parked he got out of the car?

17   A   Yes.

18   Q   Did the defendant get out of his car?

19   A   Yes, he did.

20   Q   And --

21   A   He actually got -- he parked the car in front and

22 then he got out because he had a passenger in the car.

23   Q   Okay. And before he got out of his car, did you

24 see him making any kind of gestures?

25   A   When I first saw him on 217th Street when we

1   pulled up aside him, I saw him reaching down and I kind of

2   told Wilson, let's go. Get out of here.

3   Q   So that scared you?

4   A   Yes.

5   Q   So you stopped. Wilson got out. You're still in

6   the car. Did Wilson have anything in his hands?

7   A   ' No.

8   Q   You said the defendant came over to where Wilson

9   was standing?

10   A   Yes.

11   Q   Now, who started the conversation?

12   A   Initially it was two times that they spoke.

13   Wilson started the conversation first.

14   Q   Okay.

15   A   Because they had arranged to meet down at the

16   other corner. That's where the U-turns took place.

17   Q   So they had a brief conversation while you were

18   all still in the cars?

19   A   Right.

20   Q   Then there was an agreement to go to the end of

21   the block?

22   A   Yes.

23   Q   Then Wilson and the defendant got out of the car?

24   A   Yes.

25   Q   Now, what did the defendant say at the point

1   where they're both out of the car?

2   A   He came over to the car. I apologize for what

3   'happened. Jatanya got me, called me, and she was very

4   upset.

5   Q   And what was he referring to?

6   A   He was referring to the incident that occurred.

7   MR. O'MEARA: Objection. How could she know?

8   THE COURT: Objection sustained. Objection

9   sustained.

10   Q   Had you spoken with the defendant since September

11 the 19th?

12   A   No, I haven't.

13   Q   So this was the first time you spoke with him

14 since this happened?

15   A   Yes.

16   Q   And he was apologizing to you?

17   A   Yes.

18   Q   Okay. Had he pulled a gun on you before the

19 19th?

20   A   No.

21   Q   Now, he said he was sorry. And what did he say

22 about Jatanya?

23   A   Jatanya called me very upset.

24   Q   Okay. And did he say anything else after that?

25   A   No.

A-87

1   Q   And how long would you say that conversation

2   actually lasted?

3   A   About 5, 10 minutes.

4   Q   Okay. So it was pretty fast?

5   A   Yes.

6   Q   Now, at that time were you receptive to this

7   apology?

8   A   Yes.

9   Q   And how do you mean?

10   A   I, I basically was like, yeah, okay. It's okay.

11   It's nothing. It's no problem. And I was basically

12   gesturing Wilson to come on, let's go.

13   Q   So in your heart did you really accept this man's

14   apology?

15   A   Never.

16   Q   You just wanted to get out of there?

17   A   Basically.

18   MS. BISHOP: Okay. I have no further

19   questions, Judge, at this time.

20   THE COURT: All right. Ladies and gentlemen,

21   it's almost our luncheon break so we will continue with

22   Mr. O'Meara's examination of Miss Stubbs after lunch.

23   In the meantime do not discuss this case amongst

24   yourselves nor with anybody else. Don't let anybody

25   speak to you about the case. Don't speak to the

1   lawyers, the defendant, any of his family, or any of

2   the witnesses.

3   Don't visit the scenes that have been

4   mentioned here. Don't form any opinion yet in regard

5   to this case, and do not look at or listen to any media

6   reports that may relate to this case. Have a very

7   pleasant lunch. Our court officer will tell you where

8   to meet at 2 o'clock.

9   (The jury left the courtroom.)

10   THE COURT: Okay, Miss Stubbs, you can step

11   down. You're not to discuss your testimony with

12   anybody during the luncheon recess. Be back at 2

13   o'clock. Okay. Thank you.

14   (The witness left the courtroom.)

15   COURT OFFICER: 2 o'clock Judge.

16   THE COURT: 2 o'clock.

17   THE CLERK: Second call. Step in.

18   (Luncheon recess held.)

19   * * * A F T E R N O O N   S E S S I O N * * *

20   THE CLERK: Recalling case on trial. Bring

21   the defendant out, please.

22   You want the witness back in the witness

23   stand?

24   THE COURT: Yes. Please, Miss Stubbs, come

25   up.

1   (Defendant entered the courtroom.)

2   THE CLERK: Defendant is present in the

3   courtroom.

4   THE COURT: Okay. Can we bring out the

5   jurors, please.

6   Do you have any further questions?

7   MS. BISHOP: Not at this time.

8   COURT OFFICER: Ready, Judge?

9   THE COURT: Please.

10   (The jury entered the courtroom.)

11   THE CLERK: Let the record reflect all

12   parties waive the calling of the roll and stipulate all

13   sworn jurors are present and seated in their assigned

14   seat. Counsel?

15   MS. BISHOP: Yes.

16   MR. O'MEARA: Yes.

17   THE COURT: Ladies and gentlemen, I hope you

18   had a pleasant lunch. We're now ready to continue with

19   Mr. O'Meara's examination of Miss Stubbs.

20   Miss Stubbs, you're reminded you're still

21   under the oath you took before, okay.

22   THE WITNESS: Yes.

23   THE COURT: Mr. O'Meara.

24   CROSS EXAMINATION

25   BY MR. O'MEARA:

1   Q   Now, you testified that you entered into a

2   contract with Mr. Zimmerman to lease him your extra car.

3   A   Yes.

4   Q   Now, you had only met Mr. Zimmerman two times

5   before that?

6   A   Yes.

7   Q   Briefly two times before that?

8   A   Yes.

9   Q   Never had much conversation with him?

10   A   Yes.

11   Q   Now, on September 19th at 3:00 a.m. in the

12   morning it had to be pretty dark out.

13   A   It was dark. It was nighttime.

14   Q   It was nighttime?

15   A   Yes.

16   Q   Pitch black dark. It was night.

17   A   It was night, yes.

18   Q   Now, I just have a few more questions about the

19   lease. Now, you said you leased it, leased it for one week.

20   A   Yes.

21   Q   Now, do you remember testifying at the grand

22   jury?

23   A   Yes.

24   Q   And you told the grand jury that you leased it

25   for four days.

1   A   He had it longer.

2   Q   So did you lease it to him for a week, or did you

3   lease it to him for four days?

4   A   It was under a week because I got the car back.

5   Q   You got the car back prior to the week?

6   A   No.

7   Q   So how long was the lease for?

8   A   It was supposedly for a week, but he had the car

9   for approximately four days.

10   Q   So you demanded the car back prior to the lease

11   finishing?

12   A   Yes.

13   Q   Do you remember telling any police officers or

14   anybody that you had leased him or loaned him the car for

15   two days?

16   A   No.

17   Q   Now, prior to September 19th and subsequent to

18   Mr. Zimmerman taking the car, did you have any conversations

19   with Jatanya Belnavis or Nicholas Zimmerman?

20   A   I spoke with both of them.

21   Q   Where as you demanded more money for the car?

22   A   Yes.

23   Q   Because the lease you entered into wasn't enough

24   money for you?

25   A   Right.

1   Q   Now, when -- after September 19th when you had

2   the conversation with Mr. Zimmerman and Miss Belnavis --

3   A   Yes.

4   Q   -- how often did you see Miss Belnavis after

5   that?

6   A   After the 19th?

7   Q   Yes.

8   A   I ran into her last year a few times.

9   Q   Now, you told him you weren't going to testify in

10   this case?

11 .   A   Right.

12   Q   You also told him you wouldn't do it if you got

13   something in return?

14   A   No, I never said that.

15   Q   Were you with Wilson when he approached them and

16   demand $10,000 not to testify?

17   A   No.

18   Q   Now, the next thing I'd like to speak about for a

19   minute is on September 19th at 3:00 a.m. in the morning

20   after everything happens. You drive away --

21   A   Yes.

22   Q .   -- and you see your Jeep Cherokee -- was it a

23   Jeep Grand Cherokee or Jeep --

24   A   Jeep Grand Cherokee.

25   Q   You see that behind you?

1   A   Yes.

2   Q   And then you go into a 100 mile per hour race or

3   chase?

4   A   Yes.

5   Q   Now, when you spoke to the police officers after

6   this happened, did you mention that to any of the police

7   officers?

8   A   I don't recall.

9   Q   Would you be surprised or shocked to find out

10   it's in no police report?

11   A   No.

12   Q   That you just forgot about that part of the

13   night?

14   A   No.

15   Q   Do you remember at your grand jury testimony?

16   A   A little bit. It was three years ago.

17   Q   You didn't testify that you were on a 100 mile

18   per hour chase at that time either.

19   MS. BISHOP: Objection.

20   THE COURT: Objection sustained. As to form.

21   Q   Did you testify at the grand jury?

22   A   Yes, I did.

23   Q   Did you tell the grand jury about the 100 mile

24   per hour chase?

25   MS. BISHOP: Objection.

1   THE COURT: Objection sustained as to form.

2   It's an improper way to ask the question.

3   MR. O'MEARA: Your Honor, I'd like to submit

4   to the witness her grand jury testimony.

5   THE COURT: You can show it to her.

6   (Shown to witness.)

7   THE COURT: Just read it over. Let us know

8   when you're through looking at it.

9   THE WITNESS: Okay.

10   A   Okay.

11   Q   Can you read to me the part where you spoke about

12   the 100 mile per hour chase?

13   MS. BISHOP: Objection.

14   THE COURT: Overruled. Is there anything in

15   there about it?

16   THE WITNESS: There is nothing in the

17   statement.

18   Q   Thank you. You also testified earlier that after

19   the shootings you watched Mr. Zimmerman and his two buddies

20   run to your Jeep Cherokee.

21   A   Yes.

22   Q   Did you ever tell the police that?

23   A   No.

24   Q   So you wouldn't, you wouldn't be a bit surprised

25   if on the police report that doesn't exist?

1   A   No, I wouldn't be.

2   Q   Now, I'd like to bring you back to your grand

3 jury testimony. Did you ever mention or did you ever

4 testify to the fact that Mr. Zimmerman and his friends went

5 back to his car?

6   A   I was never asked, so I never answered that.

7   Q   So your answer is no?

8   A   Yes, my answer is no.

9   Q   Now, on September 18th that night around 10

10 o'clock, where were you?

11   A   I was home.

12   Q   With?

13   A   My friend Kharisha.

14   Q   How many telephone conversations or how many

15 times did you call Mr. Zimmerman or Jatanya that night?

16   A   I called Jatanya once. I received a phone call

17 from him once. And I spoke to him again one more time.

18 Then I made about two or three more calls. So I would say

19 five times I attempted to call and twice I got through.

20   Q   You couldn't get through to him the other times?

21   A   No.

22   Q   What time that was at?

23   A   It was late approaching maybe, maybe 11:00

24 something at night. I'm not sure.

25   Q   So three and a half hours later you decide to go

1 over to his house?

2   A   Yes.

3   Q   Back to the lease. You leased the Jeep to

4 Mr. Zimmerman, but your boyfriend Wilson, he didn't want you

5 to lease the car any more.

6   A   Right.

7   Q   Now, I'd like to know where that Jeep is today.

8   A   Back at the --

9   MS. BISHOP: Objection.

10   THE COURT: What was the question? I didn't

11   hear.

12   Q   Where is that Jeep today?

13   A   I don't own it any more.

14   Q   It's not registered to your name?

15   A   No.

16   Q   If I showed you your registration from the DMV

17 and it showed a 1998, 1995 Jeep Suburban, that wouldn't be

18 yours?

19   A   No.

20   Q   Did you sell it?

21   A   No.

22   Q   What did you do with it?

23   A   I gave it back to the bank.

24   Q   Gave it back to the bank?

25   A   Yes.

1   Q   Now, you testified earlier that Wilson wanted you

2   to take it back so you could sell it?

3   A   Yes.

4   Q   Did you -- you never sold it?

5   A   No.

6   Q   Now, when you had seen Mr. Zimmerman with the

7   other girl in the Tahoe I believe?

8   A   Yes.

9   Q   Now you're saying that he apologized to you?

10   A   Yes.

11   Q   Is that when you told him you weren't going to

12   testify?

13   A   I don't know if I told him I wasn't going to

14   testify that day.

15   Q   Now, on the night in question, September 19th or

16   the morning in question, September 19th --

17   A   Yes.

18   Q   -- you decide to go over to Nicholas Zimmerman's

19   house at 2:30 in the morning --

20   A   Yes.

21   Q   -- to get your car back.

22   A   Yes.

23   Q   Because you wanted more money for the lease?

24   A   No. Because I wanted, actually wanted him to

25   return the car to me.

1   Q   You didn't want more money for the lease?

2   A   At first I did.   Then I decided I wanted the car

3   back totally.   I didn't want them to have it any more.

4   Q   To sell it?

5   A   Basically.

6   Q   Which you never did?

7   A   Right.

8   Q   Nicholas Zimmerman wasn't at home at 2:30 in the

9   morning.

10   A   No.

11   Q   So you drove over to his girlfriend's house.

12   A   Yes.

13   Q   And you didn't see the Jeep anywhere around?

14   A   No.

15   Q   Nowhere?

16   A   No.

17   Q   Did you look?

18   A   Yes.

19   Q   You looked up and down the street?

20   A   Yes.

21   Q   Then you waited in the car.   You sat in your car

22   for about a half hour.

23   A   No, I rang her bell.

24   Q   After you rang her bell --

25   A   Yes.

1   Q   -- you went back and sat in your car?

2   A   Yes.

3   Q   What were you waiting for?

4   A   I was waiting for the defendant to come.

5   Q   Now, you weren't able to contact Mr. Zimmerman at

6   11 o'clock. You tried but couldn't do it?

7   A   Right.

8   Q   Then you went to Miss Belnavis's house at 3

9   o'clock in the morning --

10   A   Or a little before, yes.

11   Q   -- looking for Mr. Zimmerman.

12   A   Yes.

13   Q   And he wasn't there?

14   A   Right.

15   Q   Then when you spoke to Miss Belnavis at her door,

16   did she tell you he wasn't there?

17   A   I didn't ask her for him.

18   Q   You just stared at one another? What happened?

19   A   No. I asked her can she have him return me the

20   car to her house now.

21   Q   You went there with three people?

22   A   Two.

23   Q   Yourself included would be three?

24   A   Yes.

25   Q   Then you claim that people ran up to you, ran

1 behind Miss Belnavis?

2   A   Yes.

3   Q   And dragged you down the street?

4   A   Yes.

5   Q   Hopped into their -- your car?

6   A   Yes.

7   Q   Then you ended up in a case.

8   A   Yes.

9   Q   You did -- but you didn't tell anything to the

10 police about them seeing your car there that night?

11   A   I wasn't the only one who spoke to the police.

12 But no, I didn't tell them that. I did tell them -- I don't

13 know if they put that in the report. I told them I saw the

14 car there.

15   Q   You just testified you don't remember if you

16 told --

17   A   I told the detective the car was there. I spoke

18 twice to the police. I went to the precinct to make the

19 report. And then later on a detective came to my house and

20 spoke to me again.

21   Q   Then the next thing -- and the chase you never

22 mentioned the chase?

23   A   I don't remember stating about the chase at all.

24   Q   Now I'd like to talk about the case where you got

25 arrested. That was in the central, Eastern District,

1   Federal Court?

2   A   Yes.

3   Q   It had to do with conspiracy to defraud?

4   A   Yes.

5   Q   Who were you defrauding?

6   A   Financial institutions.

7   Q   You were obtaining leases or financing for cars?

8   A   That's what the company did. They obtained

9   leases and finances for applicants, yes.

10   Q   You were falsifying the applicants?

11   A   No. We -- my role was that I faxed loan

12   applications over to dealerships and which had false

13   statements on.

14   Q   False?

15   A   Right.

16   Q   False documents to obtain loans for people?

17   A   False statements on the applications.

18   Q   To obtain loans?

19   A   Yes.

20   Q   And you pled guilty to conspiracy to defraud to

21   what you just said you did?

22   A   Yes.

23   Q   Because you were in fact guilty of defrauding?

24   A   I pled guilty to the charges, yes.

25   Q   And what were you obtaining in return for

1   pleading guilty?

2   MS. BISHOP: Objection.

3   A   I wasn't sentenced.

4   MS. BISHOP: Objection to the form of the

5   question.

6   THE COURT: Overruled.   Perhaps to the form.

7   Maybe you can rephrase it.

8   MR. O'MEARA: Your Honor, I will strike it.

9   Q   Now, at the time of this incident you had a new

10   Mercedes Benz?

11   A   Yes.

12   Q   And you were unemployed working part time as a

13   hairdresser?

14   A   I obtained my car, purchased my car, before I was

15   unemployed.

16   Q   And you maintained the payments while you were a

17   hairdresser?

18   A   Yes.

19   Q   And Wilson helped you, you said?

20   A   Yes.

21   Q   What does Wilson do?

22   A   Wilson currently --

23   Q   Yes.

24   A   -- or what did he do then?

25   Q   What did he do then?

```
1    A    Oh, wow.  I think he was a personal trainer then.

2    Q    What is Wilson's address today?

3    A    He lives at 218-08 100th Avenue.

4    Q    In Queens?

5    A    Yes.

6    Q    You still have this Mercedes Benz?

7    A    No, I don't.

8    Q    You don't have this Mercedes Benz?

9    A    No.

10   Q    Would you be surprised to find out that according

11   to the Department of Motor Vehicles registration that it's

12   still in your name?

13              MS. BISHOP:  Objection.

14              THE COURT:  Overruled.

15   A    Very surprised.

16   Q    And you also have a Lincoln Suburban?

17   A    No, I have a Lincoln Navigator.

18   Q    Lincoln Navigator?

19   A    Yes.

20   Q    '98?

21   A    Yes.

22              MR. O'MEARA:  Just one second, your Honor.

23              THE COURT:  Take your time, sir.

24              MR. O'MEARA:  Your Honor, I have no further

25   questions for her at this time, but I want to reserve
```

1   the right to call her after the policemen testify as to

2   who conducted the investigation.

3   THE COURT: I have no problem with that.

4   If you could still be available, okay.

5   Do you have any redirect?

6   MS. BISHOP: I do have a few questions,

7   Judge. May we step up?

8   THE COURT: Sure. Come up.

9   (Sidebar discussion off the record.)

10   THE COURT: Redirect.

11   MS. BISHOP: Yes, Judge.

12   REDIRECT EXAMINATION

13   BY MS. BISHOP:

14   Q   Miss Stubbs, you testified about a rental

15   agreement --

16   A   Yes.

17   Q   -- that you had with this, the defendant over

18   here.

19   A   Yes.

20   Q   And just so I'm clear. This rental agreement,

21   how much was he paying you for the car?

22   A   He was paying me for -- he paid me $200. I'm not

23   sure the total amount I requested.

24   Q   It was more than $200?

25   A   Afterwards, yes.

1   Q   And how many days, in other words, did the $200

2   cover?

3   A   It covered four days.

4   Q   Okay. And so in the agreement if this rental

5   agreement was going to go past four days then he owed you

6   some additional money --

7   A   Yes.

8   Q   , -- is that correct?

9   A   Yes.

10   Q   Did he ever give you any additional money?

11   A   No.

12   Q   All right. Now, you got a few questions on cross

13   examination about whether or not you told the police

14   anything about the defendant following you after he had

15   fired the shots in the air.

16   A   Right.

17   Q   You recall those questions?

18   A   Yes.

19   Q   Now let me ask you, Miss Stubbs. When you got to

20   the 105th Precinct that night was your primary focus on the

21   few seconds the defendant followed you down Brookville

22   Boulevard?

23   A   Not at all.

24   Q   What was your focus on? What information did you

25   want to get to the police right away?

1   A   I wanted to give them the description. I wanted

2   to let them know he still was driving the car. That was

3   primary, my main focus for that point.

4   Q   Did you tell the police about the gun?

5   A   Yes, definitely.

6   Q   So your main objective at that point was to get

7   the information about who had the gun, and that he had a gun

8   to the police --

9   A   Yes.

10   Q   -- is that a fair statement?

11   A   That's a fair statement.

12   Q   Okay. Now, you also testified both on direct and

13   on cross examination that you made efforts to reach the

14   defendant that evening before you went over to Jatanya's

15   house.

16   A   Yes.

17   Q   Okay. Now, what number -- not what specific

18   number, but how were you trying to get in touch with the

19   defendant?

20   A   Through a cell phone.

21   Q   You had the -- you had the cell phone number?

22   A   Yes.

23   Q   Had you actually dialed that number earlier and

24   gotten ahold of the defendant?

25   A   Yes.

1   Q   Now, when -- did you make attempts later that

2 evening to get him on that same cell phone number?

3   A   Yes.

4   Q   And you said you didn't get through?

5   A   No.

6   Q   Now, have you ever dialed a cell phone number

7 either before or after that particular night?

8   A   Yes.

9   Q   So you're familiar with how cell phones work?

10   A   Yes.

11   Q   And do you know the difference in a call not

12 going through and a call being answered and then hung up?

13   A   Yes.

14   Q   Now, please tell the jury what response you got

15 later that evening when you tried to reach the defendant on

16 his cell phone.

17   A   I didn't get -- normally if you call you would

18 get a voice mail. I never got a voice mail. I heard the

19 phone ring. Then I heard it click off.

20   Q   Okay. So what did you interpret from that sound

21 on the cell phone?

22   A   I thought I was being hung up on.

23   Q   And did you continue to try him back?

24   A   Yes.

25   Q   And did you get the same response?

1   A   Yes.

2   Q   All right. Now, at the time you -- this summer,

3   the summer of 1998. I just want to clear up something from

4   cross examination. Were you working at that time?

5   A   The summer, yes.

6   Q   Of 1998?

7   A   Yes.

8   Q   Leading up to this incident?

9   A   Yes.

10   Q   And where were you working?

11   A   I worked at a nonprofit organization as a

12   recruiter and part time I was a hair dresser.

13   Q   Now, was this recruiting job a full-time job?

14   A   Yes.

15   Q   So you did your hairdressing on the weekends or

16   in the evenings?

17   A   Yes.

18   Q   But in either event, you had income from your

19   hairdressing and from your job in human resources?

20   A   Yes.

21   Q   Now just one final question. Isn't it a fact

22   that you no longer owned the Mercedes after the year 2000?

23   A   Yes.

24   Q   And isn't it a fact that the Department of Motor

25   Vehicles has a record that you no longer own that car?

1   A   Yes.

2   MS. BISHOP: I don't have anything further at

3   this time, Judge.

4   THE COURT: Mr. O'Meara, anything else?

5   RECROSS EXAMINATION

6   BY MR. O'MEARA:

7   Q   How much was the insurance for the Mercedes Benz?

8   MS. BISHOP: Objection.

9   THE COURT: Overruled.

10   A   175 I think.

11   Q   Per month?

12   A   Yes.

13   Q   And a $650 lease?

14   A   Yes.

15   Q   And you had the other car as well?

16   A   Yes.

17   Q   How much was the insurance for the Jeep?

18   A   It was less.   I would say -- I can't really

19   recall.   I know it was under $150 a month.

20   Q   This was while you worked for the not-for-profit

21   corporation?

22   A   Yes.

23   Q   And on the side doing hairdressing?

24   A   Yes.

25   MR. O'MEARA: I have no further questions,

1   THE COURT: All right. Good morning, ladies

2   and gentlemen. We are ready to proceed with the

3   People's next witness.

4   People, your next witness, please.

5   MS. BISHOP: Yes, Judge. The People call

6   Detective Christian Kanehl.

7   C H R I S T I A N   K A N E H L, Detective, a witness called

8   on behalf of the People, after having been first duly

9   sworn and having stated his shield number as 2169

10   and his command as the Queens Warrant Squad, New York

11   City Police Department, took the witness stand and

12   testified as follows:

13   THE CLERK: Thank you. You may be seated.

14   THE COURT: Detective Kanehl, I'm going to

15   ask you to keep your voice up or move closer to the

16   mike so everybody will be able to hear you. Okay, very

17   good.

18   Miss Bishop.

19   MS. BISHOP: Thank you, Judge.

20 DIRECT EXAMINATION

21 BY MS. BISHOP:

22   Q   Good morning, Detective Kanehl.

23   A   Good morning.

24   Q   How long have you worked for the New York City

25 Police Department?

1   A   19 years.

2   Q   Now, you're assigned to the warrant squad?

3   A   Yes.

4   Q   How long have you been there?

5   A   For a year.

6   Q   Where were you prior to getting to the warrant

7   squad?

8   A   The 105 Detective Squad.

9   Q   How long were you positioned there?

10   A   13 years.

11   Q   As a detective in the 105 Squad what were your

12   duties?

13   A   Investigating crimes that happened in the past

14   from homicide to bicycle theft.

15   Q   So you investigated a whole range of crimes?

16   A   Yes.

17   Q   These were crimes that took place within the

18   105th Precinct?

19   A   Yes.

20   Q   What part of Queens does that area cover?

21   A   Queens Village, Rosedale, Laurelton, Glen Oaks.

22   Q   In September of 1998 were you working as a

23   detective in the 105 Detective Squad?

24   A   I'm sorry, what date?

25   Q   September of 1998.

1   A   Yes.

2   Q   Specifically on September 19th of 1998. Were you

3   actually working that day?

4   A   No.

5   Q   Now let me direct your attention to September the

6   23rd. Were you working that day?

7   A   Yes.

8   Q   Did you receive an assignment that day to

9   investigate an incident involving shots that had been fired

10   in the vicinity of 240-06 142nd Avenue in Rosedale, Queens?

11   A   Yes.

12   Q   And you received that assignment on September the

13   23rd?

14   A   Yes.

15   Q   Now, can you please explain to the jury why there

16   was this delay from the incident until you received the

17   assignment.

18   A   In the detective squad we are assigned cases

19   throughout the day. I was off on Friday, but they assigned

20   me the case anyway. The next two days were my days off.

21   When I came back on the 23rd that's when I picked up the

22   investigation.

23   Q   Now, on the 23rd what, if anything, did you do in

24   reference to this investigation?

25   A   I interviewed several people.

1   A   Yes.

2   Q   And let me direct your attention now to September

3   the 25th of 1998. Did you do anything in connection with

4   your investigation on that day?

5   A   Yes.

6   Q   What did you do?

7   A   I contacted a parole officer.

8   Q   A parole officer?

9   A   Yes.

10   Q   Did you have a conversation with him?

11   A   Yes, I did.

12   Q   Did you ask him some questions?

13   A   Yes.

14   Q   And were you able to set up a meeting as a result

15   of that conversation?

16   A   Yes, I was.

17   Q   And what day did you set that meeting up for?

18   A   For the September 28th.

19   Q   And who were you going to be meeting on September

20   the 28th?

21   A   Mr. Zimmerman.

22   Q   Okay. And do you see that person in the

23   courtroom today?

24   A   Yes.

25   Q   Would you please describe --

A-91

1   A   The gentleman sitting in the dark suit.

2   THE COURT: There's two gentlemen.

3   A   The darker suit with the dark shirt.

4   THE COURT: Indicating the defendant.

5   Q   Now, so on September the 25th you made an

6   appointment to meet the defendant at his parole officer's

7   for the 28th?

8   A   Yes.

9   Q   Okay. Now, on September the 28th did you do

10   anything in reference to this case?

11   A   I arrested Mr. Zimmerman.

12   Q   And where did you go in order to do that?

13   A   I went to the parole office, the office of

14   Jamaica Avenue.

15   Q   And you met with him there?

16   A   Yes, I did.

17   Q   Would you just tell the jury what you said to

18   him?

19   A   I identified myself and I told him what this was

20   in reference to. I then took him back to the 105th

21   Detective Squad.

22   Q   Now, when you got back to the 105 Detective Squad

23   do you recall approximately what time of day it was?

24   A   I think it was about 8 o'clock at night.

25   Q   And did there come a time on the 28th when you

A-92

1   advised the defendant of his constitutional Miranda

2   warnings?

3   A   Yes.

4   Q   And how did you go about doing that?

5   A   We have cards that have the warnings on them.   I

6   advised him of his Miranda warnings.   Then he signs the

7   bottom of it.

8   Q   And do you have the card that you used to advise

9   Mr. Zimmerman of his rights?

10   A   Yes.

11   MS. BISHOP: Judge, I'd ask that this card be

12   marked for identification as People's 3.

13   THE COURT: Please mark it People's 3 for

14   identification.

15   MS. BISHOP: Could you please show it to

16   defense counsel.

17   (Shown to defense counsel.)

18   (Handed to witness.)

19   (People's Exhibit 3 marked for

20   identification.)

21   Q   All right, Detective Kanehl.   Do you recognize

22   that card?

23   A   Yes.

24   Q   How do you recognize it?

25   A   I recognize it by my signature on the side.

1   Q   Okay. And is that the same card that you used to

2   advise the defendant of his constitutional warnings?

3   A   Yes.

4   MS. BISHOP: Judge, I ask that -- I'm moving

5   this card that's been identified as People's 3 into

6   evidence.

7   MR. O'MEARA: No objection.

8   THE COURT: That will be received and marked

9   as People's 3 in evidence.

10   MR. O'MEARA: Your Honor, may we approach for

11   one minute?

12   THE COURT: Sure.

13   (People's Exhibit 3 marked in evidence.)

14   MS. BISHOP: Judge, I provided him with a

15   copy of this. I just happened to have mine out.

16   THE COURT: Okay.

17   You ready for the next question?

18   MR. O'MEARA: Can I just see that copy again.

19   THE COURT: Next question, please.

20   MS. BISHOP: Yes, Judge.

21   Q   All right, Detective Kanehl, would you please

22   tell the jury what is on that card.

23   A   On the Miranda card?

24   Q   Yes.

25   A   His constitutional rights.

1   Q   Did you read each one of those rights to the

2   defendant?

3   A   Yes.

4   Q   And did he indicate to you he understood each one

5   of those rights?

6   A   Yes.

7   Q   Now, would you please read to the jury what you

8   read to him that evening?

9   A   Okay. You have the right to remain silent and

10   refuse to answer questions. Do you understand. Anything

11   you do say may be used against you in a court of law. Do

12   you understand. You have the right to consult an attorney

13   before speaking to the police and have an attorney present

14   during any questioning now or in the future. Do you

15   understand.

16   If you cannot afford an attorney, one will be

17   provided for you without cost. Do you understand. If you

18   do not have an attorney available you have the right to

19   remain silent until you have had an opportunity to consult

20   with one. Do you understand. Now that I have advised you

21   of your rights, are you willing to answer questions.

22   Q   That's what you said to Mr. Zimmerman?

23   A   Yes.

24   Q   And at the end of each question did he indicate

25   to you that he understood what you had just said?

1   A   Yes.

2   Q   How did he indicate that?

3   A   He said, yes.

4   Q   Okay. And after you completed this advisory,

5   what, if anything, did you do with that card?

6   A   I signed it. Mr. Zimmerman signed it. I dated

7   it and put the time on the top.

8   MS. NAIBERG: Judge, I ask this card be

9   published to the jury.

10   THE COURT: Ladies and gentlemen, take a look

11   at this and pass it on to your next fellow juror

12   without making any comment.

13   (People's Exhibit 3 published to the jury.)

14   THE COURT: Thank you.

15   Next question, please.

16   Q   Detective Kanehl, after you advised the defendant

17   of his warnings and you signed the card and he signed the

18   card, did you two have a brief conversation about this

19   incident?

20   A   Yes.

21   Q   And he agreed to have that conversation with you?

22   A   Yes.

23   Q   And he didn't ask for a lawyer prior to having

24   this conversation with you?

25   A   No.

1   Q   Okay. Now what, if anything, did this defendant

2 say to you about the events of September the 19th of 1998?

3   A   He denied knowing Nikia Stubbs, using her

4 vehicle. He also said he didn't go by the name of Sean and

5 he said that he doesn't remember where he was that night.

6 He could have been at a different location. He wasn't sure

7 where he was.

8   Q   And so, so he told you that he had never heard of

9 Nikia Stubbs or anything about her car?

10   A   Correct.

11   Q   And did he have anything to say about this rental

12 agreement?

13   A   He said he doesn't know what I'm talking about.

14   Q   Now, after you finished speaking with him about

15 the 19th, did you continue your arrest processing in this

16 case?

17   A   Yes.

18   Q   And would you please tell the members of the jury

19 just generally what you do to process an arrest.

20   A   Various pieces of paper. An arrest report. He

21 is photographed. He is fingerprinted. Then he is taken

22 down to central booking which is located in this building.

23   Q   So you fill out some paperwork. Then basically

24 you bring him to court?

25   A   Yes.

1   Q   Now, I'd like to direct your attention to one of

2   the pieces of paper that you fill out during the arrest

3   processing called the on-line booking sheet. Are you

4   familiar with that piece of paper?

5   A   Yes.

6   Q   And would you tell the members of the jury what

7   an on-line booking sheet is.

8   A   Anybody that's arrested, their name, their

9   address, pedigree information, and the charges are put on

10   that piece of paper.

11   Q   When you say, pedigree information, what is that?

12   A   Height, weight, aliases, place of birth, age.

13   Q   Okay. So basically just general information

14   about the individual that's under arrest?

15   A   Yes.

16   Q   Now, when you spoke with Mr. Zimmerman, what

17   address did he give you as being his home address?

18   A   253 -- I think it was 253-04. Can I --

19   Q   Would something refresh your recollection?

20   A   Yes.

21   THE COURT: Just tell us what you're looking

22   at.

23   THE WITNESS: The arrest report, your Honor.

24   A   253-40 148th Road.

25   Q   That's in Rosedale?

1   A   Yes.

2   Q   Now, Detective Kanehl, as a result of your

3   investigation into this incident did you learn that the

4   defendant used any other name other than Nicholas Zimmerman?

5   A   Yes.

6   Q   And what name is that?

7   A   Sean Zimmerman.

8   MS. BISHOP: Thank you. I have no further

9   questions at this time.

10   THE COURT: Mr. O'Meara.

11   CROSS EXAMINATION

12   BY MR. O'MEARA:

13   Q   Good morning, detective.

14   A   Good morning.

15   Q   I would like to start off first with the

16   investigation of the other witness Brathwaite. I believe

17   her name was Miss Brathwaite.

18   A   Okay.

19   Q   Now, you also interviewed her during the process

20   of your investigation?

21   A   Yes.

22   Q.   Now, how many times did you speak to her?

23   A   I believe I only spoke to her once.

24   Q   Now, when you spoke to her do you remember what

25   she told you?

1   A   She -- I --

2   MS. BISHOP: Objection if it calls for

3   hearsay.

4   THE COURT: Well, the question is, do you

5   remember. It calls for either a yes or no answer.

6   Don't tell us what you said. If you remember.

7   A   Yes, it's in my report.

8   Q   Do you remember her telling you anything --

9   MS. BISHOP: Objection.

10   THE COURT: Overruled. Let's hear the

11   question before we --

12   Q   Do you remember her telling you anything about a

13   high-speed chase?

14   A   No.

15   Q   She never mentioned it at all?

16   A   No.

17   Q   Now, when you're investigating or when you're

18   interviewing do you generally let the person being

19   interviewed do most of the speaking?

20   A   Yes.

21   Q   You let them tell you the whole story?

22   A   Yes.

23   Q   Then do you usually say, well, anything else?

24   What happened next?

25   A   Yes.

1   Q   And do you remember if you asked Miss Brathwaite

2   that when you interviewed her?

3   A   That I don't recall.

4   Q   But, regardless, the interview ended and she

5   never mentioned anything to your recollection about any

6   high-speed chase over 100 miles per hour --

7   A   Not that I recall, no.

8   Q   -- in Queens?

9   A   Not that I recall.

10   Q   Certainly not on that night in question, on

11. September 19th?

12   A   Right. Not that I recall.

13   Q   Now, during your investigation of Mr. Zimmerman

14   the allegations were that gunshots were fired?

15   A   Yes.

16   Q   Now, when there's allegations of use of a gun or

17   anything of that nature, are there possible tests you can

18   take on the defendant, Mr. Zimmerman, or any other defendant

19   for that matter, of his clothes to check whether or not

20   there was gunpowder discharged?

21   A   The paraffin test I believe it's called. It's a

22   residue test.

23   Q   Yes?

24   A   Never.

25   Q   You never take one?

1   A   Never.

2   Q   So there wasn't one taken on Mr. Zimmerman?

3   A   No.

4   Q   But the test exists?

5   A   I'm not an expert on that. The test exists, but

6 it's got to be done moments after.

7   Q   So the test does exist. Then it wasn't done on

8 Mr. Zimmerman?

9   A   No.

10   Q   Now, the Mercedes Benz that Mrs. Stubbs was

11 driving, did you check that car for fingerprints?

12   ☀ A   No.

13   Q   No you didn't check or --

14   A   I didn't check.

15   Q   You didn't find any fingerprints.

16   A   I didn't check.

17   Q   Did you conduct a search of Mr. Zimmerman?

18   A   His person?

19   Q   Yes.

20   A   That's the format when he is arrested.

21   Q   Find any gun?

22   A   He went to the parole office.

23   Q   The question was, did you find a gun on him?

24   A   No.

25   ✝ Q   Did you check his home?

1   A   No.

2   Q   You didn't search his house? .

3   A   I didn't have a warrant.

4   Q   Did you search any of these vehicles he might

5   have been traveling around in?

6   A   Didn't have a warrant.

7   Q   Leased or otherwise?

8   A   No.

9   Q   No searches done of those vehicles either?

10   A   No.

11.   Q   There was no gun found?

12   A   Not as far as I know, no.

13   Q   You're the detective on the case?

14   A   Right.

15   Q   You would have been made aware the gun had

16   actually been found, no?

17   Now, you also interviewed Miss Stubbs?

18   A   Yes.

19   Q   And you interviewed her twice?

20   A   I think I interviewed her only once.

21   Q   Only once?

22   A   On the 23rd.

23   Q   You only spoke to Miss Stubbs -- well, you met

24   with her a few other times?

25   A   She was actually only interviewed one time.

A-99

1   Q   She was only interviewed once?

2   A   Right.

3   Q   When you interviewed her and she told you this

4   story, did she never mention anything about a high-speed

5   chase?

·6   A   Not that I recall.

7   Q   She never mentioned that she had seen the Jeep

8   Cherokee there?

9   A   I just recall Miss Stubbs saying that she fled

10   when she got in her car. She fled.

11   Q   She never mentioned seeing people hop into her

12   car that she leased to Mr. Zimmerman?

13   A   I don't recall.

14   Q   She never mentioned moments later seeing that

15   same Jeep Cherokee behind her chasing her and then speeding

16   at 100 miles per hour?

17   A   All I know is she fled.

18   Q   Again, when you questioned her you gave her the

19   same opportunity to tell her full story?

20   A   Yes.

21   Q   You didn't cut her off after she said she went to

22   the car?

23   A   No.

24   Q   If she had anything more to say you certainly

25   would have listened to her?

A-100

1   ⊥ A   Yes.

2   Q   She also said there was two other guys involved

3   with this?

4   A   Yes.

5   Q   Was there anything ever found out about them?

6   A   No. She didn't know who they were.

7   Q   Were any phone records ever pulled of

8   Mrs. Stubbs's telephone calls that night?

9   ✱ A   No.

10   Q   Did you ever interview Wilson?

11   ✝ A   No.

12   Q   That -- you know who Wilson is?

13   A   I believe Wilson was Nikia Stubbs's boyfriend.

14   Q   Now, you were aware he was present during all of

15   this?

16   A   Yes.

17   Q   And nobody could find him?

18   A   I couldn't find him at the time, no. Things kind

19   of went pretty quick.

20   Q   You attempted to find him?

21   ✱A   Yes.

22   Q   Now, on the night in question, September 19th,

23   you weren't working, you weren't -- you certainly weren't at

24   the scene of the alleged crime.

25   A   Right.

1   Q   So you have no personal knowledge outside of

2   these interviews of what happened that night.

3   A   Correct.

4   MR. O'MEARA: Now, your Honor, may I present

5   the documents that we --

6   THE COURT: Go ahead.

7   Q   Detective, you have just been handed a piece of

8   paper. Can you tell me what that is?

9   A   This is when I'm interviewing somebody I take

10   notes. I put them on the back of the 61, which is the

11   complaint report. These are the notes I put on the back of

12   the complaint report while interviewing Nikia Stubbs.

13   Q   Now, at one point there I believe it's written,

14   leased.

15   A   Leased auto.

16   Q   Yes, for two days.

17   A   I believe that says, lent.

18   Q   Lent auto?

19   A   My handwriting is it's L-E-N-T.

20   Q   My handwriting is not good either.

21   A   Lent auto for two days.

22   Q   So was she telling you she lent an automobile to

23   somebody for two days?

24   A   She lent the auto, yeah, for two days.

25   Q   For two days.

1   Now, further down on the page it says, pulled up.

2   A   Right.

3   Q   At least I think it said pulled up.

4   A   Uh-huh.

5   Q   Do you have any idea what that is?

6   A   That's she pulled up in the car. She's sitting

7 in front of the car.

8   Q   She pulled up --

9   A   She's in the car.

10   Q   Not a car pulled up.

11   A   No.

12   Q   Just she pulled up.

13   A   Right.

14   Q   All right. I'm sorry. There is one more thing.

15 At the bottom it says a new Jetta, temporary tag.

16   A   I believe that was part of the description of

17 Mr. Zimmerman at the time, I believe. That had something to

18 do with him, but I didn't need that information.

19   Q   A white new Jetta, temporary tags.

20   And, now, you did testify about Mr. Zimmerman's

21 statement made to you at the 105 Precinct.

22   A   Yes.

23   Q   Basically it was he didn't have knowledge of the

24 whole incident.

25   A   Exactly.

1   Q   Said it wasn't me.

2   A   Yes.

3   MR. O'MEARA: I have no further questions.

4   THE COURT: Anything on redirect?

5   MS. BISHOP: Just a few, Judge.

6   REDIRECT EXAMINATION

7   BY MS. BISHOP:

8   Q   Detective Kanehl, you were asked about this test

9   that can be performed, a gunpowder paraffin test?

10   A   Yes.

11   Q   And your response was the test must be done

12   moments after. Moments after what?

13   A   After a shooting. Even then it doesn't work.

14   That's why it's very, very, very rarely used. When the

15   gun's fired supposedly there is some residue on the person's

16   hand. They do a test to see if there is gunpowder residue.

17   It's very inconclusive.

18   MR. O'MEARA: Objection, your Honor.

19   THE COURT: Overruled.

20   Q   Go ahead.

21   A   It's inconclusive.

22   Q   So even though we hear about these tests on T.V,

23   they don't necessarily work in real life.

24   A   I have been doing this for 13, 14 years. I have

25   never done it. I don't know of anybody who has ever done

1   it.

2   Q   Now, just to clear up something regarding your

3   interviews with Nikia Stubbs. When you conduct a formal

4   interview with a complainant in a case, it's police

5   procedure, is it not, for you to generate a piece of

6   paperwork reflecting what was said in that interview?

7   A   Yes.

8   Q   And did you do that in this case?

9   A   Yes.

10   Q   So then once that's done if you continue to speak

11   with that person about the incident, do you necessarily

12   write down every single thing that's said unless it's

13   something new?

14   A   No.

15   Q   Okay. So you continued on the 23rd to have

16   conversations with Nikia Stubbs, even though you just

17   formally interviewed her the one time?

18   A   Correct.

19   Q   Okay. Now, you testified that she didn't mention

20   this chase. She mentioned to you she fled after this

21   happened?

22   A   Yes. The complaint report was taken at the 105

23   Precinct, not at the scene.

24   Q   So, in fact, but when you interviewed her on the

25   23rd she also said that to you?

1   A   Yes.

2   Q   And even though she wasn't really focused on the

3   chase when she was talking to you, what was she focused on?

4   A   On the gunshots.

5   Q   And she definitely provided you with information

6   about that?

7   A   Yes.

8   Q   Now, you also said that you did not conduct an

9   interview with Wilson?

10   A   Correct.

11   Q   Isn't it true that you did conduct interviews

12   with two witnesses who were present, namely Nikia and

13   Kharisha Brathwaite?

14   A   Yes.

15   Q   So did you feel it was necessary to really pursue

16   Wilson once you had the information from these two women?

17   A   No.

18   MS. BISHOP: I have nothing further, Judge.

19   THE COURT: Anything else, Mr. O'Meara?

20   MR. O'MEARA: Just a few.

21   RECROSS EXAMINATION

22   BY MR. O'MEARA:

23   Q   Your interview of Miss Brathwaite, basically she

24   said that she couldn't I.D. anybody.

25   A   Yes.

1   Q   And now you wrote the complaint in this case?

2   A   I'm sorry?

3   Q   When you interviewed Miss Stubbs --

4   A   Yes

5   Q   -- you wrote down on your 61 what she said or

6   what the relevant information was?

7   A   I didn't take the 61, the complaint report.

8   Q   But when you spoke to her were you taking notes?

9   A   Yes.

10   Q   Was any of that included in any of the reports?

11   A   That's the report you showed me.   That's on the

12   back.

13   Q   That's on the back?

14   A   Yes, that's --

15   Q   I'm sorry?

16   A   That's on the back of the 61.   The photocopy you

17   just showed me, that's on the back of the 61 I have in my

18   folder.   While she is talking to me I'm taking notes on the

19   back of the complaint report.

20   Q   If she had ever mentioned about a chase, do you

21   think that's something you would have taken notice of?

22   A   It's really not significant because nobody was

23   hurt in the chase and it was just -- she was fleeing from

24   the scene.

25   Q   A 100 mile per hour chase isn't that relevant?

1   A   When somebody is shooting at somebody, 100 miles

2   an hour down the streets of Rosedale, that's kind of fast --

3   Q   When somebody is following that person, the

4   alleged person who shot at them --

5   A   Uh-huh.

6   Q   -- and then the complaining witness then

7   allegedly says she sees the car, and then says that that car

8   chased her at a 100 miles per hour --

9   A   Okay.

10   Q   -- that's not relevant information?

11   A   It's relevant. But like I said, counsel, no one

12   was hurt. There were no shots fired from the car. It

13   was -- I don't -- I don't -- I don't know. 100 miles an

14   hour down the streets of Rosedale, like I said, is highly

15   unlikely. I'm sure it wasn't 100 miles an hour. I mean

16   when your adrenaline is going --

17   Q   I'm sure it wasn't 100 miles an hour either.

18   A   Right.

19   MR. O'MEARA: I have nothing further.

20   THE COURT: Anything else?

21   MS. BISHOP: One fast thing.

22   REDIRECT EXAMINATION

23   BY MS. BISHOP:

24   Q   Detective, you described something called a 61.

25   A   Yes.

1   Q   Is that the actual complaint report that Miss

2   Stubbs filed with the precinct?

3   A   Yes.

4   Q   You didn't take down that information?

5   A   No.

6   Q   What kind of report did you put your information

7   down in after you spoke with her? What is the nature of

8   that report?

9   A   It's called a D.D.5. This is information we

10   receive through interviews is all documented on what we call

11   a D.D.5.

12   Q   That's really a compliant follow-up report?

13   A   Yes.

14   Q   That stays with the original complaint report

15   that's called a 61?

16   A   Yes.

17   MS. BISHOP: Okay.

18   MR. O'MEARA: I have nothing further, your

19   Honor.

20   THE COURT: Thank you, detective. You can

21   step down. Thank you.

22   Do we have another witness?

23   MS. BISHOP: Yes, Judge.

24   THE COURT: We will take a five-minute break

25   before the next witness so you can stretch, use the

1   Counsel?

2   MS. BISHOP: Yes.

3   THE CLERK: Counsel?

4   MR. O'MEARA: Yes.

5   THE COURT: Defendant.

6   MR. O'MEARA: I'd like to call Jatanya

7   Belnavis to the stand.

8 J A T A N Y A   B E L N A V I S, a witness called on behalf

9   of the Defendant, after having been first duly sworn

10   and having stated her residence as Queens County and

11   testified as follows:

12   THE CLERK: Thank you. You may be seated.

13   THE COURT: Miss Belnavis, I'm going to ask

14   you keep your voice up. Move that chair closer to the

15   mike so everybody can hear you. Speak right into the

16   mike. Okay.

17   THE WITNESS: Yes.

18 DIRECT EXAMINATION

19 BY MR. O'MEARA:

20   Q   Could you just state your name again.

21   A   Jatanya Belnavis.

22   Q   Now, Jatanya, can you tell me if you know

23 Nicholas Zimmerman?

24   A   Yes.

25   Q   How do you know him?

1   A   He is my boyfriend.

2   Q   Can you tell us a little bit about yourself? Do

3 you go to school?

4   A   Yes, I go York College.

5   Q   Where?

6   A   In Jamaica, New York.

7   Q   I can't really hear you. Speak up.

8   A   In Jamaica, New York.

9   Q   And do you work?

10   A   Yes, I do.

11   Q   What do you do?

12   A   I do customer service for transit.

13   Q   How long have you known Nicholas Zimmerman?

14   A   About eight years.

15   Q   How long have you dated him?

16   A   Eight years on and off.

17   Q   On and off?

18   A   Yes.

19   Q   More on than off?

20   A   Yes.

21   Q   Now, you also know Nikia Stubbs?

22   A   Yes.

23   Q   How do you know Miss Stubbs?

24   A   She was a friend of a friend that I went to

25 elementary school with. And later on you know she became my

1 hairdresser and then we became friends.

2   Q   So how long about have you known her?

3   A   I have known her for about nine or ten years.

4   Q   Now, you also know that Nikia Stubbs and

5 Mr. Zimmerman entered into some sort of contract to lease a

6 car?

7   A   Yes.

8   Q   Can you tell us about that agreement?

9   A   Well, she had the extra car she wanted to lease

10 because she couldn't make payments on both of her cars. So

11. we agreed to lease it from her while we were waiting for her

12 to get us a car.

13   Q   Who is "we"?

14   A   Myself and Nicholas.

15   Q   So you were part of this lease as well?

16   A   Not as far as the actual dollar amount but, yes.

17   Q   Now, can you tell us the terms of the leasing

18 agreement?

19   A   Well, he said that he wanted the car --

20   MS. BISHOP: Objection, Judge. It's hearsay.

21   THE COURT: I will allow it at this point.

22   A   He wanted the car for a month because we were

23 waiting on, on our, like I said, to get us a car. It had

24 already taken an extend period of time. So we went to her

25 house and he made an arrangement with her to lease the car

1   for I believe the amount of the car for the month. And she

2   gave us the keys and we had the car.

3   MS. BISHOP: Judge, may we step up?

4   THE COURT: Not at this point, no.

5   Go ahead. Next question.

6   Q   Did Nicholas Zimmerman ever pick up the car?

7   A   Yes.

8   Q   Do you know when he picked up the car?

9   A   I would say about the 10th or the 11th of

10   September.

11   Q   Do you know how long the lease was for?

12   A   One month.

13   Q   One full month?

14   A   Right.

15   Q   Were you with him when he picked up the car?

16   A   Yes.

17   Q   Now, at that time did he owe money on the car?

18   A   No.

19   Q   He had paid for the lease?

20   A   Right. He gave her the money for the note for

21   the month.

22   Q   You picked up the car.

23   A   Right.

24   Q   After the car was picked up did you hear from

25   Miss Stubbs?

1   A   Yes. About a little less than a week later. She

2   called and she said that she thought about it and she could

3   have gotten more money for the car so she wanted the car

4   back or she wanted more money.

5   Q   Who did she call?

6   A   She called myself. And once I told her that she

7   made the agreement with him, she started calling him.

8   Q   How many times did she call you?·

9   A   Me she called once. And then I don't know how

10   many times she called him. I think it was a few. I really

11 . don't remember.

12   Q   Now, do you know -- I'd like to bring your

13   attention to September 18, 1998.

14   A   Okay.

15   Q   Can you tell me what you were doing that day in

16   the later evening, let's say around 8 or 9 o'clock.

17   A   8 or 9 o'clock I was with Nicholas. He was

18   getting dressed. He had a performance that night.

19   Q   Where were you?

20   A   At his house on 148th Road in Rosedale.

21   Q   How long were you with Nicholas that day?

22   A.   Probably two or three hours.

23   Q   What time did you leave Nicholas that day?

24   A   Well, he got dressed and he dropped me off at

25   about 10:00 and then he went onto the club.

1   Q   What car was he driving?

2   A   The Cherokee.

3   Q   Now, when was the next time you spoke to

4 Mr. Zimmerman?

5   A   The 19th.

6   Q   What time?

7   A   Maybe about 8:00 in the morning.

8   Q   Now, I'd like to bring you back to what you did

9 on the 18th after Nicholas dropped you off.

10   A   I don't really remember. I probably watched T.V.

11 . and went to bed.

12   Q   Do you know what time about you went to bed?

13   A   Probably 11:00, 11:30.

14   Q   Did anything happen that night or into September

15 19th the morning that awoken you from bed?

16   A   Yes.

17   Q   What happened?

18   A   I was awakened by my father. He asked me to look

19 out the window and see if I knew a car that was parked

20 across the street because someone had been ringing on the

21 bell and banging on the door and honking the horn.

22   Q   Now, what time was this you said?

23   A   I would say about 2:30, maybe 3 o'clock.

24   Q   Did you know whose car it was?

25   A   Yes, it was Nikia's Benz.

1   Q   Nikia's what?

2   A   Nikia's Mercedes Benz.

3   Q   What did you do next?

4   A   I went downstairs and opened the door.

5   Q   What happened after that?

6   A   Well, I opened the door and Nikia was out there

7 with her boyfriend Wilson and another girl that I never seen

8 before. And she was upset. She was demanding her car. She

9 told me that I didn't -- am I allowed to curse?

10   THE COURT: Whatever she said you can say.

11   A   She said to me I didn't know who I was fucking

12 with and she wasn't one for this shit. And told me to get

13 Sean on the phone and get her car back now.

14   Q   What happened after that?

15   A   Well, I went back inside. I tried to contact

16 him. And I couldn't get through. I called his cell phone.

17 I got voice mail. I believe it was like all circuits are

18 busy one time. Then I called again and I think a girl

19 answered, but I'm not sure if that was the right number. I

20 called back again. I called voice mail again. But I never

21 got through again.

22   Q   I'd like to take you back a few minutes before

23 that, those telephone calls, while you were speaking to Miss

24 Stubbs. Were you speaking as well? Was Wilson saying

25 anything?

1   A   At that point, no.

2   Q   All right. After you make the telephone calls or

3   after you attempted to call Mr. Zimmerman, what did you do?

4   A   I went back to the door and I told them I wasn't

5   able to get in contact with him. I asked her, didn't you

6   already speak about this? Didn't he tell you he was going

7   to give you the car back tomorrow? That's when Wilson said

8   that's --

9   MS. BISHOP: Objection to hearsay.

10   THE COURT: Objection sustained.

11   You can't testify what Wilson said.

12   THE WITNESS: Okay.

13   Q   After you're at the doorstep and you're speaking

14   to Miss Stubbs -- and then Wilson said something to you?

15   A   Right.

16   Q   After Wilson spoke to you did you fear for your

17   safety?

18   MS. BISHOP: Objection.

19   THE COURT: Overruled.

20   A   Yes, I did.

21   Q   Why did you fear for your safety?

22   A   Because what he said I took as a threat and he --

23   MS. BISHOP: Objection to this.

24   THE COURT: Objection sustained.

25   A   He took off his shirt and went around the corner.

1   Q   What happened after the conversation with

2   Mr. Wilson and Nikia Stubbs?

3   A   Oh, he took off his shirt and went around the

4   corner. And I went back inside the house. I went upstairs

5   to look out the window to see if I could see where he went,

6   what he was going to do. And I didn't see him. I looked

7   through the park. I saw people in the park.

8   Q   Exactly where are you talking about?

9   A   Well, my house is around the corner from a park,

10   Brookville Park and --

11   Q   Can you hold on one second.

12   MR. O'MEARA: Can we have that map that was

13   used.

14   THE COURT: People's 1, I think.

15   Q   Using that map can you point out where your house

16   is and where Wilson went.

17   THE COURT: You can step up.

18   A   My house would be about here and Wilson went this

19   way and around there.

20   THE COURT: Indicating on -- what is the name

21   of that street?

22   THE WITNESS: On Brookville Boulevard.

23   THE COURT: On Brookville Boulevard.

24   Q   And then what happened after that?

25   A   Well, I couldn't see him. And I figured that I

1   knew the people that were in the park, or at least one of

2   them, so I made a call to another friend. And he did happen

3   to be in the park. And I asked him did he see a guy come

4   around the corner. He asked me why so I told --

5   MS. BISHOP: Objection to the hearsay.

6   THE COURT: Objection sustained. Calls for a

7   hearsay answer.

8   Q   So you had a conversation with one of your

9   friends in the park.

10   A   Yes.

11   Q   Then after that conversation, what happened?

12   A   After that conversation I went and got dressed,

13   put on some clothes, and I went outside to try to calm the

14   situation down because I didn't want any more commotion at

15   my house. My parents were upset with me. I didn't want my

16   house getting shot up.

17   Q   All right. Now, what happened after that?

18   A   After I got dressed, I went outside. And I

19   approached the car to try speak to Nikia. She ignored me.

20   And when I looked in the car, I thought I saw a gun on

21   Wilson's lap. When I turned to go back in the house, I saw

22   people coming out of the neighbor's yard and I ran.

23   Q   Just answer the questions as I ask them. So

24   you're standing outside of the car.

25   A   Right.

1   Q   Then what about the people coming?

2   A   I was standing outside the car. And I was trying

3 to talk to her. She wouldn't pay me attention. In looking

4 at the car I saw something on his lap. I believed it to be

5 a gun. So I was turning to go back into my house and that's

6 when I saw people coming out of the neighbor's yard

7 towards --

8   Q   Did you recognize those people?

9   A   I didn't stay to recognize the people.

10   Q   What did you do then?

11   A   I ran in the opposite direction. I ran up the

12 block along the cars towards 241st Street and then into a

13 yard across the street.

14   Q   Did you see any Jeep Cherokee?

15   A   No.

16   Q   And what did you do after that?

17   A   Well, after I ran into the yard I stayed there

18 for a minute. I didn't see anybody following me. And I

19 peeked out. I saw people further up the block towards 241st

20 Street. Then I ran back towards my house.

21   Q   Then what did you do?

22   A   Well, as I ran to my house my mother was in the

23 doorway telling me to get inside. And when I got up the

24 stairs through the door I heard the shots being fired.

25   Q   And did you turn to see what was going on or what

A-116

1   was happening?

2   A   No, I didn't.

3   Q   Now, what happened after that?

4   A   After that well --, my parents were upset I was

5   upset. And the police showed up at my door.

6   Q   What time did the police show up?

7   A   I would say about 4:00, 4 o'clock, 4:30.

8   Q   Did they speak to you?

9   A   Yeah, they spoke to me.

10   Q   Did you give a statement or anything?

11   A   Well, they really didn't allow me to give my

12 statement.

13   Q   What did they come to your house for?

14   A   Basically they were insinuating that my boyfriend

15 was the one who committed this act and they weren't trying

16 to hear anything other than that.

17   Q   And then where did you go or what did you do

18 after the police left?

19   A   Well, after they left I tried to contact him some

20 more and I was unable to until the morning.

21   Q   What time in the morning?

22   A   About 8:00 I think.

23   Q   And then after you spoke to him -- or let's put

24 it this way. When was the next time you had anything to do

25 with this case insofar as do you know when Nicholas was

A-117

1   arrested?

2   A   That was about a week later.

3   Q   During that time did you have any conversations

4   or did you speak to Miss Stubbs?

5   A   Not directly. We spoke with another, another

6   friend who we arranged to return the car at that point.

7   Q   When did the car get returned?

8   A   The 19th.

9   Q   Now, after the 19th did you ever speak to Miss

10   Stubbs again?

11   A   Well, I had called her on one occasion -- well, I

12   called her on a few occasions. One occasion I did get an

13   answer. Her mother answered the phone and told me that I

14   was not to call her house again. And after that I didn't

15   speak to her on the phone, but I did see her and Wilson when

16   I went by there.

17   Q   When did you see her and Wilson?

18   A   This would be about two, two days after Sean was

19   arrested.

20   Q   Now, did you have a conversation? Did you just

21   pass her by on street? What happened?

22   A   Well, we had a conversation. And at that time I

23   was made aware that --

24   MS. BISHOP: Objection to the hearsay.

25   THE COURT: Objection sustained.

1   Q   How long did the conversation last?

2   A   About -- it was short. Probably a few minutes.

3   Q   What was the general conversation about?

4   MS. BISHOP: Objection.

5   THE COURT: Just about the topic. Say what

6   the topic was.

7   THE WITNESS: Money.

8   THE COURT: Without telling us what was said.

9   A   Money to drop the charges.

10   Q   Did you know how much money was involved?

11. A   Yes.

12   Q   How much?

13   A $10,000.

14   Q   How long did this conversation last?

15   A   A few minutes.

16   Q   When was the next time you had seen Miss Stubbs?

17   A   The next time I would have seen her would be a

18   few months after that. Well, actually I'm not sure if it

19   was a few months or like the next year. I saw her at a gas

20   station.

21   Q   Did you have a conversation with her then?

22   A   No, I didn't realize it was her because she was

23   driving a different car. And you know she approached me.

24   Said hello. And I said hello. Got my gas and went on my

25   way.

1   Q   So you didn't really have a conversation about

2   this particular incident?

3   A   No.

4   Q   Now, you stated that you have known Miss Stubbs

5   for a long time?

6   A   Yes.

7   Q   Now, at any time did you ever obtain a new Jetta?

8   A   Yes.

9   Q   How did you obtain that Jetta?

10   A   Through Nikia and I guess her people get cars.

11   Q   How do you mean you obtained it through her

12   people?

13   MS. BISHOP: Objection, Judge. May we step

14   up at this time?

15   THE COURT: The objection is sustained.

16   Objection sustained.

17   MS. BISHOP: May we step up?

18   THE COURT: Come up.

19   (Sidebar discussion off the record.)

20   THE COURT: All right. Next question,

21   please.

22   Q   You obtained a Jetta?

23   A   Yes.

24   Q   Now --

25   THE COURT: Was that purchased or leased?

1   THE WITNESS: Financed.

2   Q   How was it financed?

3   A   I'm not exactly sure what you mean.

4   Q   Did you go to a bank and fill out paperwork to

5   finance it? Did you go to the car dealership and finance

6   it?

7   A   No, I went to Nikia's house.

8   Q   You went to Nikia's house to fill out paperwork?

9   MS. BISHOP: I object to the relevance of how

10   she purchased a car that has nothing to do with this

11   incident.

12   THE COURT: Overruled.

13   A   Yes.

14   Q   And do you know what happened to the paperwork

15   after that?

16   A   I believe it was submitted to the car --

17   MS. BISHOP: Objection to the speculation.

18   THE COURT: Overruled.

19   Did you get a loan based on those papers?

20   THE WITNESS: Yes.

21   THE COURT: Next question.

22   Q   Did you use that loan to obtain this Jetta?

23   A   Yes.

24   THE COURT: Who obtained this loan, you or

25   Mr. Zimmerman?

1   THE WITNESS: Me.

2   Q   How long did you have the loan?

3   A   A few months probably. About six or seven

4   months.

5   Q   I'm sorry. I meant how long did you have the

6   car?

7   A   About six or seven months.

8   Q   And then did you eventually get rid of the car?

9   A   Yes.

10   Q   How did you get rid of the car?

11   A   We sold the car.

12   Q   So why did you want to get rid of the car?

13   MS. BISHOP: Objection to the form of the

14   question.

15   THE COURT: Objection sustained.

16   Q   When, if ever, or why -- I will go back -- you

17   got rid of the car after six or seven months?

18   A   Yes.

19   Q   Was there any reason specific reason you might

20   have wanted to get rid of this car?

21   MS. BISHOP: Objection.

22   THE COURT: Overruled.

23   A   Well, I had heard from other people that --

24   MS. BISHOP: Objection to the hearsay.

25   THE COURT: Objection sustained.

1   Good morning, your Honor.

2   MR. O'MEARA: Your Honor --

3   THE COURT: Yes, sir.

4   MR. O'MEARA: I have three witnesses that are

5   present here today. One witness is here to testify in

6   rebuttal to Mrs. Stubbs' testimony about an encounter

7   she had with Mr. Zimmerman after the allegations. She

8   would testify while she was driving around she ran into

9   Mr. Zimmerman and one of his other girlfriends while

10   his other girlfriend is here and willing to testify

11. about what happened.

12   THE COURT: What else?

13   MR. O'MEARA: Your Honor, as I have mentioned

14   on Friday, the contract that was signed by

15   Mr. Zimmerman's manager and the promotor of the venue

16   where he was to perform the night of this incident. I

17   have the contract. I have both parties who signed the

18   contracts as well as promotional fliers created by one

19   of those parties.

20   Your Honor, they're not going to testify that

21   he was there that night. They're only going to testify

22   so far as these documents are the original documents.

23   They either signed them or had them created.

24   Therefore, should be allowed into evidence.

25   THE COURT: People wish to be heard?

1   MS. BISHOP: Yes. As far as the witnesses go

2   regarding this contract, they have absolutely no

3   relevance to the charges in this case. First of all,

4   they weren't a part of the alibi notice that defense

5   counsel provided, and, furthermore, they're not really

6   testifying about an alibi. They're testifying about an

7   agreement that he made to be somewhere several hours

8   before this happened.

9   So there is really no relevance to where he

10   was before 3 o'clock in the morning. And counsel just

11 .   said they're not going to be testifying that he was

12   even there. It's just going to be they had this

13   document and they put together some fliers about it.

14   So I submit that this Court should not allow those

15   witnesses to take the stand. · They will only confuse

16   the jury. They have no relevance.

17   THE COURT: It's not signed by the defendant

18   either, is it?

19   MR. O'MEARA: Your Honor, it mentions his

20   name, the contract. They can testify that was the

21   stage name he went by at the time. Furthermore, the

22   notice of alibi does state where Mr. Zimmerman was

23   going to be. That is also within the contract and the

24   fliers, your Honor. These witnesses should be allowed

25   to testify. The district attorney was given notice he

1   was, he would be at Jam Rock, a club out in Nassau

2   County. There is no prejudice so far as it is allowing

3   this contract and this material to be presented to the

4   jury. If they choose to disregard or disbelieve it, so

5   be it. That's up to the jury to decide.

6   THE COURT: What concerns me is the purpose

7   of offering this is for the purpose of showing an alibi

8   in my opinion. And because you did not produce the

9   witnesses for the defendant, for the People, that were

10   on the notice, and because these people were not on the

11   notice, it appears to the Court you're trying to get

12   through the back door what you can't get through the

13   front door. At this point we're still looking up cases

14   in regard to this. My law secretary is still checking

15   cases. So I'm going to reserve decision on that right

16 ✗ now for the moment.

17   MS. BISHOP: Judge, may I be heard as far as

18   the other witness that counsel has raised?

19   THE COURT: Yes.

20   ✗ MS. BISHOP: Your Honor, again, I haven't

21   received any kind of notice, except a few minutes ago,

22   about the name and date of birth of this person. I

23   have had no opportunity to really meet with her or

24   check into her background. And I submit she is going

25   to be talking about something that happened after this

1   incident. And I don't really know if rebuttal is the

2   proper, is the proper way to characterize what she has

3   to say. It's really more in the nature of extrinsic

4   evidence that will go -- I guess that will bear on the

5   credibility of Miss Stubbs.

6   And I submit that it's just really beyond the

7   scope of why we are here. 'That she should not be

8   allowed to testify either.

9   THE COURT: What about your offer of the

10   proof of the defendant's plea with the proviso that the

11   witness --

12   ⋆ MS. BISHOP: Wasn't prosecuted.

13   THE COURT: Yes. What was her name?

14   MS. BISHOP: Jatanya Belnavis.

15   THE COURT: The witness Belnavis was not

16   prosecuted as a part of somebody else taking the plea.

17   How is that different than what the defendant is trying

18   to offer here?

19   MS. BISHOP: They are different, Judge,

20   because during my cross examination of Miss Belnavis I

21   was precluded from confronting her with the evidence

22   that I had because it would have prejudiced the

23   defendant. That's the only reason why I was unable to

24   confront her properly while she was on the stand as a

25   witness. I think we all agree that had I done that it

1   would have very much prejudiced the defendant in an

2   unfair way.

3   So the fact that this Court may be willing to

4   let that proof come in after the fact is for a

5   different reason and under different circumstances than

6   just calling another witness to talk about something

7   else.

8   THE COURT: At this point I think they're

9   both collateral issues. And you were precluded from an

10 answer. She was not involved. It's a collateral

11 issue. I'm not going to allow you to do that. I also

12 believe that this is a collateral issue in regard to

13 what happened some months after the incident in

14 question where a meeting took place. I think it's a

15 collateral issue and the only purpose is to confuse the

16 jury. I'm not going to allow you to do that.

17 ⭑   MR. O'MEARA: Your Honor, may I be heard on

18 that?

19   THE COURT: Yes.

20   MR. O'MEARA: Your Honor, the complaining

21 witness testified to that. Testified that

22 Mr. Zimmerman reached down looking for a gun. Now we

23 brought in the witness that the complaining witness

24 herself stated was in the car. She can testify to what

25 exactly happened that day. She should be allowed to

1   testify. Mr. Zimmerman should be allowed to produce a

2   defense, your Honor. If a witness is going to get up

3   there and falsify her testimony and tell stories we

4   should be allowed to bring in the witnesses to those

5   stories and tell exactly what happened.

6   Now, she can testify that under no

7   circumstance did Mr. Zimmerman ever apologize to Miss

8   Stubbs as Miss Stubbs testified to and that he made no

9   threatening gesture. Your Honor, it's extremely

10   relevant. It goes right to Mr. Zimmerman's defense

11   that Miss Stubbs is not telling the truth.

12   THE COURT: I'm going to reserve decision. I

13   have to look that up too. So the Court will take a

14   break.

15   MS. BISHOP: Judge, may I just alert the

16   Court to Richardson's section 6-305, the last --

17   THE COURT: We looked at that.

18   MS. BISHOP: -- the last two paragraphs.

19   THE COURT: What does it say?

20   MS. BISHOP: Well, if the witness denies

21   having been convicted of a crime, the cross examiner is

22   not concluded by the witness's answer, but evidence of

23   a judgment of conviction is admissible to affect the

24   witness's credibility.

25   THE COURT: But correct. She was not

1   convicted.

2   MS. BISHOP: I understand, but the minutes

3   indicate she was never charged based on a promise and a

4   deal cut with the defendant who did plead guilty.

5   THE COURT: That only goes for convictions.

6   If an independent witness gets on the stand and denies

7   a conviction, then you can offer proof of that

8   conviction. But this is not a conviction. And I don't

9   think that that is covered by that section of

10   Richardson or any of the cases we looked up in the CPL

11   and the CPLR that are referred to by Richardson.

12   MS. BISHOP: Well, Judge, I don't mean to

13   beat a dead horse here, but it does go on to say that,

14   if you just read the very last paragraph about prior

15   immoral acts. And I would just ask the Court to

16   reconsider before making a final decision. It

17   references People -v- Bsorge --

18   THE COURT: That's my decision. As far as

19   the next witness you want to call, we will reserve

20   decision.

21   Tell the jury we're looking at issues of law.

22   They have to be patient. There are developments.

23   (A recess was taken.)

24   THE CLERK: Case on trial. Bring the

25   defendant out. All parties are present.

1   (The defendant entered the courtroom.)

2   THE CLERK: Defendant is present in the

3   courtroom.

4   THE COURT: Okay. On the issues before the

5   Court, in regard to the testimony to rebut the alleged

6   apology, I'm citing People -v- Wise 46 NY 2d 321,

7   People -v- Kent 80 NY 2d 845. The use of extrinsic

8   evidence to impeach a witness's credibility is

9   impermissible for his credibility by itself standing

10   alone is a collateral issue.

11   Evidence is not collateral, however, when it

12   is relevant to some issue other than credibility. The

13   collateral source rule does not apply where the issue

14   as to which the evidence relates is material to the

15   very issues that must be decided by the jury.

16   The People's witness alleged in her testimony

17   that at one point sometime after the incident the

18   defendant offered an apology, which is in the form of

19   an admission, which is therefore in the opinion of this

20   Court a material issue, one of the issues that the jury

21   must decide. Accordingly, I'm going to allow the

22   testimony of the witness as to the meeting subsequent

23   to the events where the alleged apology took place

24   limited only to whether there was that apology or not.

25   In regard to the People's application in

1   regard to the plea bargain that was made with the

2   defendant, even without naming the defendant, in return

3   for not prosecuting the defendant's witness, I find

4   that to be a collateral issue. It relates only to her

5   credibility. And, therefore, the People will be

6   precluded from offering such testimony.

7   In regard to the evidence of the contract,

8   it's the opinion of the Court that it is a method of

9   seeking to get evidence relating to alibi in in an

10   improper manner where the proper manner of presenting

11   the alibi has not been obtained. Accordingly, that

12   testimony will be precluded and the defendant has an

13   exception in the record for that. Okay. That's the

14   ruling of the Court.

15   MS. BISHOP: Your Honor, may I have a moment

16   to get the witness that the defense intends to call, to

17   get her information so I can call down and have someone

18   check to see --

19   THE COURT: You can get her name, address,

20   and place of work.

21   MS. BISHOP: And her date of birth.

22   THE COURT: Would you turn that over.

23   MR. O'MEARA: I can give the name and date of

24   birth right now. I can get the address.

25   THE COURT: All right.

```
 1              MS. BISHOP:  Yes.

 2              MR. O'MEARA:  Yes.

 3              THE COURT:  Ladies and gentlemen, I apologize

 4      for the lengthy delay.  We had several serious legal

 5      issues that had to be resolved requiring legal rulings

 6      by the Court.  And as you know the Court is the sole

 7      judge of the law and you're the sole judge of the

 8      facts, so they would not have been properly before you,

 9      only properly before me.  It took a while to resolve

10      them and we apologize for that.

11              We are now ready to continue with the next

12      witness.  All right.

13              Mr. O'Meara.

14              MR. O'MEARA:  I would like to call Katiuscia

15      Brifilis.

16   K A T I U S C I A   B R I F I L I S, a witness called on

17      behalf of the Defendant, after having been first duly

18      sworn and having stated her residence as Queens County,

19      took the witness stand and testified as follows:

20              THE COURT:  I'm going to ask you to move up

21      close to the mike so everybody can be able to hear you.

22      And keep your voice up.  Do you want to tap, see if

23      it's working?

24              All right, Mr. O'Meara.

25              MR. O'MEARA:  Thank you, your Honor.
```

1   DIRECT EXAMINATION

2   BY MR. O'MEARA:

3   Q   Miss Brifilis, can you tell us your education?

4   A   I'm a graduate student at Hunter College.

5   Q   Can you tell us your occupation?

6   A   I'm a social worker for St. Christopher Ottilie

7   in Brooklyn.

8   Q   Do you know Mr. Zimmerman?

9   A   Yes, I do.

10   Q   How do you know Mr. Zimmerman?

11   A   We used to date a couple of years ago.

12   Q   When?

13   A   From '94 up until '98.

14   Q   Do you know Nikia Stubbs?

15   A   Yes, I do.

16   Q   How do you know Nikia Stubbs?

17   A   Actually we went to high school together.

18   Q   Would you consider her a friend of yours?

19   A   No.

20   Q   An acquaintance?

21   A   We knew each other from school. Yes, an

22   acquaintance.

23   Q   Do you remember a time when Miss Stubbs made some

24   accusation against Mr. Zimmerman?

25   A   Yes.

1   Q   Do you know when that was?

2   A   I think it was about '97, '98.

3   Q   Do you remember after those accusations were made

4   a time when you met Miss Stubbs?

5   A   Yes.

6   Q   Was Mr. Zimmerman with you?

7   A   Yes.

8   Q   Can you tell me where you were going or where you

9   were coming from that day?

10   A   He was dropping me off home and she was pulling

11   into my block. And he pulled over. She pulled over. She

12   got out the car. He got out the car. And she did say a

13   couple of words to him.

14   Q   Now, just so we know exactly what you're talking

15   about, would you considered yourself one of Mr. Zimmerman's

16   other girlfriends in 1998?

17   A   I guess you can characterize it as that.

18   Q   Thank you. Now, were you present for the

19   conversation that happened, that was had between

20   Mr. Zimmerman and Miss Stubbs?

21   A   Yes.

22   Q   Now, at any time did Mr. Zimmerman ever apologize

23   to Miss Stubbs?

24   A   No, he did not.

25   Q   Did he ever admit any guilt to Miss Stubbs?

A-127

1   A   No, he did not.

2   MR. O'MEARA: No further questions, your

3   Honor.

4   THE COURT: Miss Bishop.

5   MS. BISHOP: Yes, Judge.

6   CROSS EXAMINATION

7   BY MS. BISHOP:

8   Q   All right, Miss Brifilis. Good morning.

9   A   Good morning.

10   Q   Now, you said you dated the defendant for a

11. while; is that right?

12   A   Yes.

13   Q   How long have you actually known him?

14   A   We met in my school. I have known him since '94

15   until we broke up.

16   Q   And okay, and when was that?

17   A   We broke up in about '98, the end of '98.

18   Q   So it's fair to say you two were together and

19   dating for that time period?

20   A   Yes.

21   Q   Isn't it true while you were together and dating

22   during that time period that you believed that you were his

23   exclusive girlfriend?

24   A   I guess sort of, yes.

25   Q   You did, right?

1   A   Yes.

2   Q   And isn't true that he was dishonest with you

3   about that? In fact he was seeing other people on the side?

4   MR. O'MEARA: Objection, your Honor.

5   THE COURT: Overruled.

6   Q   If you know.

7   THE WITNESS: What does that mean? What does

8   that mean?

9   THE COURT: Do you know if he was dating

10   anybody else?

11   THE WITNESS: Yeah, I knew he was dating

12   other people.

13   Q   But he told you it was all you, you two, in this

14   exclusive relationship?

15   A   In the beginning, yes.

16   Q   Now, you have come here to testify today on

17   behalf of the defendant; is that right?

18   A   Yes.

19   Q   And did you actually speak with the defendant in

20   the recent past before you came here today?

21   A   No, I did not.

22   Q   Did you speak with the defendant's attorney?

23   A   Yes, I did.

24   Q   Okay. And he let you know what was going on with

25   the trial and why you were needed to come in?

1   A   Yes, he did.

2   Q   Okay. And you agreed to come in and testify?

3   A   Yes, I did.

4   Q   Now, let's talk about what you just told the

5 members of the jury. You said that sometime either in 1997

6 or 1998 you became aware that the defendant had been charged

7 with committing certain crimes?

8   A   Yes.

9   Q   You remember that. You're not sure what year

10 but --

11   A   Exactly.

12   Q   -- at some point you know that.

13   A   Yes.

14   Q   Now, then you said you also -- there was some day

15 where you ran into Nikia Stubbs?

16   A   Um-hum.

17   Q   Do you remember what day that was?

18   A   I don't remember the exact day. No, I do not.

19   Q   Do you remember what time of the year it was?

20   A   I know it was in '98.

21   Q   Okay. So it was one of the 365 days in the year

22 1998?

23   A   Yes.

24   Q   You don't remember the season?

25   A   To tell you the truth, no.

1   Q   And so it's fair to say you definitely don't

2   remember the time of day?

3   A   Yes, I do. I know it was in the daytime.

4   Q   You do remember, you're certain it was in the

5   daytime, but you have no idea when.

6   A   Exactly.

7   Q   I see. Now, I'd like to know a little bit more

8   how this meeting took place.

9   A   Okay.

10   Q   You said that you were with Nicholas Zimmerman.

11   A   Yes.

12   Q   And that he was dropping you off?

13   A   Yes.

14   Q   At your house?

15   A   Yes.

16   Q   And is that over in Hollis?

17   A   Yes, it is.

18   Q   Okay. And you said that you saw Miss Stubbs?

19   A   Yes.

20   Q   And was she in a car? Was she on the street?

21   A   No, she was in her car with her boyfriend.

22   Q   Okay. And do you know her boyfriend?

23   A   I know him from the old neighborhood, yes.

24   Q   So she wasn't by herself.

25   A   No, she was not.

1   Q   Now, she wasn't driving either, was she?

2   A   I think she was. I'm not really too sure. I'm

3 not really certain, but I think she was.

4   Q   So really it's your testimony you don't remember

5 who was driving. It could have been her boyfriend?

6   A   It could have been her boyfriend, yes.

7   Q   And you were with the defendant?

8   A   Yes, I was.

9   Q   And were you driving or was he driving?

10   A   No, he was driving.

11   Q   He was driving. So and what was he driving?

12   A   He was driving a truck at the time. He had a

13 truck.

14   Q   Do you recall what kind of truck?

15   A   I think it was a Tahoe.

16   Q   Was it a Tahoe?

17   A   Yeah.

18   Q   And did there come a time when I guess you two

19 were driving onto -- driving on the street that you saw her.

20 You could see her through the glass, is that how this went?

21   A   Right. Actually my street is a two, two-way

22 street. So he was going in this way. She was going in that

23 way. So he was going towards my house. She was going out

24 from my house.

25   THE COURT: Indicating the opposite

1   direction?

2   THE WITNESS: Right, uh-huh.

3   Q   Now, was it your idea to stop?

4   A   No.

5   Q   Was it the defendant's idea?

6   A   Well, actually while we was driving past she

7   honked the horn or he honked the horn.   I don't recall who

8   was driving.

9   Q   And so after you heard this honk, he decided to

10   stop?

11   A   Right.

12   Q   Okay.   And how did you know he was making this

13   decision to stop?   Did he say anything?

14   A   No.

15   Q   He didn't indicate to you what he was doing.   He

16   just stopped the car?

17   A   Right, yes.

18   Q   Did you ask him why he was stopping?

19   A   No, I did not.

20   Q   And now you knew I guess by this time that he had

21   already been charged with certain crimes?

22   A   Yes.

23   Q   Okay.   And you testified that you knew that it

24   was Nikia Stubbs who had made these allegations, correct?

25   A   Yes.

1   Q   So you knew he was stopping to have some kind of

2   confrontation with her at this point?

3   A   I didn't know. I wouldn't say it was a

4   confrontation, but perhaps they were speaking. He was

5   pulling over to speak to her about something.

6   Q   Okay. Okay. And now, did he pull directly over

7   or did he have to go around the block?

8   A   No.

9   Q   How did that happen?

10   A   He pulled directly over. She pulled directly

11   over.

12   Q   There were no U-turns?

13   A   No.

14   Q   So you don't know anything about U-turns being

15   made?

16   A   No.

17   Q   And would you say that you stopped in the middle

18   of the block or down towards the end towards the corner of

19   the block?

20   A   Right towards the middle.

21   Q   So you don't know about U-turns and this happened

22   right in the middle of the block?

23   A   Yes.

24   Q   And now, after the cars came to a stop did you

25   stay in the car?

1   A   Yes, I did.

2   Q   And just so I understand, it's your testimony

3   that these cars were stopped right beside each other?

4   A   Yes, it was.

5   Q   And so you stayed in the car. And what did your

6   boyfriend do?

7   A   He got out the car. By that time Nikia had

8   already gotten out the car and her boyfriend got out the

9   car. I just lowered down the radio. The windows was open.

10   Q   The windows were down?

11   A   Yes, all the windows were down.

12   Q   And were the cars at that point facing in the

13   same direction?

14   A   They were facing the same direction right

15   opposite each other. Though not this way. Like that.

16   Q   Okay. I'm not really sure I understand that.

17   A   Okay. My block is a two-way block, like I said.

18   And we were going this way. They were going that way. So

19   the cars would face like that.

20   THE COURT: Opposite direction.

21   THE WITNESS: Right.

22   Q   They weren't facing the same direction?

23   A   No, they were not.

24   Q   They were in the opposite direction?

25   A   Right.

1   Q   So were you -- where you were sitting in the

2   defendant's Tahoe, were you closer to the middle of the

3   street or closer to the sidewalk?

4   A   Closer to the sidewalk.

5   Q   And when the defendant and the complainant's

6   boyfriend got out of the car, did they come around and stand

7   by your window?

8   A   No, they did not. They stood towards the

9   driver's window.

10   Q   They did?

11   A   Yes.

12   Q   And you said the radio was on.

13   A   No, I turned down -- the radio was on, but I

14   turned down the radio.

15   Q   Okay. And so now you just told the jury that

16   you're absolutely positive that he didn't apologize --

17   A   Uh-huh.

18   Q   -- for this incident. What did he say then?

19   A   Well, actually he didn't say that much.

20   Q   What did he say?

21   A   He got out the car. She got out the car. And --

22   Q   Just -- I'm just curious what he said.

23   A   You mean what -- I know she said that we

24   didn't --

25   Q   I'm asking --

1   A   Let me see if I can recall. He said that --

2   let's see. It was so long ago. He said --

3   THE COURT: If you don't recall, tell us you

4   don't recall.

5   A   I really can't recall.

6   Q   You don't recall what he said?

7   A   Right.

8   Q   Do you recall if he spoke?

9   A   I recall him speaking, yes.

10   Q   But you just don't recall what he said.

11   A   Right.

12   Q   Okay. So you know he spoke. You know that Miss

13   Stubbs and her boyfriend were there when he spoke?

14   A   Right.

15   Q   But you can't remember what he said.

16   A   Right.

17   Q   But you're certain he didn't apologize.

18   A   I'm pretty -- I'm certain he didn't apologize,

19   yes.

20   MS. BISHOP: Okay. I don't have any further

21   questions.

22   THE COURT: Anything else, Mr. O'Meara?

23   MR. O'MEARA: No, your Honor.

24   THE COURT: Okay.

25   THE WITNESS: That's it?

AFFIDAVITS

COMPLAINT - FOLLOW UP
INFORMATIONAL
PD 313-081A (Rev 4-85)-31

		Crime			PD	OCT		UF	PAGE
		CRIM POSS FORGED INS		105			Complaint No 3069	Date of This Report 3/14/97	14
Date of Orig Report 3/12/97	Date Assigned 3/12/97	Case No 71	Unit Reporting SPECIAL FRAUDS SQUAD					Follow-Up No 1	

Complainant's Name Last First M I

Victim's Name if Different

Last Name, First, M I				Address Include City, State, Zip					
Home Telephone		Business Telephone		Position / Relationship	Sex	Race	Date of Birth	Age	
Total No of Perpetrators	Wanted	Arrested	Weapon □ Used □ Possessed	Describe Weapon (if firearm give color make caliber type model etc)					

Wanted □	Arrested □	Last Name, First, M I					Address Include City, State, Zip			Apt No	Res Pct
Sex	Race	Date of Birth	Age	Height	Weight	Eye Color	Hair Color	Hair Length	Facial Hair	NYSID No	
□ Eyeglasses □ Sunglasses		Clothing Description									
Nickname First Name Alias		Scars, Marks, M D Etc									
		(Continue in ` Details')									

Wanted □	Arrested □	Last Name, First, M I					Address Include City, State, Zip			Apt No	Res Pct
Sex	Race	Date of Birth	Age	Height	Weight	Eye Color	Hair Color	Hair Length	Facial Hair	NYSID No	
□ Eyeglasses □ Sunglasses		Clothing Description									
Nickname First Name Alias		Scars, Marks, M D Etc									
		(Continue in Details)									

AREA WITHIN BOX FOR DETECTIVE / LATENT FINGERPRINT OFFICER ONLY. THIS BOX WILL BE UTILIZED BY INVESTIGATOR WHENEVER POSSIBLE AND MUST BE FULLY COMPLETED WHEN USING THIS FORM TO CLOSE A CASE "NO RESULTS"

Comp Interviewed □ Yes □ No	In Person □	By Phone □	Date	Time	Results Same as Comp Report - Different (Explain in Details) □ □
Witness Interviewed □ Yes □ No	In Person □	By Phone □	Date	Time	Results Same as Comp Report - Different (Explain in Details) □ □
Canvass Conducted □ Yes □ No	If Yes - Make Entry in Body Re Time, Date, Names Addresses, Results			Crime Scene Visited □ Yes □ No	If Yes - Make Entry In Details Re Time Date, Evidence Documented
Complainant Viewed Photos □ Yes □ Refused □ Future		Results			
Witness Viewed Photos □ Yes □ Refused □ Future		Results			
Crime Scene Dusted □ Yes □ No	By (Enter Results in Details)			Crime Scene Photos □ Yes □ No	By (Enter Results in Details)

If Closing Case "No Results," Check Appropriate Box and State Justification in Details:
□C-1 Improper Referral □C-2 Inaccurate Facts □C-3 No Evidence / Can't ID □C-4 Uncooperative Complainant □C-5 "Leads" Exhausted

DETAILS:

INVESTIGATION:
SUBJECT:

GRAND LARCENY CREDIT CARD
APPREHENSION OF SUBJECT

ON 3/13/97 THE UNDERSIGNED ALONG WITH THE CASE OFFICER, DET.
RALPH AIELLO, WERE PRESENT AT QUEENS POSTAL INSPECTIONS IN WHITESTONE, NY.
ALSO PRESENT WAS SGT. SEAN McCAFFERTY. POSTAL INSPECTORS MICHAEL CONNERS,
JEFF DE FURIA AND PAUL BURAK
     THE UNDERSIGNED WAS INFORMED BY DET. AIELLO THAT HE HAS A VALID
SEARCH WARRANT FOR THE BASEMENT OF 253-40 148 RD AND THAT THE SUBJECT OF
THE INVESTIGATION IS A NICHOLAS WILLIS, AKA SEAN ZIMMERMAN. NICHOLAS
ZIMMERMAN. THE SUBJECT IS KNOWN TO RESIDE AT THE ADDRESS LISTED ABOVE AND
IS SUSPECTED IN DEALINGS CONCERNING FRAUDULENT CREDIT CARDS.
     THE SUBJECT IS KNOWN TO DRIVE A GREEN 1992 MITUBISI WITH A NEW
YORK STATE REGISTRATION OF ~~~~~~~ IT IS UNCLEAR AT THIS TIME AS TO WHO THE
TRUE OWNER OF THIS VEHICLE IS.
     AT APPROXIMATELY 1200 HOURS THE UNDERSIGNED, ALONG WITH SGT.
McCAFFERTY RESPONDED TO THE SUBJECT LOCATION IN AUTO 8280. POSTAL
INSPECTOR JEFF DE FURIA IS TO ATTEMPT A CONTROLLED DELIVERY TO THE SUBJECT
ADDRESS.
     AT APPROXIMATELY 1300 THE CONTROLLED DELIVERY WAS MADE TO THE
SUBJECT ADDRESS. THE MAIL WAS PUT IN THE WHITE MAIL BOX LOCATED TO THE
LEFT OF THE DOOR. POSTAL INSPECTOR JEFF DE FURIA ATTEMPTED TO DELIVER THE
MAIL PERSONALLY TO THE SUBJECT BUT WAS TOLD TO PUT IT IN THE WHITE BOX ON
THE LEFT SIDE.
     AT APPROXIMATELY 1340 HOURS THE UNDERSIGNED OBSERVED THE DEFENDANT
EXIT THE RESIDENCE FROM THE FRONT DOOR ON THE LEFT HAND SIDE. HE WALKED
DOWN THE STAIRS. TURNED TO HIS RIGHT AND PROCEEDED TO THE BACK OF THE
HOUSE. THE DEFENDANT DISAPPEARED FROM VIEW FOR A COUPLE OF MOMENTS. HE
REAPPEARED A SHORT TIME LATER AT THE FRONT OF THE HOUSE AND WENT TOWARDS

CASE □ ACTIVE □ CLOSED		DATE REVIEWED / CLOSED 3/14/97		IF ACTIVE, DATE OF NEXT REVIEW	
OFFICER	RANK DET.	SIGNATURE	NAME PRINTED J. MULDOON	TAX REG NO 887133	COMMAND SFS
REVIEWING / CLOSING	CASE □ CLOSED	SUPER DESIGNATION C _____ OR B _____	SIGNATURE		COMMAND

EXHIBIT A

DETAILS

THE DRIVEWAY. A FEW MOMENTS LATER THE GREEN MITUBISI BACKED OUT OF THE DRIVEWAY AND WENT TO THE CORNER WHERE THE DEFENDANT MADE A LEFT HAND TURN. THE CAR THEN DISAPPEARED FROM VIEW.

AT APPROXIMATELY 1355 HOURS WE (SGT. McCAFFERTY AND THE UNDERSIGNED) PULLED OUT FROM OUR LOCATION. WE WERE GOING TO GO TO THE HOUSE OF THE DEFENDANT'S GIRLFRIEND ON ▓▓▓▓▓, AS WE PASSED THE DEFENDANT'S HOUSE SGT. McCAFFERTY STATED THAT HE SAW THE DEFENDANT ON THE SYDE OF THE HOUSE (LEFT HAND SIDE). THIS INFORMATION WAS PUT OVER THE AIR TO THE OTHER UNITS INVOLVED. WE PROCEEDED TO THE CORNER. MADE A LEFT AND THEN ANOTHER LEFT ONTO 148 DRIVE. AS WE DROVE UP 148 DRIVE I OBSERVED THE DEFENDANT'S CAR PARKED ON THE LEFT HAND SIDE (FACING THE WRONG DIRECTION) IN FRONT OF ▓▓▓▓▓▓ DRIVE. THE TRUNK TO THE AUTO WAS AJAR AT THIS TIME. WE WENT TO THE CORNER. MADE A U-TURN AND PULLED IN TO A PARKING SPOT APPROXIMATELY 100 TO 150 FEET FROM THE DEFENDANTS CAR. THE OTHER UNITS WERE INFORMED THAT THE AUTO HAD BEEN LOCATED.

APPROXIMATELY 3 TO 5 MINUTES LATER I OBSERVED THE DEFENDANT COMING OUT FROM THE ALLEYWAY OF 253-37 148 DRIVE. WE EXITED OUR VEHICLE AND APPROACHED THE DEFENDANT. SGT. McCAFFERTY WAS ON THE FAR SIDE AND I WAS ON THE SAME SIDE AS THE DEFENDANT. I OBSERVED THE DEFENDANT CARRYING A BLACK DUFFLE TYPE BAG THAT APPEARED TO HAVE SOMETHING BULKY INSIDE OF IT. HE WAS ALSO CARRYING A PLASTIC SHOPPING BAG. AS I APPROACHED HIM HE WENT TO THE REAR OF THE CAR AND PUT THESE ITEMS IN THE TRUNK. THE CAR HAD A TEMPORARY NEW YORK STATE REGISTRATION WHICH WAS ISSUED ON 2.23/97 AND DUE TO EXPIRE ON 8/16/97.

I ASKED THE DEFENDANT HIS NAME AND HE TOLD ME HE WAS JAMES SEAN AND HIS DATE OF BIRTH IS 2/15/75. I ASKED HIM ABOUT THE REGISTRATION. HE SAID HE DIDN'T KNOW TOO MUCH. THE CAR BELONGS TO HIS SISTER LINDA. I TOLD HIM THERE IS A PROBLEM WITH THE CAR. I ASKED HIM IF HIS NAME WAS NICHOLAS WILLIS. NICHOLAS ZIMMERMAN OR POSSIBLY SEAN ZIMMERMAN. HE SAID NO. THAT HIS NAME IS JAMES SEAN. HIS FATHER'S NAME IS NICHOLAS. NOT HIS. SGT. McCAFFERTY ASKED HIM IF HE HAD ANY IDENTIFICATION ON HIM. HE SAID, "NO". THE UNDERSIGNED ASKED, "WHAT IS YOUR REAL NAME. I KNOW YOU LIED TO ME BEFORE". HE SAID, "MY NAME IS NICHOLAS ZIMMERMAN AND DATE OF BIRTH IS 2/18/76". SGT. McCAFFERTY THEN ASKED HIM IF HE HAD ANY IN THE CAR? THE DEFENDANT SAID HE WASN'T SURE. SGT. McCAFFERTY ASKED HIM TO CHECK. THE DEFENDANT WENT AROUND TO THE PASSENGER SIDE OF THE VEHICLE AND OPEN THE DOOR. HE THEN WENT INTO THE GLOVE COMPARTMENT. THE GLOVE COMPARTMENT WAS FILLED WITH MUSIC COMPACT DISKS. THE DEFENDANT SAID THAT HE WAS NERVOUS AND ASKED SGT. McCAFFERTY TO LOOK IN THE GLOVE COMPARTMENT. SGT. McCAFFERTY TOLD HIM TO TAKE THE STUFF OUT OF THE GLOVE COMPARTMENT AND LOOK THROUGH IT. THE DEFENDANT DIDN'T FIND ANY IDENTIFICATION IN THERE. HE THEN SAID, "IT MIGHT BE IN MY HOUSE". I ASKED HIM WHERE HE LIVED. HE SAID THAT HE LIVES AROUND THE CORNER. I ASKED 253-40 148 ROAD. HE SAID, "YEA. 253-40 148 ROAD". SGT. McCAFFERTY ASKED WHERE IN THE HOUSE HE LIVED? HE SAID. "UPSTAIRS". SGT. McCAFFERTY ASKED WHAT ABOUT IN THE BASEMENT? HE SAID, "NO. I DON'T KNOW WHO LIVES DOWN THERE. I LIVE UPSTAIRS". SGT. McCAFFERTY THEN ASKED THE DEFENDANT IF WE COULD LOOK IN THE TRUNK OF THE CAR FOR HIS IDENTIFICATION. THE DEFENDANT SAID. "SURE". SGT. McCAFFERTY WENT TO THE REAR OF THE CAR WITH THE DEFENDANT. THE DEFENDANT HAD THE KEYS IN HIS RIGHT HAND. AS I WAS MOVING TOWARDS THE REAR OF THE CAR THE DEFENDANT BENT DOWN AS IF TO PICK SOMETHING UP. SGT. McCAFFERTY WAS AT THE REAR OF THE CAR WITH THE DEFENDANT AND I WAS NEAR THE LEFT REAR FENDER. SGT. McCAFFERTY ASKED. "WHAT IS THAT"? SGT. McCAFFERTY THEN BENT DOWN AND PICKED UP A PLASTIC BUS PASS TYPE OF A WALLET. IN THE WALLET WERE NUMEROUS CREDIT CARDS SOME OF WHICH HAD THE NAME OF NICHOLAS ZIMMERMAN AND OTHERS WHICH HAD OTHER NAMES ON THEM. THE DEFENDANT WAS PLACED UNDER ARREST FOR CRIMINAL POSSESSION OF STOLEN PROPERTY AT THAT TIME. THE TRUNK WAS THEN OPENED AND FOUND TO CONTAIN A REENCODING DEVICE. ADDITIONAL CREDIT CARDS. BLANK CREDIT CARD STOCK AND BLANK CHECK STOCK. WE RETURNED TO 253-40 WITH THE DEFENDANT AND THE CAR. THE DEFENDANT'S SISTER WAS AT HOME AND TOLD US TO COME UPSTAIRS. SGT. McCAFFERTY AND THE ASSIGNED IDENTIFIED OURSELVES AND WENT UP TO INFORM THE DEFENDANT'S SISTER LINDA THAT HE HAD BEEN ARRESTED AND SGT. McCAFFERTY ASKED HER WHO OWNS THE GREEN DIAMONTE. SHE STATED THAT THE CAR BELONGS TO NICHOLAS'S GIRLFRIEND ▓▓▓▓▓ WE ASKED IF SHE KNEW IF HE HAD ANY IDENTIFICATION IN THE HOUSE. SHE ▓▓▓▓▓▓▓▓▓▓▓▓▓▓▓▓▓▓▓▓▓▓▓▓▓▓▓▓▓▓▓▓▓ ▓▓THAT WAS ▓▓. SHE CAME OUT A SHORT TIME LATER STATING THAT SHE COULD NOT FIND ANYTHING BECAUSE THERE ARE NO LIGHTS IN THERE ▓▓▓▓A THEN ASKED IF WE HAD A SEARCH

CASE ☒ACTIVE ☐CLOSED			DATE REVIEWED/CLOSED 3/16/97		IF ACTIVE DATE OF NEXT REVIEW		
REPORTING OFFICER	RANK DET	SIGNATURE		NAME PRINTED J. MULDOON		TAX REG NO 882735	COMMAND SFS
REVIEWING/CLOSING SUPERVISOR	RANK	FULL PRESENTATION	OR	SIGNATURE		CO INITIALS	

1ST COPY CRIMINAL RECORDS SECTION

Pg. 2

COMPLAINT FOLLOW-UP INFORMATIONAL
PD 313-081A SECOND SHEET (Rev. 4-89) 21

Page	of	Pages
Pct	Complaint No	Date of This Report

DETAILS

| 105 | 3069 | 3/14/97 |

WARRANT? SHE WAS INFORMED THAT WE DID NOT HAVE A WARRANT FOR UP HERE BUT DID HAVE ONE FOR DOWN IN THE BASEMENT. SHE SAID THAT SHE DID NOT WANT US LOOKING AROUND. SHE WAS THEN INFORMED THAT WE WERE GOING TO THE JUDGE TO GET THE WARRANT AMENDED TO LOOK UP HERE IN THIS APARTMENT.

CASE ACTIVE.........

		DATE REVIEWED-CLOSED			IF ACTIVE DATE OF NEXT REVIEW		
ACTIVE CLOSED		3/16/97					
REPORTING OFFICER	RANK DET.	SIGNATURE			NAME PRINTED J. MULDOON	TAX REG NO 882735	COMMAND 87B
REVIEWING / CLOSING SUPERVISOR	CASE CLOSED	ENTRY DESCRIPTION		OR B	SIGNATURE	CO INITIALS	

1ST COPY CRIMINAL RECORDS SECTION

Pg. 3

Complaint Follow Up		Add'l Compl Codes No				4 Dr. of Report	UCCB No	12 Complaint No	File No
PD 3?4 58 - Rev 9-80			00		4	105		3069	

Date of this Report	Day of Week	Date Orig Report	Date Assigned	Last Number	Unit Reporting	
3/17/97	MON.	Mo 3 Da 13 '97	3/13/97	71F	SPECIAL FRAUDS SQD.	

Victim's Last Name First Name etc
POSTAL/ HOUSEHOLD SERVICES (JOHN CROWE)

CRIM.POSS.FORGED INSTRU.(OPEN) 729

CRIM.POSS.FORGED INSTRU.(CLOSED) 105 Q97013152

		Case Status	
		Open X Closed	

Completion Costs — Follow Up No 9

Make	License No	State	Exp	Type	No Of Plates	Vin No	
		NY	8/16/9?	PAS	2		

Year	Make	Model	Style	Color	Value	Ins Code	Policy No	
92	MITSU.	DIAMANTE SEDAN	GREEN		999			

Invoice No	Vehicle was	Alarm No	Pct	Time	Date	
A82139OV	X Used in Crime ☐ Rec v'd	NONE				

Vehicle Obtained At	Prec vinct	Towed by	Rotation Tow	Location Stored	
F/O 253-37-148DRIVE	105		☐ Yes ☐ No	WHITESTONE POUND	

Property Summary

				Item		66 Value Shown	Value Recovered
				Motor Vehicle	01		
				Container	04		
				Furs Clothing	06		
				Firearms	07		
				Once Liquid	08		
				Consumables	11		
				Misc	12		

Total No of Perpetrators	Wanted 1	Arrested 1	Weapon ☐ Used X Possessed	Describe Weapon (if firearm give color make calibre type model etc) #P018B58 .32 CAL. SEMI-AUTO,CHROME,

Wanted	Arrested X	Last Name First Name	Address Include City State Zip DAVIS INDUST	Apt No	Pers Pct
		WILLIS,NICHOLAS		2nd	105

Sex	Race	Date of Birth	Age	Height	Weight	Eye Color	Hair Color	Hair Length	Facial Hair	NYSID No
M	B			5 11	160	brown	black	short	mustache	72150130

☐ Eyeglasses ☐ Sunglasses — Clothing Description RED,WHITE,&BLACK SHIRT,BLUE JEANS,WHITE SNEAKERS
Nickname First Name Alias "ZIMMERMAN" — Scars Marks M O etc

INVESTIGATION:C.P.F.I.C.P.FORGED DEVISE,SC.TO DEFRAUD,C.C./CK.FRAUD.
SUBJECT: SEARCH WARRANT AND ARREST CLEARANCE.

On 3/12/97 based on the information provided in follow-ups #4 through
#8 I applied for and recieved a search-warrant for 253-40-148th rd.,
basement apt.(Sea.ch Werrant #201).

On 3/13/9/ myself,P.I.Defuria,P.I.Sureck,P.I.Connors, and S.A.Sautner,
Sgt.McCafferty,and Det.Muldoon were present in the vicinity of the ab-
-ove location. The suspect, Willis answered the door and stated to Defuria
-trolled delivery of the creditcards in the names of _____ ,and
_____. The suspect, Willis answered the door and stated to Defuria
that those persons lived in the basement apt. and that he should leave
the mail in the mail-box. _____ then did this and left. We then
continued to conduct surveillance and a short time later the suspect
was observed leaving the subject location. A short time later the sus-
-pect was apprehended by Sgt.McCafferty and Det.Muldoon(CONT'D ON PG.2)

Complaint Report Prepared By	SAME	Title	
DET		SFS RALPH AIELLO 908957	

ACUS

Pg. 4

the details of this are listed in Det.Muldoon's Follow-up #1. Shortly after the suspect was stopped myself, and P.I.'S Defuria and Burack arrived, this was in F/O 253-37-148th drive. At this point the suspect was asked what he had in the trunk. He then walked to the rear of the car and started to open the trunk. I then heard Sgt. McCafferty say "what's that"? The suspect then handed Sgt.McCafferty a clear plastic purse which contained credit cards in the names of Nick Zimmerman and other person's names. (2) white plastic cards w/ mag stripes, Hilton guest pass. I then arrested the above named deft. at 1405 hours in F/O the above location for the crimes of C.P.F.I.,C.P.FORGED DEVICE, C.P.S.P., and Schemeing to Defraud. Upon looking in the trunk of the above described vehicle, we discovered a re-encoding machine and a white plastic bag and a grey plastic bag which later on revealed to be containing several other credit-cards,stolen checks,counterfeit checks, blank check stock and several other documents.including people's names and addresses.

At 1445 hours the perp. was secured outside in RMP 8398. Myself,Sgt.McC--afferty,S.A.Sautner,P.I.Defuria,P.I. Connors then executed the Search Warrant(#201) in the basement apt. A thorough search of the premises was done with negative results. At 1510 hours a female identifying herself as ▓▓▓▓▓▓▓▓▓▓▓▓▓▓▓▓▓▓▓▓▓▓ apt. and wanted to know what we were doing. Myself and Sgt. McCafferty then explained to M▓▓▓ s▓▓

After the deft. was arrested, a short time later Sgt. McCafferty was in--formed by the deft's ▓▓▓▓▓▓▓ identified as ▓▓▓▓▓▓▓▓▓▓▓ that Nicholas did in fact live in the second floor apt. Based on this I then went back to ADA Peress's office where I re-applied for a 2nd search warrant, this time for the 2nd floor apt. At 1925 hours I was granted this warrant(#208).

At 2025 hours I executed the 2nd warrant(#208), along with P.I. Connors as my recorder,Sgt.McCafferty,Lt.Synan,Det.Muldoon, P.I.Defuria,p.i. Burack. and S.A. Sautner. All the items seized as a result of this warrant are listed on the attached vouchers and Queens search warrant reciept. Amongst these items were the aforementioned .32 semi-auto pistol and ammunition, another re-encoding machine,additional blank check stock, blank grey credit cards with names and mag stripe, mitsubishi credit card, I.D. with deft's photo and other perso 's names, computer terminal,keyboard, additional names addresses. and c.c. #'s.

On 3/18/97 I obtained this deft's rap-sheet,(attached) it indicates this deft. is currently on probation in Queens. I am also informed that 180.80 has been waived by the deft. A "CRIMS" search indicates this deft's. next court date is 4/1/97.(CRIMS printout attached).

| Reporting Officer's Rank/Name/Signature | Name Printed DET DFS R. AIELLO | Tax Registry No 908957 | Supervisor's Signature | Command |

A.C.C.U.

Pg. 5

THE PEOPLE OF THE STATE OF NEW YORK

v.

NICHOLAS WILLIS AKA
NICHOLAS ZIMMERMAN

DEFENDANT

STATE OF NEW YORK
COUNTY OF QUEENS

97C012139

POSTAL INSP JEFFREY DEFURIA OF USPIS, SHIELD 5048, BEING DULY SWORN,
DEPOSES AND SAYS THAT APPROXIMATELY BETWEEN MAY 1 1995 12:01 AM AND MARCH
13 1997 2:05 PM AT 253-40 148 ROAD, AND 240-06 142 AVENUE,ROSEDALE, AND
ELSEWHERE IN THE COUNTY OF QUEENS, STATE OF NEW YORK,

THE DEFENDANT COMMITTED THE OFFENSES OF:
PL 155.40-1 GRAND LARCENY IN THE SECOND DEGREE
PL 165.52 CRIMINAL POSSESSION OF STOLEN PROPERTY IN THE SECOND DEGREE
PL 170.25 CRIMINAL POSSESSION OF A FORGED INSTRUMENT SECOND DEGREE (10
          COUNTS)
PL 170.40-2 CRIMINAL POSSESSION OF FORGERY DEVICES (2 COUNTS)
PL 165.45-2 CRIMINAL POSSESSION OF STOLEN PROPERTY IN THE FOURTH DEGREE
          (15 COUNTS)
PL 190.65-1A SCHEME TO DEFRAUD IN THE FIRST DEGREE
PL 265.01   CRIMINAL POSSESSION OF A WAEPON IN THE FOURTH DEGREE

IN THAT THE DEFENDANT, ACTING IN CONCERT WITH OTHERS, DID: KNOWINGLY AND
UNLAWFULLY STEAL PROPERTY WITH A VALUE EXCEEDING FIFTY THOUSAND DOLLARS;
KNOWINGLY POSSESS STOLEN PROPERTY, THE VALUE OF WHICH EXCEEDS FIFTY
THOUSAND DOLLARS, WITH INTENT TO BENEFIT HIM/HERSELF OR A PERSON OTHER
THAN AN OWNER THEREOF OR TO IMPEDE THE RECOVERY BY AN OWNER THEREOF; WITH
INTENT TO DEFRAUD, DECEIVE OR INJURE ANOTHER AND WITH KNOWLEDGE THAT THE
INSTRUMENT WAS FORGED, UTTER OR POSSESS A FORGED INSTRUMENT OF A KIND
SPECIFIED IN SECTION 170.10 OF THE PENAL LAW; WITH INTENT TO USE, OR TO
AID OR PERMIT ANOTHER TO USE, THE SAME FOR PURPOSES OF FORGERY, MAKE OR
POSSESS A DEVICE, APPARATUS, EQUIPMENT OR ARTICLE CAPABLE OF OR ADAPTABLE
TO SUCH USE; KNOWINGLY POSSESS STOLEN PROPERTY CONSISTING OF A CREDIT
CARD, DEBIT CARD OR PUBLIC BENEFIT CARD WITH INTENT TO BENEFIT HIM/HERSELF
OR A PERSON OTHER THAN THE OWNER THEREOF OR TO IMPEDE THE RECOVERY BY THE
OWNER THEREOF; ENGAGE IN A SCHEME CONSTITUTING A SYSTEMATIC ONGOING COURSE
OF CONDUCT WITH INTENT TO DEFRAUD TEN OR MORE PERSONS OR TO OBTAIN
PROPERTY FROM TEN OR MORE PERSONS BY FALSE OR FRAUDULENT PRETENSES,
REPRESENTATIONS OR PROMISES, AND SO DID OBTAIN PROPERTY FROM ONE OR MORE
OF SUCH PERSONS; POSSESS A FIREARM.

THE SOURCE OF DEPONENT'S INFORMATION AND THE GROUNDS FOR DEPONENT'S
BELIEF ARE AS FOLLOWS:

DEPONENT STATES THAT ON OR ABOUT MARCH 13, 1997, HE AND MEMBERS OF THE

Pg. 6

NYPD, US POSTAL INSPECTION SERVICE ("USPIS") AND US SECRET SERVICE
("USSS") EXECUTED SEARCH WARRANTS #201/97 AND 208/97 AT 253-40 148 ROAD,
ROSEDALE, QUEENS, WHICH WERE SIGNED BY THE HON. JUDGE STEVEN PAYNTER ON
MARCH 12 AND 13, 1997, RESPECTIVELY.

DEPONENT FURTHER STATES THAT PURSUANT TO THE SEARCH OF THE
ABOVE-MENTIONED LOCATION, THE DEFENDANT'S PERSON, AND A 1992 MITSUBISHI
DIAMANTE DRIVEN BY THE DEFENDANT AT THE TIME OF HIS ARREST AND WHICH
DEPONENT HAS SEEN THE DEFENDANT DRIVING AND HAS SEEN PARKED AT THE 148
ROAD LOCATION'S DRIVEWAY IN THE COURSE OF SURVEILLANCE CONDUCTED BY HIM IN
1997, DEPONENT RECOVERED PROPERTY INCLUDING IN EXCESS OF TWENTY-FIVE
VISA, MASTERCARD, AMERICAN EXPRESS, JC PENNEY AND OTHER CREDIT CARDS IN
THE NAMES OF INDIVIDUALS OTHER THAN THE DEFENDANT; PHOTO IDENTIFICATION
CARDS BEARING THE PHOTO OF THE DEFENDANT IN NAMES OTHER THAN THAT OF THE
DEFENDANT; PLASTIC CARDS PURPORTING TO BE CREDIT CARDS IN VARIOUS STAGES
OF COMPLETION; BLANK PLASTICS; TWO ENCODING MACHINES; PERSONAL AND COMPANY
CHECKS IN THE NAMES OF INDIVIDUALS OTHER THAN THAT OF THE DEFENDANT;
DOCUMENTS PURPORTING TO BE BUSINESS CHECKS IN VARIOUS STAGES OF
COMPLETION; REAMS OF BLANK BASKET WEAVE CHECK STOCK PAPER; DOCUMENTS
BEARING THE NAMES AND PERSONAL AND/OR FINANCIAL INFORMATION, INCLUDING
SOCIAL SECURITY NUMBERS, OF MORE THAN 200 INDIVIDUALS; CONVENIENCE AND
PERSONAL CHECKS OF INDIVIDUALS OTHER THAN THE DEFENDANT; MERCHANT RECEIPTS
IN NAMES OTHER THAN THAT OF THE DEFENDANT BEARING THE CREDIT CARD NUMBERS
AND SIGNATURES OF NUMEROUS CREDIT CARD HOLDERS; COMPUTER AND DISKS BEARING
PERSONAL AND FINANCIAL INFORMATION OF INDIVIDUALS OTHER THAN THE
DEFENDANT; CHECK ENDORSEMENT STAMP; CREDIT CARD, FINANCIAL AND PERSONAL
MAIL ADDRESSED TO INDIVIDUALS OTHER THAN THE DEFENDANT;AND A.32 CALIBER
SEMI-AUTOMATIC FIREARM, ONE LOADED MAGAZINE, AND IN EXCESS OF 40 ROUNDS OF
AMMUNITION.

DEPONENT FURTHER STATES THAT AS A US POSTAL INSPECTOR, HE HAS RECEIVED
TRAINING AND IS EXPERIENCED IN THE DETECTION OF COUNTERFEIT CHECKS AND
CREDIT CARDS. DEPONENT FURTHER STATES THAT SINCE JUNE, 1995, HE HAS BEEN
ASSIGNED TO AN INVESTIGATION OF STOLEN AND COUNTERFEIT CHECK FRAUD AND
CREDIT CARD FRAUD AND THAT PURSUANT TO THAT INVESTIGATION, HE HAS
CONDUCTED SURVEILLANCE OF THE DEFENDANT, HIS RESIDENCE AND THE MAIL
DELIVERED TO HIS RESIDENCE. DEPONENT STATES THAT BETWEEN JULY, 1996
AND MARCH 13, 1997, MAIL IN THE NAMES OF MORE THAN FORTY INDIVIDUALS,
INCLUDING ENVELOPES CONTAINING CREDIT CARDS, WERE DELIVERED TO THE
DEFENDANT TO THE DEFENDANT AT HIS 148 ROAD ADDRESS.

DEPONENT IS INFORMED BY NANCY LUCAS, FRAUD INVESTIGATOR FOR BANK ONE,
THAT NICK ZIMMERMAN WAS LISTED AS THE SECONDARY ACCOUNT USER ON AT LEAST
TEN ACCOUNTS WHICH WERE OPENED AT THE REQUEST OF AN INDIVIDUAL NAMED NICK
ZIMMERMAN AND THAT CREDIT CARDS WERE SENT TO SAID INDIVIDUAL 148 STREET
ADDRESS OR AT 240-06 142 AVENUE, JAMAICA BETWEEN DECEMBER, 1996 AND
JANUARY, 1997 AND THAT ALL OF THE APPLICATIONS USED TO OPEN THESE CREDIT
CARDS CONTAIN FALSE INFORMATION AND THAT AS A RESULT OF ISSUING SAID
CREDIT CARDS, BANK ONE HAS SUFFERED LOSSES IN EXCESS OF $25,000.00
DEPONENTIS FURTHER INFORMED THAT THE DEFENDANT DID NOT HAVE THE PERMISSIO
OR AUTHORITY OF BANK ONE TO POSSESS THESE CARDS OR USE THEM AND THAT THE
TOTAL CREDIT VALUE OF SAID CARDS EXCEEDS $30,000.00. DEPONENT FURTHER
STATES THAT SIX OF THE ABOVE-MENTIONED CREDIT CARDS WERE RECOVERED
PURSUANT TO THE ABOVE-MENTIONED SEARCH AND ARREST ON MARCH 13, 1997, AND
THAT THE OTHER BANK ONE CARDS IN THE SAME NAME WERE RECOVERED FROM THE

Pg. 7

Exhibit C

Defendant: WILLIS, NICHOLAS   Page 3

DEFENDANT PURSUANT TO HIS JANUARY, 1997 ARREST IN NEW YORK COUNTY.

DEPONENT IS INFORMED BY TIM HALE, FRAUD INVESTIGATOR FOR HOUSEHOLD CREDIT
SERVICES THAT TWO CREDIT CARD ACCOUNTS WERE OPENED IN JULY, 1996 AND
SEPTEMBER, 1996 RESPECTIVELY FOR GEORGE LEWIS AND MICHAEL ALLEN, ONE AT
THE 148 ROAD ADDRESS AND THAT AS A RESULT, HOUSEHOLD HAS SUFFERED LOSSES
IN EXCESS OF $7500.00. DEPONENT STATES THAT TWO CREDIT CARDS IN THE NAMES
OF GEORGE LEWIS AND MICHAEL ALLEN AND A HANDWRITTEN LIST BEARING THOSE
NAMES AND PERSONAL INFORMATION OF THOSE INDIVIDUALS WAS RECOVERED
PURSUANT TO THE ABOVE-MENTIONED SEARCH AND ARREST ON MARCH 13, 1997.

DEPONENT IS INFORMED BY HILTON BROOKS, FRAUD INVESTIGATOR FOR ATT
UNIVERSAL CREDIT CARD SERVICES THAT THREE ACCOUNTS IN THE NAMES OF NICK
ZIMMERMAN AND JATANYA BELNAVIS WERE OPENED AND THAT ATT SUFFERED LOSSES IN
EXCESS OF $21,000.00. DEPONENT STATES THAT THE ATT CREDIT CARD IN THE NAME
OF BELNAVIS AND DOCUMENTS CONTAINING OTHER PERTINENT INFORMATION WERE
RECOVERED PURSUANT TO THE ABOVE-MENTIONED SEARCH AND ARREST ON MARCH 13,
1997.

DEPONENT STATES THAT THE CREDIT CARDS RECOVERED PURSUANT TO THE
ABOVE-MENTIONED SEARCH AND ARREST INCLUDED SEVEN MITSUBISHI CREDIT
CARDS IN THE NAMES OF LINCOLN STEWART , ALIMI BANJOKO, SANIEL SAMANIEGO,
MALVALENE HURSEFIELD, VARNEL FOUCAULT, ROBERT BRYAN, AND BRENTON BARETT.
DEPONENT IS INFORMED BY JOHN CROWE, INVESTIGATOR FOR HOUSEHOLD CREDIT
SERVICES THAT HOUSEHOLD IS THE CREDIT CARD INSTITUTION WHICH ISSUES SAID
CARDS FOR INDIVIDUALS WHO APPLY FOR CREDIT AT "THE WIZ" APPLIANCE STORES.
DEPONENT IS FURTHER INFORMED BY MR. CROWE THAT THE DEFENDANT DID NOT HAVE
THE AUTHORITY OR PERMISSION OF HOUSEHOLD TO POSSESS OR USE SAID CREDIT
CARDS AND THAT THE TOTAL CREDIT VALUE OF SAID CARDS EXCEEDS $35,000.00.

DEPONENT STATES THAT THE CREDIT CARDS RECOVERED PURSUANT TO THE
ABOVE-MENTIONED SEARCH AND ARREST INCLUDED TWO CORPORATE AMERICAN EXPRESS
CARDS IN THE NAMES OF CARUSO AND MORANCIE. DEPONENT FURTHER STATES THAT
HE RAN FIVE OF THE CARDS RECOVERED THROUGH A BANK IDENTIFICATION READER,
INCLUDING A THIS-END-UP CARD, THREE SONY BANK OF NEW YORK CARDS, ONE
BLANK WHITE PLASTIC CARD, AND A FIRST CARD AND OBSERVED THAT THE
MAGNETIC STRIPES ON SAID FIVE CARDS WERE ENCODED WITH CREDIT CARD ACCESS
NUMBERS WHICH BASED ON HIS TRAINING AND EXPERIENCE, DEPONENT IS AWARE THAT
THEY BELONG TO AMERICAN EXPRESS, WHICH BEGIN WITH THE NUMBERS 37...
DEPONENT FURTHER STATES THAT PURSUANT TO THE ABOVE-MENTIONED SEARCH
WARRANT, HE RECOVERED AN PORTABLE ENCODER AND FROM HIS TRAINING AND
EXPERIENCE, HE KNOWS THAT SAID DEVICE IS USED TO ERASE AND REENCODE
COUNTERFEIT AND ALTERED CREDIT CARDS WITH LEGITIMATE CREDIT CARD NUMBERS
ASSIGNED TO LEGITIMATE CREDIT CARDHOLDERS, AND THAT IN THE NORMAL COURSE
OF BUSINESS, CREDIT CARD COMPANIES DO NOT USE PORTABLE ENCODERS TO ENCODE
OR DECODE CREDIT CARDS. DEPONENT IS INFORMED BY DENNIS MACMANMON, FRAUD
INVESTIGATOR FOR AMERICAN EXPRESS THAT THE DEFENDANT DID NOT HAVE THE
PERMISSION OR AUTHORITY OF AMERICAN EXPRESS TO POSSESS SAID CARDS AND THAT
SAID CARDS WERE APPLIED FOR USING THE DEFENDANT'S 148 ROAD ADDRESS, OR
ENCODE ANY CARDS WITH NUMBERS BELONGING TO AMERICAN EXPRESS.

DEPONENT STATES THAT BASED ON THE ABOVE, THE DEFENDANT HAS STOLEN IN
EXCESS OF FIFTY THOUSAND DOLLARS USING STOLEN AND FRAUDULENTLY OBTAINED
CREDIT CARDS AND THAT AT THE TIME OF HIS ARREST, POSSESSED CREDIT CARDS
WITH AN AGGREGATE CREDIT VALUE OF IN EXCESS OF $100,000.

Pg. 8

Exhibit C

Defendant : WILLIS, NICHOLAS   Page 4

DEPONENT FURTHER STATES THAT PURSUANT TO THE ABOVE-MENTIONED SEARCH
WARRANT, HE RECOVERED EIGHT GREY PLASTIC CARDS EMBOSSED WITH THE NAMES OF
LEGITIMATE INDIVIDUALS WHOSE NAMES AND PERSONAL INFORMATION ARE LISTED ON
DOCUMENTS ALSO RECOVERED FROM SAID LOCATION AND THAT SAID PLASTIC CARDS
ALSO CONTAIN VISA NUMBERS AND EXPIRATION DATES. DEPONENT FURTHER STATES
THAT BASED ON HIS TRAINING AND EXPERIENCE HE IS AWARE THAT THE NUMBERS,
WHICH BEGIN WITH A 4.., ARE CREDIT CARD ACCESS NUMBERS OF VISA AND THAT
SAID GREY PLASTIC CARDS ARE COUNTERFEIT VISA CARDS WHICH CAN BE USED WITH
COLLUSIVE MERCHANTS OR MAIL ORDER COMPANIES DESPITE THE FACT THAT THEY AF
NOT COMPLETED INSTRUMENTS.

DEPONENT FURTHER STATES THAT IN THE COURSE OF THE ABOVE-MENTIONED
INVESTIGATION, HE HAS RECOVERED COUNTERFEIT CHECKS AND COPIES OF
COUNTERFEIT CHECKS WHICH SINCE AT LEAST MAY 1, 1995 HAVE BEEN
NEGOTIATED AND INCURRED LOSSES IN EXCESS OF $60,000.00 TO LEGITIMATE
COMPANIES AND ACCOUNT HOLDERS OF THE BANK ACCOUNTS REPRESENTED ON THOSE
CHECKS AND THAT SEVERAL OF THE CHECKS WERE MADE OUT TO AND ENDORSED BY
JATANYA BELNAVIS. DEPONENT IS INFORMED BY THE DEFENDANT THAT JATANYA
BELNAVIS IS HIS GIRLFRIEND. DEPONENT IS INFORMED BY JATANYA BELNAVIS THA
SHE IS THE DEFENDANT'S GIRLFRIEND AND THAT SHE LIVES AT 240-06 142 AVENU
IN ROSEDALE. DEPONENT FURTHER STATES THAT OTHER CHECKS WERE MADE OUT TO
AND CASHED BY COMPUTER COMPANIES FOR $33,000.00 IN COMPUTER EQUIPMENT
WHICH WAS DELIVERED TO SEVERAL QUEENS AND BROOKLYN LOCATIONS WHICH ARE
INDICATED IN DOCUMENTS RECOVERED PURSUANT TO THE SEARCH AND ARREST ON
MARCH 13, 1997. DEPONENT FURTHER STATES THAT BASED ON HIS TRAINING AND
EXPERIENCE AND PURSUANT TO SAID SEARCH, HE RECOVERED A PORTABLE DEVICE
WHICH ENCODES THE BANK ACCOUNT NUMBERS, TRANSIT NUMBERS AND OTHER REQUIF
NUMBERS ON THE BOTTOM OF CHECKS, AND IS CAPABLE OF ENCODING THE AMOUNT C
THE CHECKS AS FOR EXAMPLE ON PRINTED PAYROLL CHECK, DOCUMENTS WHICH
PURPORTED TO BE CORPORATE CHECKS IN VARIOUS STAGES OF COMPLETION, AN
ENDORSEMENT SIGNATURE STAMP AND GREEN INKPAD AND HAS OBSERVED THAT SEVEF
OF THE PURPORTED CHECKS BEAR COMPANY NAMES, BANK ACCOUNT NUMBERS AND THP
ENDORSEMENT STAMP. DEPONENT FURTHER STATES THAT HE RECOVERED SEVERAL REJ
OF BASKET WEAVE CHECK STOCK CONTAINING THE SAME PAPER AS THAT USED TO
CREATE THE ABOVE-MENTIONED PURPORTED CHECKS, AND THAT THE PAPER IS THE
SAME AS THAT USED IN RECOVERED NEGOTIATED COUNTERFEIT CHECKS FROM THE
ABOVE-MENTIONED INVESTIGATION. DEPONENT IS ALSO INFORMED BY JEANETTE
FELDER THAT SHE LIVES AT THE 148 ROAD ADDRESS AND THAT IN MAY, 1995, BL
CHECKS ON HER PERSONAL ACCOUNT WERE STOLEN FROM THE MAIL AND THAT CHECK
WERE COMPLETED AND NEGOTIATED ON THAT ACCOUNT WITHOUT HER AUTHORITY OR
PERMISSION AND THAT THE DEFENDANT DOES NOT HAVE HER PERMISSION OR
AUTHORITY TO POSSESS HER MAIL AND CHECKS. DEPONENT FURTHER STATES THAT
PURSUANT TO THE ABOVE-MENTIONED SEARCH, HE RECOVERED MAIL IN THE NAME O
JEANETTE FELDER, ADDRESSED TO HER AT THE 148 ROAD ADDRESS, FROM THE
DEFENDANT'S POSSESSION AS WELL AS MAIL ADDRESSED TO OTHER TENANTS OF TH
148 ROAD RESIDENTIAL BUILDING. DEPONENT IS FURTHER INFORMED THAT HE
PROVIDED A COPY OF A CHECK WHICH PURPORTS TO BE A CHECK OF MC&R MAJESTI
AUTO SALES IN BROOKLYN, NEW YORK TO MR. MOSHE, SALES MANAGER OF THAT
BUSINESS AND IS INFORMED BY MR. MOSHE THAT SAID CHECKS WERE COUNTERFEI
THAT THEY BORE THE NAME, BANK ACCOUNT AND ADDRESS OF SAID BUSINESS BUT
FORM APPEARANCE AND STYLE OF THE CHECKS ARE UNLIKE COMPANY CHECKS EVER
USED BY SAID BUSINESS AND THAT THE DEFENDANT DID NOT HAVE PERMISSION OF
AUTHORITY TO POSSESS, USE OR DUPLICATE CHECKS OF SAID BUSINESS.

FALSE STATEMENTS MADE IN THIS DOCUMENT ARE
PUNISHABLE AS A CLASS A MISDEMEANOR PURSUAN'

Pg. 9

SUPREME COURT OF THE STATE OF NEW YORK
COUNTY OF QUEENS

—————————————————————————X

PEOPLE OF THE STATE OF NEW YORK

NOTICE OF ALIBI
INDICTMENT NO.: 3296/98

-against-

NICHOLAS ZIMMERMAN
                    Defendant

—————————————————————————X

SIR/MADAM:

PLEASE TAKE NOTICE that the above named Defendant intends to offer a defense at the trial of this action that at the time of the commission of the crime charged that he was at some place or places other than the scene of the crime, to wit: At the Club Jamrock, located on Fulton Street in Hempstead, NY.

PLEASE TAKE FURTHER NOTICE that the Defendant intends to call the following witnesses in support of such defense:

Andre Dallyrymple	10 York Drive, Wyandanch, NY	(914) 738-3050
Brian Dallyrymple	10 York Drive, Wyandanch, NY	(914) 738-3050
Chris Dallyrymple	10 York Drive, Wyandanch, NY	(914) 738-3050

Dated: Bronx, New York -
       11/23/01

Yours,

Brendan O'Meara, Esq.,
Attorney for Defendant
O'Meara & Associates
304 Grand Concourse
Bronx, New York 10451
Tel. (718) 585-2315

TO: CLERK, CRIMINAL COURT
      CRIMINAL COURT
      QUEENS COUNTY

      OFFICE OF THE DISTRICT ATTORNEY
      QUEENS COUNTY

Barry "Sidiq" Alexander, being duly sworn deposes and says:

1. On August 18, 1998, my partner, Theophulus Brown and I, Barry "Sidiq" Alexander signed a contract with Haron Wilson, acting as management for Nicholas Zimmerman (Puzz Pacino) to perform at Jamroc Nightclub (45 Main Street, Hempstead, New York 11550), on September 18, 1998.

2. In keeping with the contract agreement, Mr. Zimmerman and Mr. Wilson arrived at the club around 2:00am in the morning of September 19, 1998. At which point they were escorted to the V.I.P section ot the club where my partner and I, had a brief conversation with Mr. Zimmerman about his performance schedule. At which point, Mr. Zimmerman performed at his scheduled time of 2:30am, until 3:00am.

3. Afterwards, Mr. Zimmerman had brief conversations with other artists and media executives. At some time after the show, Mr. Zimmerman and I discussed doing other venues together in the future.

4. About two weeks later rumors were circulating that Mr. Zimmerman had been arrested. Approximately two months after that Mr. Zimmerman contacted my office about doing some other venues in the area. I told him that I did not feel comfortable doing venues with him because if he were to get sentenced to any jail time behind the allegations, then it would be my company that would lose out on any promotions for events we would do together.

5. On or about December 6, 2001, I received a call from Jatanya Belnavis asking me to testify on Mr. Zimmerman's behalf about his whereabouts that morning, September 18, 1998, and I agreed.

6. I called Brendan O'Mears, the following day, and explained to him that I was with Mr. Zimmerman on September 19, 1998 around 3:00am and he said

Pg. 11

I would not be able to testify because he forgot to add my name to the alibi list.

Subscribed and sworn to
before me, this 4 day of
November, 2002.

_____
NOTARY-PUBLIC
LENNOX A. BOUYEA
NOTARY PUBLIC, State of New York
No. 52-4662133
Qualified in Suffolk County
Commission Expires April 30, 2003

Barry Alexander

Pg. 12

Exhibit F

AFFIDAVIT

On September 18, 1998, I, Latina Boyd, was scheduled to perform at Jamroc Nightclub (45 Main Street, Hempstead, NY 11550). In keeping with the contract agreement with the club promoter I arrived at the club around 1:00am on September 19, 1998. At this point I was escorted to the V.I.P section of the club. I then had a brief conversation with the promoters of the event and they informed me that I would be performing after Mr. Zimmerman (Puzz Pacino), which would be around 3:00am.

I paid close attention to the stage when they announced Mr. Zimmerman because I was told that he had a very good stage performance. According to schedule I watched Mr. Zimmerman (Puzz Pacino) perform on stage around 2:30am until 3:00am. After my performance, I met Mr. Zimmerman (Puzz Pacino) backstage and he said he liked my performance and I said I liked his. We then exchanged phone numbers and both agreed that we would work together in the future.

About a week later I heard through media reports that Mr. Zimmerman (Puzz Pacino) had been arrested for a robbery that happened the same night of the performance. I asked him about it and he denied it was him and said it was all a big misunderstanding. On or about December 6, 2001, Mr. Zimmerman (Puzz Pacino) called me and told me that he needed me to give an affidavit to the Court in relation to that night, and I agreed. He gave me his lawyer's phone number and I called him later that evening and explained to him that I was with Mr. Zimmerman (Puzz Pacino) on the night of the incident. He told me that he had enough witnesses to win the case and if he needed me he would call me, but he never called.

Subscribed and sworn to
before me, this 31 day of
October, 2002.

Latina Boyd

Jason L. Russo, Notary Public
State of New York
Qualified in Suffolk County
Reg. No. 02RU6025589
Commission Expires 20 07
June 1, 2007

Pg. 13

Exhibit G

Affidavit

Samuel Belnavis, being duly sworn deposes and says:

On September 19, 1998 around 3:00am a young lady I've come to know as Nikia Stubbs came to my house ringing my bell repeatedly. When I came to the door I heard her yelling something about a car she had rented to my daughter's boyfriend, Nicholas Zimmerman. My daughter then informed Miss Stubbs that Nicholas wasn't there; he had a performance that night and would not be back until early morning. Nikia then said she would wait outside until he came back. After putting on clothes, which took no longer than ten minutes, my daughter went outside to the car to talk to Nikia. I was standing in my doorway

At some point during the conversation my daughter turned away from the car and started to run back towards the house. At the same time two men walked from Brookville Boulevard passing directly in front of my house and stopped a few houses behind where Nikia's car was parked. I then saw a man I have since learned was Wilson Barnes emerge from Nikia's car with pistol in hand and walk down towards the two men. At some point during the conversation one of the three men holding a gun in his hand fired the gun into the air several times while yelling profanity and threats at my daughter. Nikia sped off. From my house doorway, to the sidewalk, I could clearly see the men that walked by.

None of the men were Nicholas Zimmerman. Since Mr. Zimmerman has been dating my daughter for the past 9 years I would be able to spot him instantly. That night he was not one of the three men in the conversation or the man who fired the gun.

Subscribed and sworn to
before me, this _14_ day of
N o v e m b e r , 2002.

_____
Notary Public

_____
Samuel Belnavis

HERBERT C. ROSEMAN
Notary Public, State of New York
No. 01RO4612601
Qualified in Kings County
Certificate Filed in New York County
Commission Expires Dec 31, 2005

Pg. 14

AFFIDAVIT

Natasha Dockery, being duly sworn deposes and says:

On September 19, 1998 I arrived at my house (240-07-142nd Ave) around 2:30am after being out on a date. When I got in I took a shower and got ready for bed. While I was dressing I heard a loud conversation outside. When I looked outside I noticed two of my friends (Nikia Stubbs and Jatanya Belnavis) along with Nikia's boyfriend Wilson. I paid the conversation no mind because I was tired and I didn't feel like going back outside.

The conversation started getting louder and louder so I went back to my window to see what was going on. When I got to the window I saw Wilson with two other men across the street yelling and cursing about a car. Wilson turned and began to fire several shots in the air. I then ducked to the floor of my bedroom. After the shots were over I went back to window and I saw Nikia Stubbs car making a left turn at the corner.

Around the time of the trial for Mr. Zimmerman, Jatanya and Nicholas contacted me to testify on his behalf and I agreed. They said that a lawyer was going to contact me to get a statement but no lawyer ever called.

Subscribed and sworn to
before me, this 9th day of
_____, 2002.

_____
NOTARY PUBLIC

Natascha Dockery

REISEL R DEUTSCHER
Notary Public, State of New York
No. 01DE4903427
Qualified in Nassau County
Commission Expires Aug 24, 2005

Pg. 15

Exhibit I

Affidavit

I Nikia Stubbs make the following statement of my own free will. I have not been threatened or promised anything in exchange for this statement and swear to its truthfulness.

On the morning of September 19, 1998, I filed a complaint with the 105th precinct alleging that a male by the name of Sean who reportedly lived in Rosedale NY had forcefully pulled me from my car brandishing a gun. I was thrown to the ground and during the confrontation approximately nine (9) shots were fired into the air while he was threatening to kill me. She told the police she knew Sean's address and thought he might have been convicted of a crime. At the 105th precinct she looked at over a 1000 photographs on the computer and saw many that resemble Sean but she wasn't sure if any of them were him. Ultimately I didn't pick out anyone. The detectives drove her home but came back later that same night, this time with just one photograph. One of the Detectives said "Is this the guy?" and she responded "Yeah, that looks like him". They told me the person in the picture was named Nicholas Zimmerman but he also used the name Sean

Several days later the detectives from the 105th pct. called me. They advised me that Nicholas Zimmerman had been arrested and I would be contacted by the District Attorney's Office to testify before the Grand Jury.

A few weeks later I got a call to come to the Grand Jury and testify and I did, telling them the story about what happened. A few weeks after I testified Jatanya Behavis contacted me. She asked me to drop the charges against Sean because I had identified and implicated the wrong man. The person that had been arrested turned out to be her boyfriend. Having been convinced by the detectives that I had identified the right person I ignored the request. In the three years between the day of the incident and the trial I was receiving a lot of information from family and friends that I might have identified and had the wrong person arrested. I even heard a rumor that another male name Sean was confessing to the crime to a few of his friends. Nicholas Zimmerman even approached me one day and said he was sorry for what happened to me but couldn't understand why I was saying it was him who did it. He told me he had nothing to do with it.

When the District Attorney contacted me and informed me of their readiness to prosecute the case I was not cooperative in the beginning. I had my own issues to deal with. I had an open Federal case and was out on $150,000 bail. When the District Attorney wasn't able to find me they contacted my father in Florida because he used to work for them as an investigator and he told me to get in touch with the ADA who was handing the case which she did. The District Attorney told me that if I refused to cooperate I would be arrested on a Material Witness Order and held in jail until I testified. After continually telling the District Attorney that I didn't want to testify I was persuaded to pursue the

Pg. 16

conviction. I reluctantly testified at the trial that Nicholas Zimmerman was the person who committed the crime and he was convicted.

I have since contacted Jatanya Belnavis and apologized for what I believe might have been a grave error. She accepted my apology and said that Nicholas' attorney would contact me to get a full statement.

I would like to express my deepest regrets to the courts and Mr. Zimmerman for having possibly accused the wrong man. The day the incident occurred I was extremely scared by what happened and was only 50 to 60 percent sure that it was Sean who committed the crime. I had actually only seen Sean on two (2) occasions prior to the incident and that was months earlier for about 5 minutes each time. I never spent any period of time in his company. I associated him with Jatanya Belnavis. At the time of the trial I was nervous about my own situation (Federal case) and when the District Attorney threatened to have me arrested on a Material Witness Order I thought it would impact my bail status so I testified even though I thought I might have been mistaken about it being Zimmerman who fired the shots.

Although I testified truthfully about the scenario that happened the day of the incident I wasn't absolutely certain then that it was Nicholas Zimmerman who committed the crime against me then. When the detectives came back to my house with just one photograph and it resembled the person involved I told the police I thought it was him. I never viewed a line-up and the first time I saw Zimmerman face to face after the incident was when he spoke to me in the street and apologized for what happened to me but said it wasn't him who did it.

I respectfully recant any and all testimony I provided at Nicholas Zimmerman's trial that indicated that I was certain that it was Nicholas Zimmerman who committed the crime against me.

I have read the above statement prepared by Mr. Kevin W. Hinkson, a NYS Licensed and Bonded Private Investigator with offices at 32 Court Street suite 707, Brooklyn NY, 11201, (718) 625-2634. He has made no promises to me in exchange for this statement.

Nika Stubbs _Nika Stubbis_   3/24/03
Nika Stubbs   Date

Subscribed to me this ___24th___ day of March 2003

signature
Notary Public

Pg. 17

January 5, 2002

To: Honorable Judge R. Rosengarten
      125-01 Queens Blvd
      Supreme Court, K-20
      Kew Gardens, NY 11415

From: Haron Wilson
      334 Blake Ave
      Brooklyn, NY 11203

Dear Mr. Rosengarten:

I am a personal friend and manager to Nicholas Zimmerman, since 1996 I have helped Mr. Zimmerman with music production, legal work, and performances. On the afternoon of August 18, 1998, I signed a contract with D-UP Entertainment to have Mr. Zimmerman perform at the Jam Roc Nightclub located at 45 Main Street, Hempstead NY 11701. In keeping our contract agreement with D- UP Entertainment, Mr. Zimmerman and I arrived at the Jam Roc NightClub around 2:00 am on Sept. 19, 2001 at which Mr. Zimmerman performed on stage around 2:40 to about 3:00am. After the performance, Mr. Zimmerman took pictures, signed autographs, and did television interviews for another hour or so after the event.

I can testify that I was with Mr. Zimmerman from 1:00 am to about 4:30 am on the morning of Sept 19, 1998, when I attempted to offer this evidence at trial it was ruled that the alibi notice was recieved late and my testimony would not be allowed. Mr. Zimmerman's lawyer has tried to contact me, but I changed my number in the last couple of months and it took a little longer to find me. I asked the courts in charge of this matter to understand that Mr. Zimmerman only had a couple of days to locate me and bring me to court to testify and they had to go through a few channels to find me. If Mr. Zimmerman was given a new trial I would be more happy to testify on his behalf.

If there are any questions and you need to talk to me please feel free to contact me at 1. 917. 204. 8509. Thank You

Sincerely Yours,

Heron Wilson

Pg. 18

Exhibit K

AFFIDAVIT

Theophulus Brown, being duly sworn deposes and says:

1. On August 18, 1998 I signed a contract with Haron Wilson to have Mr. Zimmerman perform at Jamroc nightclub on September 18, 1998.

2. In keeping with the contract agreement, Haron Wilson and Nicholas Zimmerman arrived at Jamroc nightclub (45 Main Street, Hempstead, New York 11550) around 2:00am on September 19, 1998. When they arrived the two of them were escorted to the V.I.P. section of the club where I had a brief conversation with Mr. Zimmerman about his performance time.

3. Mr. Zimmerman performed at his scheduled time of 2:30am and closed his performance around 3:00am. Afterwards Mr. Zimmerman did television interviews that I had arranged for him for about another hour or so.

4. About a week later I heard through media reports that Mr. Zimmerman had been arrested for an incident that allegedly happened the same night he performed for me. I paid the coverage no mind because I figured it would be resolved once they found out where he was that night.

5. On or around December 6, 2001, I got a call from Jatunya Belnavis asking me to testify on behalf of Mr. Zimmerman and I agreed. She gave me his lawyer's (Brendan O'Meara) telephone number, which I called and left two messages. Either that night or the following day he called back and I told him the story and he said he would call me back if I had to testify.

Pg. 19

6. The next time I heard from Brendan was on December 15, 2001 and he asked me if I was willing to come in and testify the next day, as to my knowledge of Mr. Zimmerman's whereabouts the night in question. I arrived at the Courthouse the next day and was told I would not be allowed to testify in the case.

7. I was never called as a witness in Mr. Zimmerman's case.

Subscribed and sworn to
before me, this 31 day of
October , 2002.

_____
NOTARY PUBLIC

Theophulus Brown

Jason L. Russo, Notary Public
State of New York
Qualified in Suffolk County
Reg. No. 02RU6025569
Commission Expires 20 07
June 1, 2007

Pg. 20

'MY OWN WOMAN'

"When I go home, I'm not the DA. I talk to my son about his day, I talk to my daughter about her day. ... I don't talk about my day because nobody's interested."

Pirro defends her record in an explosive interview

NEW YORK'S RISING Republican superstar Jeanine Pirro is once again fielding questions about her husband's associates, and this time the furious.

CAPO: W'CHESTER DA'S HUBBY TOLD GAMBINOS OF PROBE

Pirro in hot seat?

A MOBSTER CLAIMED that the husband of Westchester District Attorney Jeanine Pirro once told him sensitive information about one of her ongoing cases, according to FBI documents.

Albert Pirro, husband of Westchester District Attorney Jeanine Pirro (right), denied any wrongdoing after reputed capo Greg DePalma (photo left) said on tape that Pirro shared information on one of his wife's cases.

Albert Pirro at a glance

Pg. 22

Exhibit N

Form 2168 (Rev. 5/93)
(Copy locally as needed)

STATE OF NEW YORK — DEPARTMENT OF CORRECTIONAL SERVICES

Shawangunk _____ Correctional Facility

Check One [X] **ADMINISTRATIVE SEGREGATION RECOMMENDATION**

            □ **INVOLUNTARY PROTECTIVE CUSTODY RECOMMENDATION**

1. Inmate Name ZIMMERMAN, NICHOLAS _____ DIN 02-A-1663 Cell SH-1

2. Reason for this recommendation:

You are under investigation for an escape attempt at Sing Sing Correctional

Facility. Your presence in population represents a risk to Facility

order, safety and security.

5/16/03   12:00PM   W. Lutz _____ [signature] _____ Sergeant
Date   /   Time   Name of Person Making Recommendation   Signature   Title

3 Is inmate confined pending a determination on this recommendation?   [X] Yes   □ No

4 If Yes,

   a Housing Unit of present confinement _Special Housing Unit_   Cell SH-1

   b Authorized by J. Maly, Deputy Superintendent for Security

Notice to Inmate: A hearing will be conducted within 14 days of this recommendation in accordance with the provisions of Part 254 of Chapter V. You will be entitled to call witnesses on your own behalf, provided that doing so does not jeopardize institutional safety or correctional goals.

If restricted pending a hearing on this recommendation, you may write to the Deputy Superintendent for Security or his/her designee prior to the hearing to make a statement on the need for continued confinement

Served by C.O. Flynn, Jan'g on 5/17/03
_at II: 13 pm_

Distribution Original — Inmate
         Copy — Disciplinary Office

Pg. 23

N.J. school workers go on strike

BLAIRSTOWN, N.J. — Teachers in the North Warren regional school district went on strike early yesterday, several hours after contract talks broke down.

The northern New Jersey district planned to ask a judge to order the teachers back to work.

Karen Joseph, a spokeswoman for the New Jersey Education Association, said the talks ended around 1:15 a.m., when negotiators failed to reach an agreement on salary and health benefits issues. The union represents 109 teachers, secretaries, custodians and school aides.

Union members have been working without a contract for a year, Joseph said.

Classes were canceled in the district yesterday, but most students had come to school before the strike was called.

"We did have a full house that showed up," said Superintendent of Schools John Toleno. "We housed them for about an hour until we could get the buses back here."

The district serves about 1,000 students from Blairstown, Frelinghuysen, Hardwick and Knowlton townships.
AP

Sing Sing 'bust-in' was bid to bust out

A man who allegedly tried to sneak into Sing Sing in a prison employee's uniform last month has been arrested and at least two inmates have been transferred as part of an investigation into an apparent escape attempt, officials said yesterday.

The probe is continuing and could involve several more prisoners, said State Police Investigator Darren Daughtry.

He refused to say whether any employees were involved, but said the arrested man is not an employee and the uniform was not authorized by the Department of Correctional Services.

Sing Sing, in Ossining, was locked down May 7 after the uniformed man tried to get in, the department said.

Officers were suspicious of him but let him leave when he said he was new on the job and

RON KUBY
Inmate-client transferred.

"dangerous items," the investigator said.

Neither Daughtry nor Linda Foglia, a department spokeswoman, would identify the man arrested or provide more details about the alleged escape attempt.

A call to the inspector general's office under Attorney General Eliot Spitzer was referred back to Foglia.

Foglia confirmed, however, that one of the prisoners transferred out of Sing Sing was Nicholas Zimmerman, 27, of Queens, who has served one year of a 14-year stretch for weapons possession.

He and an unidentified inmate were sent to the Shawangunk Correctional Facility in Wallkill "because of the intrusion attempt," she said.

He was charged with promoting prison contraband for allegedly trying to enter with

would get "the appropriate paperwork" from his car, spokesman Mike Houston said at the time. The man did not return.

He was tracked to New York City and arrested there May 12, Daughtry said.

Ron Kuby, said Zimmerman is under investigation for attempted escape.

Zimmerman is appealing his weapons conviction and "knows nothing of any escape attempt," Kuby said.

As for the man who tried to get into the prison, Zimmerman "doesn't know who this person is or why he would enter the prison and certainly never attempted to escape," Kuby said. "That's what he has a lawyer for."

Kuby said Zimmerman was transferred May 16 and is under "administrative segregation," in his cell 23 hours a day with sharply limited access to his lawyer.

Sing Sing, on the Hudson River waterfront, spawned the phrase "up the river" and housed the state's electric chair for many years.
AP

MH:bc

COUNTY COURT
STATE OF NEW YORK : WESTCHESTER COUNTY
THE PEOPLE OF THE STATE OF NEW YORK

     -against-   **INDICTMENT NO.**
                             04-0960-01-02

NICHOLAS ZIMMERMAN & STEVEN FINLEY,

                Defendant(s)

COUNT 1   **PL 200.00   DFO NW**

THE GRAND JURY OF THE COUNTY OF WESTCHESTER, by this Indictment, accuses the defendants of the crime of **BRIBERY IN THE THIRD DEGREE,** committed as follows:

The defendants, in the County of Westchester and State of New York, on or about and between November 2002 and May 2003, while aiding and abetting and acting in concert with each other and several other individuals, did confer and offer and agree to confer, any benefit upon a public servant upon an agreement or understanding that such public servant's vote, opinion, judgment, action, decision or exercise of discretion as a public servant would thereby be influenced.

Pg. 25

<u>**COUNT 2**</u>   **PL 110/205.15   01   DF1 NW**

THE GRAND JURY OF THE COUNTY OF WESTCHESTER, by this Indictment, accuses the defendants of the crime of **ATTEMPTED ESCAPE IN THE FIRST DEGREE**, committed as follows:

The defendants, in the County of Westchester and State of New York, on or about April 24, 2003, while aiding and abetting and acting in concert with each other and several other individuals, and having been charged with and convicted of a felony, did attempt to escape from a detention facility.

<u>**COUNT 3**</u>   **PL 110/205.15   01   DF1 NW**

THE GRAND JURY OF THE COUNTY OF WESTCHESTER, by this Indictment, accuses the defendants of the crime of **ATTEMPTED ESCAPE IN THE FIRST DEGREE**, committed as follows:

The defendants, in the County of Westchester and State of New York, on or about May 6, 2003, while aiding and abetting and acting in concert with each other and several other individuals, and having been charged with and convicted of a felony, did attempt to escape from a detention facility.

Pg. 26

COUNT 4   PL 110/205.15   01   DF1 NW

THE GRAND JURY OF THE COUNTY OF WESTCHESTER, by this indictment,
accuses the defendants of the crime of **ATTEMPTED ESCAPE IN THE FIRST
DEGREE**, committed as follows:

The defendants, in the County of Westchester and State of New York,
on or about May 7, 2003, while aiding and abetting and acting in concert
with each other and several other individuals, and having been charged
with and convicted of a felony, did attempt to escape from a detention
facility.

COUNT 5   PL 205.25   01   DF1 NW

THE GRAND JURY OF THE COUNTY OF WESTCHESTER, by this indictment,
accuses the defendants of the crime of **PROMOTING PRISON CONTRABAND IN THE
FIRST DEGREE**, committed as follows:

The defendants, in the County of Westchester and State of New York,
on or about April 24, 2003, while aiding and abetting and acting in
concert with each other and several other individuals, did knowingly and
unlawfully introduce dangerous contraband into a detention facility, to
wit: a loaded nine millimeter (9mm) handgun.

Pg. 27

COUNT 6   PL 205.25   01   DF1 NW

THE GRAND JURY OF THE COUNTY OF WESTCHESTER, by this Indictment,
accuses the defendants of the crime of **PROMOTING PRISON CONTRABAND IN THE
FIRST DEGREE,** committed as follows:

The defendants, in the County of Westchester and State of New York,
on or about April 24, 2003, while aiding and abetting and acting in
concert with each other and several other individuals, did knowingly and
unlawfully introduce dangerous contraband into a detention facility, to
wit: a loaded .38 caliber handgun.

COUNT 7   PL 205.25   01   DF1 NW

THE GRAND JURY OF THE COUNTY OF WESTCHESTER, by this Indictment,
accuses the defendants of the crime of **PROMOTING PRISON CONTRABAND IN THE
FIRST DEGREE,** committed as follows:

The defendants, in the County of Westchester and State of New York, on or
about April 24, 2003, while aiding and abetting and acting in concert with
each other and several other individuals, did knowingly and unlawfully
introduce dangerous contraband into a detention facility, to wit: a
canister containing pepper spray.

Pg.   28

COUNT 8   PL 205.25   02   DF1 NW

THE GRAND JURY OF THE COUNTY OF WESTCHESTER, by this Indictment,
accuses the defendants of the crime of **PROMOTING PRISON CONTRABAND IN THE
FIRST DEGREE,** committed as follows:

The defendants, in the County of Westchester and State of New York,
on or about April 24, 2003, while aiding and abetting and acting in
concert with each other and several other individuals, and being confined
in a detention facility, did knowingly and unlawfully make, obtain, and
possess dangerous contraband, to wit: a loaded nine millimeter (9mm)
handgun.

COUNT 9   PL 205.25   02   DF1 NW

THE GRAND JURY OF THE COUNTY OF WESTCHESTER, by this Indictment,
accuses the defendants of the crime of **PROMOTING PRISON CONTRABAND IN THE
FIRST DEGREE,** committed as follows:

The defendants, in the County of Westchester and State of New York,
on or about April 24, 2003, while aiding and abetting and acting in
concert with each other and several other individuals, and being confined
in a detention facility, did knowingly and unlawfully make, obtain, and
possess dangerous contraband, to wit: a loaded .38 caliber handgun.

Pg. 29

PL 205.25   02   DF1 NW

THE GRAND JURY OF THE COUNTY OF WESTCHESTER, by this Indictment,
accuses the defendants of the crime of **PROMOTING PRISON CONTRABAND IN THE
FIRST DEGREE**, committed as follows:

The defendants, in the County of Westchester and State of New York,
on or about April 24, 2003, while aiding and abetting and acting in
concert with each other and several other individuals, and being confined
in a detention facility, did knowingly and unlawfully make, obtain, and
possess dangerous contraband, to wit: a canister containing pepper spray.

COUNT 11   PL 205.25   01   DF1 NW

THE GRAND JURY OF THE COUNTY OF WESTCHESTER, by this Indictment,
accuses the defendants of the crime of **PROMOTING PRISON CONTRABAND IN THE
FIRST DEGREE**, committed as follows:

The defendants, in the County of Westchester and State of New York, on or
about May 7, 2003, while aiding and abetting and acting in concert with
each other and several other individuals, did knowingly and unlawfully
introduce dangerous contraband into a detention facility, to wit: a
loaded nine millimeter (9mm) handgun.

Pg. 30

COUNT 12   PL 205.25   01   DF1 NW

THE GRAND JURY OF THE COUNTY OF WESTCHESTER, by this Indictment,
accuses the defendants of the crime of **PROMOTING PRISON CONTRABAND IN THE
FIRST DEGREE,** committed as follows:

The defendants, in the County of Westchester and State of New York,
on or about May 7, 2003, while aiding and abetting and acting in concert
with each other and several other individuals, did knowingly and
unlawfully introduce dangerous contraband into a detention facility, to
wit: a canister containing pepper spray.

COUNT 13   PL 205.25   02   DF1 NW

THE GRAND JURY OF THE COUNTY OF WESTCHESTER, by this Indictment,
accuses the defendants of the crime of **PROMOTING PRISON CONTRABAND IN THE
FIRST DEGREE,** committed as follows:

The defendants, in the County of Westchester and State of New York,
on or about May 7, 2003, while aiding and abetting and acting in concert
with each other and several other individuals, being confined in a
detention facility, did knowingly and unlawfully make, obtain, and possess
dangerous contraband, to wit: a loaded nine millimeter (9mm) handgun.

Pg. 31

COUNT 14   **PL 205.25   02   DF1 NW**

THE GRAND JURY OF THE COUNTY OF WESTCHESTER, by this Indictment, accuses the defendants of the crime of **PROMOTING PRISON CONTRABAND IN THE FIRST DEGREE**, committed as follows:

The defendants, in the County of Westchester and State of New York, on or about May 7, 2003, while aiding and abetting and acting in concert with each other and several other individuals, and while being confined in a detention facility, did knowingly and unlawfully make, obtain, and possess dangerous contraband, to wit: a canister containing pepper spray.

COUNT 15   **PL 110/265.03   02A   CF2 NW**

THE GRAND JURY OF THE COUNTY OF WESTCHESTER, by this Indictment, accuses the defendants of the crime of **ATTEMPTED CRIMINAL POSSESSION OF A WEAPON IN THE SECOND DEGREE**, committed as follows:

The defendants, in the County of Westchester and State of New York, on or about and between April 24, 2003, and May 7, 2003, while aiding and abetting and acting in concert with each other and several other individuals, did attempt to possess a loaded firearm, to wit: a loaded nine millimeter (9mm) handgun, with intent to use the same unlawfully against another person.

Pg. 32

COUNT 16   PL 110/265.03   02A   CF2 NW

THE GRAND JURY OF THE COUNTY OF WESTCHESTER, by this Indictment,
accuses the defendants of the crime of **ATTEMPTED CRIMINAL POSSESSION OF A
WEAPON IN THE SECOND DEGREE**, committed as follows:

The defendants, in the County of Westchester and State of New York,
on or about and between April 24, 2003, and May 7, 2003, while aiding and
abetting and acting in concert with each other and several other
individuals, did attempt to possess a loaded firearm, to wit: a loaded
.38 caliber handgun, with intent to use the same unlawfully against
another person.

COUNT 17   PL 105.10   01   EF4 NW

THE GRAND JURY OF THE COUNTY OF WESTCHESTER, by this Indictment,
accuses the defendants of the crime of **CONSPIRACY IN THE FOURTH DEGREE**,
committed as follows:

The defendants, in the County of Westchester and State of New York,
on or about and between November 2002 and May 2003, with intent that
conduct constituting a class "C" felony be performed, to wit: Criminal
Possession of a Weapon in the Second Degree, agreed with one or more
persons to engage in and cause the performance of such conduct.

Pg. 33

PL 105.05   01   AMS NW

THE GRAND JURY OF THE COUNTY OF WESTCHESTER, by this Indictment,

accuses the defendants of the crime of **CONSPIRACY IN THE FIFTH DEGREE,**

committed as follows:

The defendants, in the County of Westchester and State of New York,

on or about and between November 2002 and May 2003, with intent that

conduct constituting a felony be performed, to wit: Escape in the First

Degree, agreed with one or more persons to engage in and cause the

performance of such conduct.

OVERT ACTS (in support of Counts 17 and 18):

1.   On or about and between November 2002 and May 2003, defendant
Zimmerman directed Jatanya Belnavis, Tamara Johnson and Latrina Boyd to
pay cash to NYS Correction Officer Quangtrice Wilson on several occasions
to bring in various items, including cellular telephones, into the Sing
Sing Correctional Facility in Ossining, New York, to inmates Zimmerman and
Finley.

2.   On or about and between November 2002 and May 2003, defendants
Zimmerman and Finley made numerous telephone calls utilizing their
cellular telephones from inside the Sing Sing Correctional Facility to
Jatanya Belnavis, Latrina Boyd, Tamara Johnson, Barry Alexander,
Quangtrice Wilson and others to discuss and carry out activities in
furtherance of the escape plan.

3.   On or about and between November 2002 and May 2003, NYS
Correction Officer Quangtrice Wilson brought three (3) cellular telephones
into the Sing Sing Correctional Facility and provided two (2) to inmate
Nicholas Zimmerman and one (1) to inmate Steven Finley.

4.   On or about and between November 2002 and May 2003, NYS
Correction Officer Quangtrice Wilson provided her NYS correction officer
identification card to Tamara Johnson and Jatanya Belnavis in order for
them to produce fake/bogus NYS correction officer identification cards to
be used in the planned escape.

5.   On or about and between November 2002 and May 2003, NYS
Correction Officer Quangtrice Wilson provided Jatanya Belnavis and

defendants Zimmerman and Finley with information on the physical layout and operations of the Sing Sing Correctional Facility for use in the planned escape.

6. On or about and between November 2002 and May 2003, Jatanya Belnavis, Tamara Johnson and Latrina Boyd obtained various correction officer uniform items and badges from a law enforcement uniform and equipment supply store in the Bronx, New York for use in the planned escape.

7. On or about and between November 2002 and May 2003, defendant Zimmerman directed Jatanya Belnavis to obtain handguns in order to bring those items into inmates Zimmerman and Finley for their use during the planned escape from Sing Sing Correctional Facility.

8. On or about April 24, 2003, Jatanya Belnavis, an individual identified as "Roc", and other individuals, including Tamara Johnson and Barry Alexander, drove to the Sing Sing Correctional Facility to carry out the planned escape of Sing Sing inmates Zimmerman and Finley.

9. On or about April 24, 2003, in the early afternoon hours, Tamara Johnson made an inmate visit to defendant Zimmerman at the Sing Sing Correctional Facility to carry out the planned escape of Sing Sing inmates Zimmerman and Finley.

10. On or about April 24, 2003, in the early afternoon hours, Barry Alexander made an inmate visit to defendant Finley at the Sing Sing Correctional Facility to carry out the planned escape of Sing Sing inmates Zimmerman and Finley.

11. On or about April 24, 2003, Jatanya Belnavis and an individual identified as "Roc", both dressed as NYS correction officers, entered the Sing Sing Correctional Facility carrying a 9mm automatic handgun, a .38 caliber handgun, pepper spray and various NYS correction officer uniform items, identification cards and badges, to meet up with inmates Zimmerman and Finley in or near the inmate visit room inside the facility to carry out the escape plan.

12. On or about May 6, 2003, Jatanya Belnavis, Tony Dubose, Tamara Johnson, Barry Alexander, Keisha Moore, Tiana Payne and Kira Scott drove to the Sing Sing Correctional Facility to carry out the planned escape of Sing Sing inmates Zimmerman and Finley.

13. On or about May 6, 2003, in the early afternoon hours, Tiana Payne and Kira Scott made an inmate visit to defendant Zimmerman at the Sing Sing Correctional Facility to carry out the planned escape of Sing Sing inmates Zimmerman and Finley.

14. On or about May 6, 2003, in the early afternoon hours, Keisha Moore made an inmate visit to defendant Finley at the Sing Sing Correctional Facility to carry out the planned escape of Sing Sing inmates Zimmerman and Finley.

Pg. 35

15. On or about May 6, 2003, Tony Dubose brought a motorcycle to the Village of Ossining in the vicinity of the Sing Sing Correctional Facility for use by defendants Zimmerman and Finley to leave the area following the planned escape.

16. On or about May 6, 2003, Jatanya Belnavis, Tony Dubose, Tamara Johnson, Barry Alexander, Keisha Moore, Tiana Payne and Kira Scott, upon deciding that they arrived too late to carry out the escape plan that day departed from the Sing Sing Correctional Facility and returned to New York City.

17. On or about May 7, 2003, Jatanya Belnavis, Tony Dubose, Tamara Johnson, Barry Alexander, Keisha Moore, Tiana Payne and Kira Scott drove to the Sing Sing Correctional Facility to carry out the planned escape of Sing Sing inmates Zimmerman and Finley.

18. On or about May 7, 2003, in the early afternoon hours, Tiana Payne and Kira Scott made an inmate visit to defendant Zimmerman at the Sing Sing Correctional Facility to carry out the planned escape of Sing Sing inmates Zimmerman and Finley.

19. On or about May 7, 2003, in the early afternoon hours, Keisha Moore made an inmate visit to defendant Finley at the Sing Sing Correctional Facility to carry out the planned escape of Sing Sing inmates Zimmerman and Finley.

20. On or about May 7, 2003, Tony Dubose, dressed as a NYS correction officer, entered the Sing Sing Correctional Facility carrying a 9mm automatic handgun, pepper spray and various NYS correction officer uniform items, identification cards and badges, to meet up with inmates Zimmerman and Finley in or near the inmate visit room inside the facility to carry out the escape plan.

21. On or about and between May 7, 2003 and May 15, 2003, Jatanya Belnavis, Latrina Boyd, Tamara Johnson, Barry Alexander and several other individuals, met up at a "Days Inn" Hotel in New York City to discuss the failed escape plan and what to do if approached and questioned by law enforcement authorities. While there, they spoke about this topic with defendants Zimmerman and Finley by cellular telephone.

22. On or about May 12, 2003, defendant Zimmerman spoke with Tony Dubose and Barry Alexander by cellular telephone in an attempt to provide money and transportation to Dubose to assist him in leaving the New York City metropolitan area to avoid questioning, apprehension and arrest by law enforcement authorities.

Pg.36

PL 205.20   02   AM2 NW

THE GRAND JURY OF THE COUNTY OF WESTCHESTER, by this Indictment, accuses the defendant, **NICHOLAS ZIMMERMAN**, of the crime of **PROMOTING PRISON CONTRABAND IN THE SECOND DEGREE**, committed as follows:

The defendant, in the County of Westchester and State of New York, on or about November 2002 and May 2003, did while being a person confined in a detention facility, knowingly and unlawfully make, obtain and possess contraband, to wit: a cellular telephone.

COUNT 20

PL 205.20   02   AM2 NW

THE GRAND JURY OF THE COUNTY OF WESTCHESTER, by this Indictment, accuses the defendant, **NICHOLAS ZIMMERMAN**, of the crime of **PROMOTING PRISON CONTRABAND IN THE SECOND DEGREE**, committed as follows:

The defendant, in the County of Westchester and State of New York, on or about November 2002 and May 2003, did while being a person confined in a detention facility, knowingly and unlawfully make, obtain and possess contraband, to wit: a cellular telephone.

Pg. 37

PL 205.20   02   AM2 NW

THE GRAND JURY OF THE COUNTY OF WESTCHESTER, by this Indictment, accuses the defendant, **STEVEN FINLEY**, of the crime of **PROMOTING PRISON CONTRABAND IN THE SECOND DEGREE**, committed as follows:

The defendant, in the County of Westchester and State of New York, on or about November 2002 and May 2003, did while being a person confined in a detention facility, knowingly and unlawfully make, obtain and possess contraband, to wit: a cellular telephone.

All contrary to the form of the statute in such case made and provided and against the peace and dignity of the People of the State of New York.

                    /s/ Jeanine Pirro
                District Attorney of Westchester County

GRADING SCHOOLS

The Journal News.com

Crime/Public Safety

Home Design

Search our site [GO]

Past 7 Days
·Advanced search tips

SERVICES
Subscriber Services
E-Newsletter Signup
Greater NY Wine & Food Expo
NEWS
Westchester
Rockland
Putnam
New York
Newswatch: Iraq
Crime/Public Safety
Education
Environment
Gov't&Politics
Health
Religion
Transportation
Obituaries
Weekly Publications

SHOPPING
Shopping
Coupons
Local Stores

PHOTOS
Daily gallery
Local sports
Special galleries
Order reprints

SPORTS
NY report
Varsity Central:
· HS Sports
Outdoors
All-Stars
· Rockland
· West.-Putnam
Columnists
· Rick Carpiniello
· Jane McManus
· Ian O Connor
· Glenn Sapir
50 seconds
Behind the · · nes
National
Sub · can Goli

BUSINESS

☑ E-mail this story to a friend   ☑ View printer-friendly version

Sing Sing escape plot foiled

By JONATHAN BANDLER
THE JOURNAL NEWS
(Original publication: February 4, 2004)

WHITE PLAINS — Two inmates tried to bust their way out of Sing Sing last year in a scheme that involved impersonating officers, smuggling guns and fake uniforms into the maximum security prison, and bribing a correction officer, authorities said yesterday.

The plot led to the arrests of seven people — the inmates, the officer and four accused accomplices — during an eight-month investigation, they said.

The probe began after the prison was locked down May 7, when one of the accomplices tried to get into the prison, they said. It was revealed yesterday that the group had twice before gone to the prison to spring the inmates.

On May 6, two of the plotters got inside with loaded handguns but left when one got too nervous to go through with it, Westchester County District Attorney Jeanine Pirro said. The group also had gone there in April.

"This was a very orchestrated attempt to get two career felons out of Sing Sing," Pirro said yesterday. "A catastrophe was absolutely averted here."

The mastermind was identified as Nicholas "Puzz" Zimmerman, a rapper convicted of gun possession in 2001, who was trying to escape with fellow inmate Steven Finley, Pirro said. She said Zimmerman recruited two of his girlfriends, Jatanya Belnavis and Latrina Boyd, and bribed Correction Officer Quangtrice Wilson to help. The girlfriends offered two Brooklyn men, Tony Dubose and Barry Alexander, $5,000 each to help them plan the breakout, with a promise of $10,000 more if it were successful, authorities said.

The plan was foiled when guards became suspicious of Dubose on May 7, when he entered Sing Sing with a fake ID and claimed he was a correction officer transferred from Fishkill. Dubose fled after saying he was going to his car to get his transfer papers, authorities said, but he left behind a bag with pepper spray and fake uniforms, prompting officials to lock down the prison.

Dubose was identified as a suspect because Ossining Police Officer Donald Farrell had gotten his license information after ticketing a motorcycle Dubose and Alexander left that day near the prison. The motorcycle was to be Zimmerman and Finley's getaway vehicle, Pirro said.

The plot relied on the confusion during afternoon shift change to get the fake correction officers into the prison. It was first attempted on April 24, Pirro said, but Belnavis and Alexander aborted the plan because they got to the prison too late.

On May 6, Belnavis and a man who has yet to be arrested reached the second floor of the prison wearing wigs and dressed as correction officers. They had two loaded handguns and a bag

More News
·Widow says husband's killer is known, but free
·Chief of Teamsters local in Scarsdale ousted
·Murder trial starts today
·17-year-old dies in crash
·Cop's suspension extended
·Fire Prevention Week
·3 suspects arrested in beating, carjacking
·Man arrested after chase from New Jersey
·The case against two New Rochelle men accused in the fatal assault of a New Rochelle man August 28 was adjourned to Oct. 14 yesterday.
·Robbery attempt victim, then suspect charged
·Woman charged in con attempt

Local stocks
Real estate
Technology
David Schepp

Life & Style
Antiques
Day in the Life
Calendar
Travel

ENTERTAINMENT
Dining
For kids
Games
Movies
Music
Theater
THE LINE
Celebrations
The Bridal Book

WEEKLIES
The Item
The Patent Trader
Review Press
Standard Star
The Star
The Times

OPINION
Editorials
Letters
Matt Davies
 • The Pulitzer Prize
Community Views
Columnists
 • Bob Baird
 • Arthur Gunther
 • Laurie Nikolski
 • Phil Reisman

CLASSIFIED
Jobs
Homes
Cars
Grocery Coupons
Local Classifieds
Local Stores

FYI
Corrections
News Standards
About us
Contact Us
FAQ
Subscribe
How to advertise

... ... prison identification cards. Pirro said they left when Belmavis suffered a "panic attack."

By mid-May, authorities had arrested Dubose, 25, and transferred Zimmerman and Finley to other prisons. The inmates were later charged with first-degree attempted escape. Belnavis, 28, of Queens, Boyd, 26, of Manhattan and Alexander, 34, were arrested over the summer on the same charge Dubose is facing, first-degree promoting prison contraband. Wilson, 31, resigned following her arrest last week on charges of first-degree promoting prison contraband and third-degree bribe receiving. She had been a correction officer since 1993, the last four years at Sing Sing.

Pirro said Wilson had a relationship with Zimmerman and accepted several thousand dollars in bribes in exchange for providing details about operations and security at Sing Sing, as well as information about the guards' uniforms. She also smuggled a cellular telephone to Zimmerman that he used to communicate with the others, Pirro said.

The investigation, conducted by state police, the state Department of Correction and the District Attorney's Public Integrity Bureau, is continuing, and additional arrests and charges were expected.

Zimmerman, 27, is serving a 14-year sentence for weapon possession. Finley, 26, was sentenced in 2001 to 20 years for attempted murder in Nassau County. Both can get an additional four years if convicted of the escape attempt. The others face up to seven years in prison if convicted.

Zimmerman's lawyer, Ronald Kuby, suggested that his client would not have tried to get out because his appeal of the gun-possession conviction was pending.

"Why would he try to break out of prison when I'm his lawyer?" Kuby said yesterday. "There was no reason for him to break out. That's why he's got a lawyer. Jeanine Pirro tells a good story."

Send e-mail to Jon

Pg. 40

Exhibit R

Westchester County, New York
District Attorney's Office

Jeanine Pirro, D.A.

FOR IMMEDIATE RELEASE
DATE: February 03, 2004

ARRESTS MADE IN ATTEMPTED SING SING JAIL BREAK

Site
Map

Contact
The D.A.

Recent
Press
Releases

Domestic
Violence

Homeland
Security

Specialized
Prosecution
Units

Crime
Stoppers

Community
Programs

Consumer
Info

Victims
Assistance

Professional
Opportunities

Kid's
Corner

Westchester's
Most
Wanted

Reaching
Other
Agencies

Search the Site

Search

Westchester County District Attorney Jeanine Pirro, joined by representatives of the New York State Police and Ossining Police announced today the arrests of seven individuals including a corrections officer, two inmates and four civilians following an eight month investigation into the foiled break-out attempt at the Sing Sing Maximum Security Correctional Facility on May 7, 2003. On May 7, 2003 it is alleged that Tony Dubose, DOB 12/7/78, of 1240 Sutter Avenue, Brooklyn, New York, attempted to enter the Sing Sing Correctional Facility posing as a "new transfer" corrections officer. Dubose had been offered $15,000 in cash to carry out the escape plan by the other participants in the scheme. This defendant wore a fraudulent correction's officer uniform and carried counterfeit identification credentials, including a fake correction officer badge. In addition, he carried a canister of aerosol pepper spray which is illegal to posses inside the facility. Dubose's attempt was foiled when officials at the facility questioned his identity and his transfer claim. While Dubose was able to flee before being apprehended, he left behind a bag containing fake uniform items and the pepper spray. Corrections authorities immediately locked-down the facility and the ensuing investigation revealed two additional escape attempts to break-out two long-term inmates being housed at Sing Sing. The inmates are Nicholas Zimmerman aka Puzz, DOB 2/18/76, currently of Shawangunk Correctional Facility, Walkill, New York, and Steven Finley, DOB 7/7/77, currently of Attica Correctional Facility, Attica, New York. They are both charged with Attempted Escape in the First Degree. Both inmates were immediately transferred from Sing Sing to the upstate facilities after the escape plot was uncovered. Sing Sing Correction Officer Quangtrice Wilson, DOB 9/14/72, of 920 Trinity Avenue, New York, New York was arrested for allegedly accepting several thousand dollars in bribes from the participants to bring in contraband including a cell phone to the inmates. She is also alleged to have assisted in the escape plan by providing information on the Sing Sing physical plant, operations, security and uniform and identification information. Both Wilson and Dubose are charged with Promoting Prison Contraband in the First Degree. Wilson is also charged with Bribe Receiving in the Third Degree. In addition to the May 7, 2003 attempt, it is

11

alleged that on April 24, 2003, Jatanya Belnavis, DOB 5/8/75, of 240-06 142nd Avenue, Rosedale, New York, and a male accomplice (as yet uncharged) entered Sing Sing Correctional Facility wearing phony correction officer's uniforms and wigs. The pair carried a bag containing fake badges and identification cards for the inmates they intended to break-out of the facility. In addition, they possessed loaded 9mm and .38 caliber handguns. The attempt was aborted when Belnavis suffered a panic attack and had to exit the facility before the escape plan could be carried out. On May 6, 2003 another alleged attempt was aborted when the defendants, Belnavis, Alexander and possibly others realized that they were late arriving to the facility and had missed the shift change. In all three attempts, the defendants hoped to utilize the confusion of a change of shift when approximately 300 correction officers enter and exit the Sing Sing facility in order to carry out the escape plan. Barry Alexander aka Sidiq, DOB 2/16/69, of 17 East 17th Street, Apt. 3D, Brooklyn, New York, and Latrina M. Boyd, (DOB 2/28/77) of 120 West 138th Street, New York, New York, have been charged with Promoting Prison Contraband in the First Degree for their roles in allegedly assisting the attempted break-outs. Boyd is alleged to have assisted in the escape planning as well as obtaining the bogus identification, badges and uniform items. Alexander, who assisted in the planning of the escape attempts, was allegedly present at the facility during the break-out attempts and brought a motorcycle to the vicinity of the correctional facility in the Village of Ossining to be used by the inmates to flee the scene once outside of the facility. Early on the morning of May 7, 2003, prior to the escape attempt that day, an alert Ossining police officer, P.O. Donald Farrell, stopped Alexander and Dubose in the vicinity of the Sing Sing facility while they were moving the motorcycle closer to the facility. P.O. Farrell questioned the two males and obtained NYS driver license and other pedigree information from them. The next day, after learning of the attempted escape at the facility, P.O. Farrell contacted investigators of the New York State Police and advised them of the suspicious activity he observed the day before and provided them the names and pedigree information of the individuals he had stopped and questioned. This information was the break investigators were looking for. The investigation was conducted by the Public Integrity Bureau of the District Attorney's Office in conjunction with the New York State Police and the New York State Department of Correctional Services Inspector General's Office. District Attorney was joined by Captain Frank Kohler, Lt. James H. Murphy and Senior Investigator Robert Bennett and Investigator Darren. D. Daughtry all of the NYS Police and Chief Joseph Burton and PO Donald Farrell of Ossining Village Police Department. Attempted Escape in the First Degree is a class "E" felony and is punishable by a maximum of 4 years in state prison. Bribe Receiving in the Third Degree and

DA: Inmates tried 3 escapes

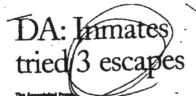

The Associated Press

White Plains – An inmate at Sing Sing used three girlfriends – including a correction officer – to try to break him and a friend out of prison on three occasions with a scheme that involved impersonating guards, smuggling guns and using a getaway motorcycle, prosecutors said.

Though there was no escape, District Attorney Jeanine Pirro said the plot could have become a "catastrophe" if successful and demonstrated problems with security at the prison.

On the first attempt, on April 24, a woman dressed as a guard and carrying two handguns got past security and up to the second floor of the famous fortress-like prison in Ossining but suffered a "panic attack" and fled, Pirro said.

The second try on May 4, was foiled when the plotters arrived too late to take advantage of the guards' shift change, a key element in their plans.

And the third try, on May 7, eventually led to the arrest of the inmates, the three women and two other men who a fake guard was stopped at the entrance and the motorcycle was ticketed outside the prison, Pirro said.

Those arrested were:

▶ The inmates, Nicholas Zimmerman, 27, and Steven Finley, 26. Pirro said Zimmerman, who had the three girlfriends, was the mastermind.

▶ The correction officer, Quangtrice Wilson, 31, of Manhattan.

▶ The other girlfriends, Jatanya Belnavis, 28, of Queens, and Latrica Boyd, 26, of Manhattan.

▶ Tony Dubose, 25, and Barry Alexander, 34, both of Brooklyn.

Cons' great escape foiled

Two inmates from Brooklyn planned a "Mission: Impossible"-style escape from Sing Sing with guns, disguises, female help and even a motorcycle, but they got busted in the last road.

Westchester County District Attorney Jeanine Pirro said yesterday that ringleader Nicholas Zimmerman, 27, a rap singer serving two to 15 years for weapons crimes, parole violations and bail jumping, sweet-talked three girlfriends – one a correction officer – into helping him.

Zimmerman and pal Steven Finley, 26, hatched a plot that involved impersonating guards and using guns smuggled into the famous lockup in Ossining. Pirro said two handguns got past security, but the purpose of a shootout, in the event that such was needed," adding, "it could have been an equation for catastrophe."

She said the charismatic Zimmerman persuaded two girlfriends on the outside to help and also developed a relationship with guard Quangtrice Wilson, 31.

Wilson allegedly accepted several thousand dollars to provide information about shift changes, the prison layout and more, Pirro said. She was arrested, too.

Sing Sing ding-a-ling uses gal-pal guard in breakout bid: DA

Pirro's Comments Prompt Action By Defense Group

BY ANTHONY LIN

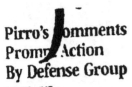

Jeanine Pirro

...defendants and suspects in high-profile cases...

...A professional and judicial complaint letter of the defense lawyers group cited in a letter to the grievance committee of the Ninth Judicial District several comments Ms. Pirro had made to the news media concerning the indictments of two accused sex offenders and an alleged murderer.

Among the matters cited by the law group was the case of Eddie N. Concern, who was charged Feb. 1 with kidnapping, rape, child endangerment and other charges. That day Ms. Pirro told the 1010 WINS radio station that Mr. Cordero "likes the idea of hurting children and treating them like prey."

She continued, "We're naive if we think that when we send these predators to prison that they come out and they're better."

Ms. Pirro also told The New York Times that she could not by law reveal whether Mr. Cordero was HIV-positive. Asked by the paper if she knew his condition, she said, "Yeah, I do, and that's what makes me so angry."

Ms. Pirro's office released a statement yesterday that said: "The District Attorney is proud of her record leading the fight against child molesters, serial rapists and murderers. She will continue to protect the people of Westchester County despite the rantings of these critics, who would be embarrassed by their callous indifference to innocent crime victims."

Daniel N. Arshack, a lawyer who is secretary to the prosecutorial complaint center, said Ms. Pirro's comments went far beyond the prosecutor's duty to inform the public and would make it harder for the accused to receive fair trials.

"Our view is these sorts of comments serve no real law-enforcement purpose," said Mr. Arshack. "They serve only to increase the public opprobrium for those accused."

The defense lawyers' complaint says that Ms. Pirro's comments are in violation Disciplinary Rule 7-107, which states that lawyers involved in criminal matters should not make extrajudicial comments they should reasonably know will prejudice the adjudicative process.

Jeff Fogel, the legal director of the Center for Constitutional Rights, said prosecutors had been pushing the envelope with...

Lawyers File Complaint Against DA Pirro

Continued from page 1

...complaints for years.

"This is a longstanding problem of prosecutors," he said, "and they rarely are taken to task by ethics committees."

...recently... Attorney... made in a June 2000 press conference concerning the case of accused Al...

...admitted... comments of his... political...

Disciplinary Committee of the Appellate Division, First Department, was later withdrawn and filed with the Department of Justice's ethics office.

Disciplinary committee proceedings are generally confidential and can take years to resolve. Complaints can consume resources, both publicity and anxiety, and in extreme cases can tarnish reputations of disbarment.

Prosecutors who make statements about their cases that may become construed as prejudicial may also jeopardize their cases with judges who...

...charges being dismissed...

...judge's own conduct or statements...

may have been made even before they were assigned to the case.

The complaint against Ms. Pirro is the first referred to a disciplinary committee by the Prosecutorial and Judicial Complaint Center which was formed last May.

...the First Department's Disciplinary Committee said disciplinary complaints do not produce statistics for time but said have teeth.

He recalled that Garrett Heidinan, the former Brooklyn district attorney, was censured by the Tenth Judicial District's grievance committee for informing a judge at a press conference she applauded the censure as it... by the Court of Appeals which unanimously upheld it.

Continued from page 1

regulation of informant testimony in a number of forms. In the 2000 decision of *Dodd v. State*, 993 P2d 778, 784 (Okla. 2000), for instance, the Oklahoma Supreme Court adopted expanded discovery rules in all cases involving jailhouse informants. In order to provide defense counsel with adequate information to use in cross-examination. Noting that "[t]he judicial process is tainted and justice cheapened when factual testimony is purchased, whether with leniency or money," see id. at 784 n. 7, the court found that "complete disclosure" was required with respect to "all jailhouse informant testimony not specifically excluded by the United States Constitution."

The additional discovery required by *Dodd* includes: (1) the informant's complete criminal history, (2) any deal or benefit that the informant has been provided or may be provided in the future, (3) the specific statements allegedly made by the defendant and the time, place and manner in which the informant disclosed them, (4) all other cases in which the informant testified or offered to testify, (5) whether the informant recanted at any time, and (6) "all other information relevant to the informant's credibility." See id. at 784.

The *Dodd* court also adopted another prophylactic measure used in several states: a cautionary jury instruction. The court prescribed a pattern instruction in all cases where

may have benefitted from his testimony). The Louisiana Court of Appeal in *State v. Divers*, 889 So2d 335, 352-53 (La. App. 2004), likewise approved an instruction stating that jailhouse informants' testimony must be weighed with "great caution" if it is not materially corroborated.

Judicial Reliability Hearing

Yet a fourth approach, albeit one which has thus far been rejected by the courts, is a judicial reliability hearing. Such a hearing would involve a vetting process similar to that used in Canada, except under the supervision of the courts and with defense counsel able to conduct cross-examination. In the *Dodd* case, the Oklahoma Supreme Court initially mandated such hearings, but subsequently recalled that ruling and substituted the expanded discovery rules on the basis that juries rather than courts should determine witnesses' credibility. See *Dodd*, 993 P2d at 786-786 (Strubhar, J. specially concurring). In a partial dissent, however, two judges argued persuasively that the courts already perform pre-admission "gatekeeping" functions with respect to expert witnesses, and should therefore be permitted to do so in circumstances as fraught with potential prejudice as the admission of jailhouse informants' testimony. See id.

consists of the uncorroborated testimony of an accomplice or an informant. See *Divers*, 889 So2d at 352-53. Mississippi also mandates a "caution and suspicion" instruction for any "state's witness who has received a reduced sentence to testify," whether that witness is an accomplice or a jailhouse informant. See *McViest*, 551 So2d at 158-59. The same court has indicated in dicta that the testimony of either would not be sufficiently "direct" evidence to obviate the need for a special instruction where the evidence is otherwise circumstantial. See id. at 159. Moreover, at least one California judge has argued that the corpus delicti of an offense should not be established by the uncorroborated testimony of a jailhouse snitch. See *People v. Jones*, 949 P2d 890, 917 (Cal. 1998) (Mosk, J., concurring).

The New York courts should accordingly follow Justice Lawton's suggestion and equate the testimony of jailhouse informants with that of accomplices for corroboration purposes. In addition, New York should consider adopting some or all of the regulatory measures instituted in other states, such as expanded discovery, reliability hearings or special jury instructions. In this way, the "increasing problem [of jailhouse informants] throughout the American justice system" can be alleviated in New York.

Lawyers File Complaint Against DA Pirro

Continued from page 1

potentially prejudicial comments for years.

"This is a longstanding problem of prosecutors," he said, "and they rarely are taken to task by ethics committees."

Mr. Fogel's group recently launched an effort to have former Southern District U.S. Attorney and now Deputy Attorney General James Comey disciplined for comments he made in a June 2004 press conference concerning the case of accused Al Qaeda operative Jose M. Padilla.

The center's complaint alleged that Mr. Comey violated DR 7-107 when he claimed that Mr. Padilla had admitted being a terrorist in the course of his interrogations. The complaint, originally filed with the

Disciplinary Committee of the Appellate Division, First Department, was later withdrawn and filed with the Department of Justice's ethics office.

Disciplinary committee proceedings are generally confidential and can take years to resolve. Committees can censure lawyers, both publicly and privately, and, in extreme cases, recommend suspension or disbarment.

Prosecutors who make statements about defendants that could be construed as prejudicial may also jeopardize their cases with judges who have various measures at their disposal, including gag orders, sanctions and the possibility of charges being dismissed.

But Mr. Fogel said most judges did not see it as their role to enforce ethical rules governing statements that

may have been made even before they were assigned to the case.

The complaint against Ms. Pirro is the first referred to a disciplinary committee by the Prosecutorial and Judicial Complaint Center, which was formed last May.

Thomas Cahill, chief counsel to the First Department's Disciplinary Committee, said disciplinary complaints against prosecutors are rare but could have teeth.

He recalled that Elizabeth Holtzman, the former Brooklyn district attorney, was censured by the Tenth Judicial District's grievance committee for criticizing a judge in a press conference. She appealed the censure all the way to the Court of Appeals, which unanimously upheld it.

— *Anthony Lin can be reached at alin@nln.com.*

Pirro's Comments Prompt Action By Defense Group

BY ANTHONY LIN

THE NEW YORK State Association of Criminal Defense Lawyers has filed a disciplinary complaint against Westchester County District Attorney Jeanine Pirro over what it claims is her "pattern and practice of making inappropriate extra-judicial comments concerning defendants and suspects in high-profile cases."

The Prosecutorial and Judicial Complaint Center of the defense lawyers' group cited in a letter to the grievance com-

Jeanine Pirro

mittee of the Ninth Judicial District several comments Ms. Pirro had made to the news media concerning the indictments of two accused sex offenders and an alleged murderer.

Among the matters cited by the bar group was the case of Eddie W. Cordero, who was charged Feb. 1 with kidnapping, rape, child endangerment and other charges. That day, Ms. Pirro told the 1010 WINS radio station that Mr. Cordero "likes the idea of finding children and treating them like prey."

She continued, "We're naive if we think that when we send these predators to prison that they come out and they're better."

Ms. Pirro also told The New York Times that she could not by law reveal whether Mr. Cordero was HIV-positive. Asked by the paper if she knew his condition, she said, "Yeah, I do, and that's what makes me so angry."

Ms. Pirro's office released a statement yesterday that said: "The District Attorney is proud of her record leading the fight against child molesters, serial rapists and murderers. She will continue to protect the people of Westchester County despite the rantings of these critics, who should be embarrassed by their callous indifference to innocent crime victims."

Daniel N. Arshack, a lawyer who is secretary to the prosecutorial complaint center, said Ms. Pirro's comments went far beyond the prosecutor's duty to inform the public and would make it harder for the accused to receive fair trials.

"Our view is these sorts of comments serve no real law enforcement purpose," said Mr. Arshack. "They serve only to increase the public opprobrium for those accused."

The defense lawyers' complaint says that Ms. Pirro's comments are in violation Disciplinary Rule 7-107, which states that lawyers involved in criminal matters should not make extrajudicial comments they should reasonably know will prejudice the adjudicative process.

Jeff Fogel, the legal director of the Center for Constitutional Rights, said prosecutors had been pushing the envelope with

Continued from page 1

potentially prejudicial comments for years.

"This is a longstanding problem of prosecutors," he said, "and they rarely are taken to task by ethics committees."

Mr. Fogel's group recently launched an effort to have former Southern District U.S. Attorney and now Deputy Attorney General James Comey disciplined for comments he made in a June 2004 press conference concerning the case of accused Al Qaeda operative Jose M. Padilla.

The center's complaint alleged that Mr. Comey violated DR 7-107 when he claimed that Mr. Padilla had admitted being a terrorist in the course of his interrogations. The complaint, originally filed with the Disciplinary Committee of the Appellate Division, First Department, was later withdrawn and filed with the Department of Justice's ethics office.

Disciplinary committee proceedings are generally confidential and can take years to resolve. Committees can censure lawyers, both publicly and privately, and, in extreme cases, recommend suspension or disbarment.

Prosecutors who make statements about defendants that could be construed as prejudicial may also jeopardize their cases with judges who have various measures at their disposal, including gag orders, sanctions and the possibility of charges being dismissed.

But Mr. Fogel said most judges did not see it as their role to enforce ethical rules governing statements that may have been made even before they were assigned to the case.

The complaint against Ms. Pirro is the first referred to a disciplinary committee by the Prosecutorial and Judicial Complaint Center, which was formed last May.

Thomas Cahill, chief counsel to the First Department's Disciplinary Committee, said disciplinary complaints against prosecutors are rare but could have teeth.

He recalled that Elizabeth Holtzman, the former Brooklyn district attorney, was censured by the Tenth Judicial District's grievance committee for criticizing a judge in a press conference. She appealed the censure, all the way to the Court of Appeals, which unanimously upheld it.

— *Anthony Lin can be reached at alin@alm.com.*

ARE YOU TIRED OF BEING RAILROADED BY THE

CRIMINAL INJUSTICE SYSTEM?

WELL THEN IT'S TIME YOU GET F.O.C.I.S.ED !

THE F.O.C.I.S MOVEMENT LEGAL SERVICES
A grassroots organization dedicated to educating the families of the innocent or the wrongfully convicted prisoner.

COMING SOON! ! !

The Families Oppressed by the Criminal Injustice System

The F.O.C.I.S Movement is subsidiary of Madison Avenue Entertainment Group. For more information:
Call 877-507-5841 or email at: MadisonAvenue07@aol.com

ARE YOU IN PRISON FOR A CRIME YOU DIDN'T COMMIT?

WERE YOU WRONGFULLY CONVICTED?

IS YOUR LIFE STORY AS INTERESTING AS NICHOLAS
ZIMMERMAN'S

Then Madison Avenue Entertainment Group would like to hear from you.

CALL: 877-507-5841
EMAIL: MadisonAvenue07@aol.com
WRITE: P.O. BOX 908
Roosevelt, NY 11575

Send a self-addressed stamped envelope and a 1-2 page letter explaining
how you are innocent and wrongfully convicted and a company
representative will mail you an information packet.

ARE YOU AN ASPIRING AUTHOR LOOKING TO PUBLISH A BOOK

-OR-

ARE YOU SKILLED IN LITERARY ARTS AND THINK YOU HAVE
WHAT IT TAKES TO BECOME AN INVESTIGATIVE AUTHOR LIKE
KENDRA LYNEIGH HUGHES?

Then Madison Avenue Entertainment Group would like to hear from YOU.

CALL 877-507-5841

-OR-

Email us at MadisonAvenue07@aol.com

We are currently seeking authors to investigate cases of actual innocence
and Wrongful convictions. Also seeking novels, true stories, and
biographies, etc....

PUZZ PACINO

PRESENTS

NEW YORK'S ILLEST
RE-RELEASED

COMING SOON ! !

ON
MADISON AVENUE ENTERTAINMENT GROUP CD'S CASSETTES AND VINYL

Made in the USA
Middletown, DE
24 May 2019